The Irrational David

The Irrational David

The Power of Poetic Leadership

Ken Evers-Hood

Foreword by Jenny Warner

CASCADE *Books* · Eugene, Oregon

THE IRRATIONAL DAVID
The Power of Poetic Leadership

Cascade Books
An Imprint of Wipf and Stock Publishers
199 W. 8th Ave., Suite 3
Eugene, OR 97401

www.wipfandstock.com

PAPERBACK ISBN: 978-1-5326-3622-6
HARDCOVER ISBN: 978-1-5326-3624-0
EBOOK ISBN: 978-1-5326-3623-3

Cataloguing-in-Publication data:

Names: Evers-Hood, Ken, author. | Warner, Jenny, foreword.

Title: The irrational David : the power of poetic leadership / Ken Evers-Hood ; foreword by Jenny Warner.

Description: Eugene, OR : Cascade Books, 2019 | Includes bibliographical references.

Identifiers: ISBN 978-1-5326-3622-6 (paperback) | ISBN 978-1-5326-3624-0 (hardcover) | ISBN 978-1-5326-3623-3 (ebook)

Subjects: LCSH: Poetry. | Religion and poetry. | Pastoral theology. | Church work.

Classification: BV4012.2 .E93 2019 (paperback) | BV4012.2 .E93 NUMBER (ebook)

Manufactured in the U.S.A.   03/19/19

I dedicate this work to pastors and poets—and to all the irrational fools who, like me, dare to dream of a world in which there lies no difference between the two.

Contents

Permissions

Foreword

When I get stuck, I call Ken Evers-Hood. And when you read this book, you'll know why he's on my speed dial of advisers.

Ken and I met as Presbyterian pastors in the same presbytery in Oregon. As a new pastor, serving three hours from the hub of most other churches, I had few true colleagues. Ken invited me to sit in the back row of presbytery meetings with him, included me in the irreverent commentary of the younger pastors (by which I mean, those under 55), all the while sharing with me a great love of the presbytery and its process.

I learned to trust Ken's perspective, and so when he invited me to join him in a yearlong leadership cohort with the poet David Whyte in 2015, I said yes. The experience changed both of us. We found a community and a construct that took us further in ministry, our lives, and our future. Our collective engagement with David's work taught us to bring our whole selves to bear in our vocation. We learned to trust where vulnerability leads us, which is perhaps the most radical move a leader in contemporary America can make, religious or not.

Ken found another companion in this wholehearted journey in David of the Bible—a shepherd, king, musician, poet, friend, lover, and full-throated human. In this book, you will see David with a lens that opens fresh possibilities of being faithful, not perfect.

It's no wonder Ken feels such a kinship with the David of the Bible. He also is a man with many hats (and shoes and suits!)—a respected leader, mentor, scholar, father, husband, preacher, poet, pastor, outdoorsman, fly-fisherman, musician. He seems too good to be true. But I can tell you that Ken is also a welcoming, gracious, humble, and generous friend, and because of that, I forgive him his shining brilliance and am just grateful that he shares himself with me, and now, with you.

In his first book, *The Irrational Jesus,* Ken offered his doctoral research on decision-making and leadership in the church. In this book, *The Irrational David,* Ken dives deep and has "a real conversation," as David Whyte would say. He brings Scripture, philosophy, theology, poetry, literature, and psychology into a conversation that puts us all at ease because of Ken's profound vulnerability.

For those who are struggling to articulate a faith that is not either/or in the aftermath of the liberal/fundamentalist battles, Ken masterfully articulates a faith that honors the complexity of postmodern understandings in a way that is grounded and undefended. He doesn't let either side get away with defended polarities and invites us into faithfulness and wholeness instead.

My copy of this book will be full of underlining and coffee stains as I return over and over to see what Ken has to say about the text I'm preaching on. His words often say what I intuit, but am not yet able to articulate. As a gift to preachers, he brings along references from literature, history, and life that will make Scripture come alive week after week. This book is a trusted dance partner in the rhythm of life with God.

Rev. Jenny Warner
Pastor of Valley Presbyterian Church
Portola Valley, California

Acknowledgments

While poets and their words give shape to the world, even more are poets themselves shaped by the world. So many have influenced the person I have become and the words I offer. Chief among them is David Whyte. I wasn't quite sure what I was getting myself into the first time I crossed the sound from Mukilteo to Whidbey Island to join Invitas, Whyte's Institute for Conversational Leadership. Thankfully, I still don't and am loving the ongoing journey of discovery. David, you awakened aspects of my soul that had fallen dormant, invited me into real conversations, and encouraged me to step into the world, as you say, half a shade braver. Along with David Whyte, I'm grateful for the leadership team of Invitas: Libby (LFW!) Wagner, Craig Fleck, Mitch Saunders, and Maryliz Smith.

Of course, so much of the learning at Invitas happened among the cohort itself. Jenny Warner and Cyndi Wunder, here's to the three Presbyterian musketeers! Thanks also to Angela Bossie, Robin Bryant, Natalie Caine, Jonathan Cook, Sharon Connors, Casey Cummings, Matt Dockerty, Anders Engen, Ann Helmke, Libby Hoffman, Rory Holland, Jim Huling, Catherine Humphrey, Bob Lambert, Lori Lennox, Nicola McDowell, Sarah Steel, Jules Swales, Kate Woodland, and Bob Wright. You all inspired me, encouraged me, and pushed me—and I learned from each one of you.

But where would a poet be without a place to practice and grow? I continue to be head over heels for the great-hearted people of Tualatin Presbyterian Church. You not only allow me to be myself and try new things, but you demand it. So many of these poems were first heard in the sanctuary of TPC. Few places of worship welcome their pastor to experiment like this; few pastors have ever known a more nurturing pulpit.

I'm also incredibly grateful for the 2016 Duke DMin cohort, whom I have had the privilege of mentoring the past couple of years. Every afternoon together, when the last place you wanted to be was stuck in a classroom, you put up with my relentless onslaught of poetry. Sometimes you yawned. Sometimes you snapped. (OK, just Jennifer.) My hope is that some of it got inside of you and that you remembered to care for your soul while you were renewing your minds. I'm incredibly proud of your class and am thankful for each of you: Chris Aho, Jacob Buchholz, Jason Butler, Santino Cantalupo, Shameka Coleman, Shane Comellas, Fr. Craig Giera, Carol Harston, Julio Hernandez, Sarah Johnson, Uiyeon Kim, Logan Kruck (House Kruck!), Russ Lackey, Lesley McClendon, Amanda Olson, Yvette Pressley, Adam Shoemaker, and Jennifer Strickland.

Many thanks also go to those who took time to read and comment on the manuscript, offering invaluable feedback and suggestions for improvement. You helped me see where I could write more clearly and made the book better in every way. I'm especially grateful to Ashley Goff, Cyndi Wunder, Laura Everett, Sarah Moore-Nokes, and Eric Barreto. And finally, a huge and massive thanks to Jean and John Martin who really didn't need another book to edit and organize, but nevertheless gave tirelessly of their time and talent. This project would not have been possible without you. Thank you!

Introduction

In *The Irrational Jesus: Leading the Fully Human Church*, I made the case that behavioral theology, an interdisciplinary fusion of theology and behavioral economics, helps us to better understand Jesus' full humanity and our own.[1] Leaning on Dan Ariely's notion of people as "predictably irrational" beings, I explored how God created us with brains that perceive the world in two different ways: a fast, emotional system; and a much slower, rational one. We are, as psychologist Jonathan Haidt puts it, something like small, rational riders, sitting astride powerful, emotional elephants. Working through cognitive heuristics, or mental shortcuts, our fast, emotional brains send impressionistic summaries to our reflective, rational awareness. Sometimes these heuristics work well, and we can move quickly through our days, trusting we see the world accurately enough. But other times, especially when swayed by strong emotion or confronted with the specter of loss, these heuristics create blind spots known as cognitive bias, ensuring that for now we see through a very dim mirror indeed.

Cognitive bias, unlike other forms of bias such as motivational bias or racial bias, stems from how God made us through eons of evolution. Just as sighted human beings can't physically see a complete range of 360 degrees, fully human people can't avoid experiencing cognitive bias. But even though we can't avoid having blind spots, we can learn about them. Just as drivers of unfamiliar vehicles adjust their mirrors, we can use our awareness as figurative rear and side view mirrors to help us adjust for these biases. Given that God created us with blind spots, I argued cognitive bias isn't sin just as our inability to see through the back of our head is not sinful. This is simply human finitude, or limitation. It is how God created us to be. Sin, I would

1. Evers-Hood, *Irrational Jesus*, 79.

argue, is arrogantly pretending not to have these blind spots, or defensively refusing to listen to others when they point them out to us. Consider the conversation Jesus has with the Pharisees regarding the man born blind: "Some of the Pharisees near him heard this and said to him, 'Surely we are not blind, are we?' Jesus said to them, 'If you were blind, you would not have sin. But now that you say, "We see," your sin remains'" (John 9:40–41).

Looking back at *The Irrational Jesus*, I largely wrote about our predictable irrationality as something to be handled with great care. While I lifted out what Ariely refers to as the "upside of irrationality" in the sermons I shared and the section I wrote about game theory, Paul, and our irrational desire for fairness and justice, I was mostly cautionary about cognitive bias. To use the language of Harry Potter, I offered a Defense Against the Dark Arts Class, describing the various expressions of cognitive bias and how to ward them off. And this was important work that needed to be done. But learning how to avoid the traps of our irrationality is only one side of the equation for leaders. If we look again at Haidt's metaphor of the rider and elephant, we see that learning to adjust for our biases is a way of reasoning with our rider. This kind of humbling work, checking ourselves for bias, is incredibly important. But, reasoning with our rational riders is not nearly enough. Leaders must also learn how to sing to our emotional elephants.

Because of the way we are made, our fully human bodies respond to story, poetry, and music in ways prose can never touch. The emotionally cool language of logic and reason helps us tease through complicated, multilayered challenges. But it takes emotionally evocative language to compel us to action once a reasonable course comes into view. In terms of church leadership the difference between these two languages is easy to spot: it's the difference between delivering a paper about some interesting aspect of Jesus and preaching the good news of the open tomb. The paper might intrigue us, but ultimately, we will move on largely unchanged. A good sermon disturbs, challenges, and inspires us—working on us at a level octaves below the plane of our rational mind. To return to the world of Harry Potter, irrational leaders use language to cast spells to lift up our hearts, something along the lines of Hermione's levitation charm (Levi-O-sa, not Levi-o-SA!), at the same time as they reason with our minds.

[handwritten marginal note: irrational leadership]

When it comes to a fully human leader who knows how to reason with riders and sing to elephants, no biblical figure embodies this talent more than King David. As Baruch Halpern puts it in the fantastically titled *David's Secret Demons: Messiah, Murderer, Traitor, King*: "David, in a word, is human, fully, four-dimensionally, recognizably human. . . . He is the first human being in world literature."[2] On the one hand, David could be incredibly calculating. Just as George Washington established the capital in Washington DC as a compromise between Hamilton's northern hope and Jefferson's southern dream, David's choice of Jerusalem pragmatically balanced the desires of the northern and southern tribes. In his love life David's marriages with Michal, the daughter of Saul, and the wealthy Abigail were as (or more) strategic as they were romantic. David could even be strategic in his religious observance. The second David realized his display of grief and humility would not move God to save the first child he conceived with Bathsheba, he immediately moved on with life.

On the other hand, while David was often shrewd, he is probably most famous (and infamous) for his wild irrationality. Sometimes his deep, passionate nature led the people around David to hate him. When David brought the ark of the covenant into Jerusalem, he paraded before it like Mick Jagger, much to the disgust of his forsaken wife Michal. And in David's perhaps best known and lowest moment, his inability to control his desire for Bathsheba caused David to betray and murder Uriah, one of his most loyal soldiers—all in an effort to cover his sin.

But David's powerful emotion inspired deep love and loyalty, too. When David casually expressed his thirst for the waters of a well at Bethlehem, three of his warriors risked their lives to bring him a drink. In disbelief at their loyalty and sacrifice, David poured the water out as a sacrifice before God, unwilling to gratify his own desire at his men's expense. While today some may wonder if David was not dishonoring the men's sacrifice by pouring out their gift, Walter Brueggemann rightly notes: "In an act of simple majesty and nobility, David refuses to drink water secured at the risk of his men's lives, even though they went into risk in utter devotion to him. David's response is not one of rejection, but of solidarity. His act of pouring water out on the ground could have been read as refusal of the gift. But David's men knew better. They knew it was a sacramental act because words would fail to speak about the binding between them."[3]

And through it all David sings. David sings to Saul to soothe his darkest demons. David sings a lament over Saul upon his death. And while David clearly didn't write all the psalms (it would have been hard for David to write about the Babylonian exile in Psalm 137 when it didn't happen for another five hundred years), it does not mean that David didn't write any of them. I see no good reason not to accept David's hand in the great song book of the Bible. Yes, David knew how to strategize, but what makes him

2. Halpern, *David's Secret Demons*, 6.

3. Brueggemann, *David's Truth*, 116.

the amazing leader we still talk about thousands of years later is that he knew when to think and when to sing.

At the same time I was beginning to connect the Irrational Jesus with the Irrational David, I met another David who also knows how to sing. In the fall of 2015 and spring of 2016, I traveled to Washington's beautiful Whidbey Island off the coast of Seattle to study conversational leadership with poet David Whyte as part of the work of his Invitas institute. Conversational leadership, as I understand it from Whyte, hinges on being robustly vulnerable enough to show up and have real, courageous conversations with the people around us. How many times, Whyte wonders aloud, have you been part of a meeting where everyone talks around and over one another, but no one is brave enough to say what they really feel and think? (Yeah, actually, that's most meetings, isn't it?) The worst meetings, Whyte argues, aren't meetings that go off script or where conflict emerges. The worst gatherings occur when everyone is physically present, but no one actually shows up in any real or honest way.

Now, while David Whyte works with massive organizations like Boeing and NASA, I found myself nodding my head and thinking how relevant actually showing up is to congregational leadership, as well. Whether it's a pastor leading worship or listening to a couple in trouble, a congregational board facing a changing, daunting landscape, or a denominational leader caring for a congregation mired in conflict, all congregational leadership at some point comes down to showing up for real, honest, and sometimes difficult conversations. All congregational leadership comes down to people mustering the courage to show up with all we are and all we are feeling—and then sharing our real and honest selves with love.

One night when our group was gathered at David Whyte's house in the company of the "arrogant cooking pots"[4] hanging in his kitchen, I asked him why corporations like Boeing would hire a poet. I wasn't trying to be insulting. I was honestly curious. Now, I love poetry, but when I think of multinational corporations, verse doesn't spring to mind. With a presence and intensity only Whyte has, he asked me a series of rhetorical questions in his Irish-tinged lilt: "What's leadership but the ability to see things other people don't? Well, that's poetry, isn't it? What's leadership but putting this vision into language that cuts to the bone? That's poetry. What's leadership but being courageous enough to show up and say what you really think regardless of how you may be perceived? That's poetry."

And he had me.

4. Whyte, "Everything Is Waiting," 359.

I was already impressed with Whyte's presence, the power of his words, and his ability to recite not only his own work but Wordsworth, Dante, and Rilke. (Of course, Whyte recites Dante in Italian and Rilke in German.) Whyte's core conviction—that the poetic imagination isn't merely something nice yet ultimately unnecessary to organizational life, but the very ground for real life together—struck a deep chord in me. How can organizations move into new and more spacious ways of being unless someone first dreams what new and spacious might look like? And how can groups of people begin to negotiate these new pathways unless someone discovers words that are both true and stirring? In ancient Greek, the word *poieo* means to make or create. Through spending time with David Whyte, I understood in a new way how poets are the ones who see and by their seeing help create the conditions for others to walk into a new future.

One of the primary reasons King David captivated so many people was his sense of vision and ability to see things that others did not. David Wolpe, in *David: The Divided Heart*, paints this portrait of King David:

> David throughout his life is ever capable of enlarging the image, seeing perspectives that a more blinkered view cannot imagine. When it is clear that Goliath cannot be felled with armor and sword, he envisions another possibility. Later, when Saul's pursuit makes his continued existence in Israel impossible, he flees to the enemy. When Jerusalem is a backwater, he will see it as a capital; when worship in Israel is nomadic, he will envision a Temple. David's reputation as a musician and poet reinforces this quality; he is someone who does not follow the normal paths but brings into being, conjuring solutions and possibilities from the void: In the seventeenth century, English poet Abraham Cowley wrote in his epic *Davideis*, "From the best Poet, the best of Kings did grow."[5]

So, largely because of these two Davids in my life, I started integrating poetry into my own work on Sunday mornings in new and different ways. I have always loved and valued poetry in liturgy and have offered up a poem to open or close a sermon now and then. (Three points and a poem, anybody?) But for the most part I read these pieces rather than reciting them, and they were more garnish than meal. The way I saw King David and David Whyte living with poetry was something new to me. Poetry is not ornamental for them, something beautiful and tasteful to wrap up a sermon with a little literary bow. Poetry is the work itself. Poetry stops aimless conversations we've been having with ourselves for years with a powerful ruthlessness.

5. Wolpe, *David*, 13.

Poetry poses terrible, beautiful questions—questions that, as Whyte puts it "have no right / to go away."[6] In poetry, we encounter a presence that in the most subtle of ways slips past our defenses.

As a preacher, I started to see poetry as a way into the biblical text far below the level of the rational. I am grateful for the logical, rational, exegetical training I received in seminary, and of course I agree it is important to study the language, context, history, and scholarship of a lectionary text. But, particularly in my Presbyterian tradition, we are so good at reasoning with our rational riders, we have all but forgotten how to sing to the emotional elephants driving us underneath. In a brilliant and scathing piece advocating "incarnational language," preacher and poet Kathleen Norris is right when she laments the weak way in which so many church leaders use language.[7] Norris stands tall among the many voices who have helped me drop down below the level of the intellect over the years. Here are a few other voices who have encouraged me to unleash my emotional intuitions: Craig Barnes, *The Pastor as Minor Poet*; Bob Dykstra, *Personal, Pastoral Preaching*; Anna Carter Florence, *Preaching as Testimony*, and the poetry of J. Barrie Shepherd and Jan Richardson.

Indeed, through the poetic imagination I have learned that eisegesis, reading oneself into the text, is not only acceptable but a vital practice and impossible to avoid. Yep, I said it. I'm defending eisegesis, that most dreaded of homiletical sins. Eisegesis is simply how preachers, honest preachers anyway, begin. Of course, we should also practice exegesis and attempt to gain outside perspectives, but we cannot help but begin with ourselves. Because we are mysteries to ourselves, though, practices like poetry help us discover who and what we really are. To borrow the language of Rilke, in poetry preachers find a way to "go within and scale the depths of your being from which your very life springs forth."[8] Or, as David Whyte frames this dialectic in "Start Close In": "To hear / another's voice, / follow / your own voice, / wait until / that voice / becomes a / private ear / that can / really listen / to another."[9]

As a good Presbyterian I was taught to distrust my voice and intuition and rely on objective analysis of the text, lest I impose myself and distract from the Word. But while I value solid exegetical practice and the contributions scholarship offers in understanding the social, historical, and cultural nuances of the text, I long ago stopped believing that preachers should begin with this kind of logical, rational thinking. We should

6. Whyte, "Sometimes," 53.

7. Norris, "Incarnational Language," 699.

8. Rilke, *Letters to a Young Poet*, 12.

9. Whyte, "Start Close In," 360–61.

start, rather, with the irrational, emotional conversation that occurs when our curious, wondrous, imaginative selves encounter the text honestly, unsure where this meeting will lead.

In this book, I share some of the conversations I've been overhearing between the Scriptures and poetry, and some of the exchanges I've been having between the Scriptures and me and between me and the world. These are essays in the truest sense: attempts to find another's voice by listening closely to my own. Every poem collected here stems from a conversation between me and a scriptural passage or biblical narrative. I first offer a poem and then share how this poem intersects with my own life. You may hear something entirely different than I intended, of course, and I welcome your insight. But I have found great meaning in hearing the story of how poets stumble upon their words. Next, I draw out the biblical connection more explicitly and speak to the exegetical points of interest at which the poetry hints. When it's appropriate, I also lift out any theological truth the poetry and Scripture embody that may not be entirely evident upon first blush. Finally, I've structured this work around four aspects of King David's life: David as a believer; David as beloved; David as a beautiful mess; and David as broken-hearted. The first chapters in each of the four sections are short essays, which set up these four themes. For those readers familiar with *The Irrational Jesus*, the structure in *The Irrational David* differs significantly. These four aspects of David provide a thematic architecture that organizes my own poetry and interpretive work but are not always centered on either King David or David Whyte. So, while the essays that open each section focus heavily on King David, think of these pieces as jumping off points for further exploration.

My hope is that you will feel inspired by my irrationality and start writing and exploring the Scriptures in ways that honor your unique self and voice, too. It's not only good for the church, but it's life-giving for those of us with the gift and burden of preaching. It is the best way I have discovered to stay interested and engaged. One of the rules that has guided my preaching is if I'm not interested and passionate about what I'm saying, then why would anyone else be? Once, I heard Bob Dykstra lecture about being riveted by a Nobel prize-winning scientist, Barbara McClintock, give an amazing talk on corn. Corn. From this experience he learned that interesting people are interested people. Interesting people are interested people! Dykstra couldn't care less about corn, but he was carried away by this woman's passion. People in love with something, people who are passionate, engage us naturally. And people in love with something remain vital for the long haul.

David the Believer

1

David's Faith through Doubt
and Brokenness

For all his massive faults—and they are breathtaking—faith marks the
biblical portrayal of David from beginning to end. The most stable relationship in David's life is the one between him and God. Indeed, David
Wolpe points out that one of the few sins David appears to avoid is the
sin of idolatry, a fundamental betrayal of God. Wolpe writes: "Not only is
David free from the stain of idolatry, his relationship with God is steady and
assured throughout the story. A staunch believer and a worshiper, David
prays, offers thanks, and most importantly, hopes to build the Temple. His
being credited with the Psalms solidifies the traditional depiction of David
as the most devotional figure in the Bible."[1]

And yet, I bristle at the idea of David being some kind of superhuman,
"staunch," wizard of faith. Part of my bristling is personal, and part of it
comes from the faith expressed in the Psalms. While the songs of faith are
steadfast and resolute in the Psalms, they aren't devotional in any conventional, stained-glass, Christian bookstore kind of way. They are often dark,
raw, and riddled with apparent doubt.

Consider Psalm 22, a great psalm made even more famous by Jesus'
later remix: "My God, my God, why have you forsaken me? Why are you
so far from helping me, from the words of my groaning? O my God, I cry

1. Wolpe, *David*, 139.

3

by day, but you do not answer; and by night, but find no rest" (22:1–2). While it's true that Psalm 22, like other lament psalms, concludes on a note of trust, it's impossible for me to hear David's sense of being forsaken and unheard as a traditional expression of faith. Forsaken? No answers? No help or rest? These words express David's faith, but it is not how most people imagine someone with a staunch, devotional faith should sound.

Part of my seminary education included a stint at Robert Wood Johnson Hospital in New Brunswick, New Jersey, for something called Clinical Pastoral Education, or CPE for short. This unique "joy" entailed, in the first week, heading down to the morgue. While the young physician cut into the corpse on the table, he casually talked to us about his weekend plans. I was feeling okay about this encounter, until he actually lifted the skin from the deceased man's torso and placed it over the man's head like a grotesque form of peekaboo. Of course, he did this to expose the internal organs. "See that?" the doctor said, pointing to some dark yellow clumps. "That fat? That's the kind of fat you'll never get rid of no matter what you do. So anyway, what are you guys doing over the weekend?"

As horrifying as the autopsy was, it was just the beginning. CPE emphasizes listening and verbalizing feelings. One of the supervisors, I'll call him "Bill," would ask class members what they were feeling. After a while it became kind of game. Bill allowed for only four feelings: mad, sad, glad, and afraid. If you didn't come up with one of these words, or something very close, he would yell in his thick Jersey accent: "That's nawt a feeling! Whaddya feeling?" For me, after Bill's relentless accosting, the right answer about my feelings would have been a mix between anger and fear.

The hardest part for me personally was a colleague, a woman I will call "Greta." Greta arrived in America as a refugee from Hungary soon after the communist revolution there. She often led music for us in the chapel in the mornings. I'm not exactly sure what songbook she learned from, but I'm pretty sure the word "dirge" was in the title. They were the darkest, slowest, saddest songs I had ever heard in my life. One time, Greta and I were paired up to do these faith evaluations where we had to listen to one another at a deep level and then report back on how faith seemed to impact the life of our partner. When it came time for Greta to report on me, she proudly announced to the class: "Ken has an *unshakable* faith. He trusts in God and Jesus Christ always. He has no doubts, and his faith is just *unshakable*." Everyone in that group knew me pretty well at that point. And anyone acquainted with me knows unshakable is about the last word one would use to describe my faith. Most days, I have nine doubts before breakfast, and I am more than happy to share them with you. No, Greta said my faith was unshakable because that's what she believed it was supposed to be and probably what she desired hers to be. But unshakable is not how I experience faith, nor is it how I see David experiencing faith in the biblical account. The faith I know and read about in the Psalms is faith *with* doubt, rather than faith *without* doubt.

I am able now to agree with Wolpe that David's faith can be rightly called staunch, but not because it was unshakable. David knew periods of intense doubt where God felt absent, silent, and dark as night to him. Faith did not solve that experience or make it magically better. Rather, faith enabled David to name this darkness in song. The evidence of David's faith is the singing of the song itself—even singing about God's absence establishes a kind of connection with the Holy. This is the kind of faith I know and hear in David Whyte as well:

FAITH

I want to write about faith,
    about the way the moon rises
        over cold snow, night after night,

faithful even as it fades from fullness,
    slowly becoming that last curving and impossible
        sliver of light before the final darkness.

But I have no faith myself,
    I refuse it the smallest entry.

Let this then, my small poem,
    like a new moon, slender and barely open,
        be the first prayer that opens me to faith.[2]

2. Whyte, "Faith," 94.

2

Resurrection Is Not an Argument

Mark 16:1–8

RESURRECTION IS NOT AN ARGUMENT

For all of us with questions

Resurrection is not an argument
not an idea to which you might agree
or not and move on unchanged.

Resurrection is a weed
her roots cracking into concrete
finding a way where there is no way.
Resurrection is resistance
the thin man, white shirt
facing down four machines of war
vulnerability his only weapon.

Resurrection is the dwarf mountain hemlock
fighting through rime ice
growing sideways
stunted by howling wind
but growing anyway.

And resurrection is you
showing up one more time
to a place you don't understand
to a love you know you don't deserve
but bringing everything you have
hoping she is right
when she says you never disappoint.

Resurrection is not an argument.
It is a song sung in another tongue
that somehow still brings tears to flow
the warm hand finding your shivering shoulder
on the coldest night when you have turned away.
Resurrection is life
when all you know for sure
is the shadow of death.

THE STORY BEHIND THE POEM

I loved E. B. White's writing as a boy; *Charlotte's Web* and *The Trumpet of the Swan* were among my favorite books growing up. It came as a surprise later in life to learn White wasn't only a gifted writer for young people but a talented essayist as well. And, while a person of faith, White was also uneasy with belief. In his essay "Bedfellows," he discusses his concern regarding Dwight Eisenhower's advocacy for prayer. Arguing that a president should pray and be led by faith, White also thought presidents should not, at the same time, advertise for prayer either. He writes: "I hope that belief never is made to appear mandatory."[1] E. B. White, I think, was a man of faith, but he was a man who was nervous about belief, especially when the powerful seek to make certain beliefs unquestionable.

I feel the same way, and this has made being part of the church a challenge for me at times. The church so often becomes a place less of faith ("I believe, help my unbelief") and more of belief, spelled out in official creeds and statements that often feel less like guidelines and more like requirements. This is especially true of the resurrection.

For me the question "Do you believe in the resurrection?" is entirely different than "Do you trust in the resurrection?" When resurrection becomes a matter of belief, I can feel my curiosity, wonder, and intellect begin to shut down. I can feel the binary narrowness of *yes* and *no*. And I can also feel the threat implied by supplying the wrong answer. Do I trust in the resurrection, though? This is an entirely different question. Trust already indicates a certain level of unknowing. Trust is never required when you are absolutely certain about a matter. Absolute certainty in the resurrection means you don't trust it; you know it. So, asking me if I trust in the resurrection opens up my mind and heart. Asking me if I trust in the resurrection prompts me to wonder how I've experienced resurrection. Asking me if I trust in the resurrection causes me to reflect on where I've seen it in others.

A pastor friend of mine experiencing a period of doubt inspired this poem. He came to faith in an evangelical, theologically conservative tradition, attended a well-known conservative seminary, but then wound up drifting away from this mooring over time. In a way, his story is a reverse mirror to mine. I grew up in an extremely liberal family who loved Marcus Borg and John Dominic Crossan. While I continue to be grateful for this foundation, encountering thinkers like Karl Barth and Miroslav Volf pushed me toward a more complicated, centrist view. One of the things my

---

1. White, "Bedfellows," 107.

friend and I have bonded over is our shared joke that he was a bad evangelical and I had turned into a bad liberal.

At the time, we were part of a group that met weekly to talk about the Scriptures and preaching and what boneheaded things our congregations (or more often, ourselves) were up to. As Easter was fast approaching, our sights were set on the resurrection. But my friend was clearly distraught. How can you lead a Christian body with integrity when you have questions about this core truth? How do you preach on something you aren't quite sure you believe?

None of us around that circle were able to answer these questions, of course. We just sat with the weight of them pressing down upon us. My ultimate response is this poem. I've always been uncomfortable with the evangelical right wing that so often wants to treat the resurrection like a fact: the Bible says it, I believe it, and that settles it. But I've become equally concerned about projects such as the Jesus Seminar, which, in my view, elevates human reason above all else as if we can reason our way to faith. If the right is sure that the resurrection is a settled fact, the left seems equally sure dogs dined on Jesus' mangled body and we're all just celebrating a kind of wishful thinking.

Today I would say I trust in the resurrection. I trust in the resurrection not because we can prove it by belief or disprove it relying on scholarly criticism: for me the resurrection is true because we experience it. The resurrection is true because we have seen it.

Through natural imagery—a weed cracking through concrete or these absurd trees we have at the timberline in the Pacific Northwest, growing where the mountain and the wind clearly do not want them to be—I see hints of a vital power that will not be conquered by adversity or death. And through human imagery—the unknown Chinese man who stared down tank after tank at Tiananmen Square (ironically in Chinese translated as meaning "the gates of heavenly peace") and in my friend showing up to worship and lead when he wasn't quite sure what he was doing—I see a glimpse of resurrection.

One of the surprises for me in the poem came when the language of Psalm 23 invaded the last stanza. This was not something I planned on using in the poem, but I love this language. It reminds me of celebrating countless memorials at which we read and hear these words that both acknowledge the reality and the pain of death, but also the hope of a love stronger than death as well.

I believe E. B. White would have resonated with this view of the resurrection. White's wife, Katharine, was also a writer as well as a gardener. Katharine battled a terrible skin disease that finally took her life. One of her ways of coping with her illness was by putting her hands in the dirt and feeling the peace of her wild garden. In the introduction to her book, *Onward and Upward in the Garden*, E. B. White writes: "As the years went by and age overtook her, there was something comical yet touching in her bedraggled appearance on this awesome occasion—the small, hunched-over figure, her studied absorption in the implausible notion that there would be yet another spring, oblivious to the ending of her own days, which she knew perfectly well was near at hand, sitting there with her detailed chart under those dark skies in the dying October, calmly plotting the resurrection."[2]

E. B. White didn't believe in the resurrection. He had seen it.

THE SCRIPTURE: MARK 16:1–8

When the sabbath was over, Mary Magdalene, and Mary the mother of James, and Salome bought spices, so that they might go and anoint him. And very early on the first day of the week, when the sun had risen, they went to the tomb. They had been saying to one another, "Who will roll away the stone for us from the entrance to the tomb?" When they looked up, they saw that the stone, which was very large, had already been rolled back. As they entered the tomb, they saw a young man, dressed in a white robe, sitting on the right side; and they were alarmed. But he said to them, "Do not be alarmed; you are looking for Jesus of Nazareth, who was crucified. He has been raised; he is not here. Look, there is the place they laid him. But go, tell his disciples and Peter that he is going ahead of you to Galilee; there you will see him, just as he told you." So they went out and fled from the tomb, for terror and amazement had seized them; and they said nothing to anyone, for they were afraid.

THE STORY BEHIND THE SCRIPTURE

Mark's account is probably the earliest story of resurrection in the four Gospels, written around AD 70. I'll write more about how the Gospels came to be constructed later on in the book. The importance of Mark being the earliest account is that the original ending of Mark lacks a resurrection appearance. To spell that out a bit more: in the earliest ending of the earliest

2. White, "Introduction," xix.

Gospel, Jesus dies and the disciples are presented with an empty tomb. There is no witness of the resurrected Jesus himself.

Something pastors are taught but sometimes don't share with their congregations is that no one actually possesses the original manuscripts for any of the books of the Bible. There is no library you can visit, no museum you can enter to discover the original version of Mark or any of the other Gospels. Rather, what we have are thousands of scraps of papyri and other documentary evidence from different ages. In order to piece together a reliable Greek translation, scholars have to compare thousands of different scrolls, papyri, and manuscripts. Sometimes, when scholars compare these different versions they discover variances. Now, to be fair, many of these differences are tiny and insignificant. Some of them, such as doubled words and lines, make sense given that human scribes copied the manuscripts and sometimes made mistakes. But in the case of Mark, the appearance of additions feels like the product of a church anxious about a Gospel with an embarrassing lack of textual proof for the resurrection.

In the very earliest traditions, Mark's Gospel stops at verse eight with the women fleeing and saying nothing to anyone because they were afraid. As the years went by, however, the church began to "help" Mark out by adding first a shorter ending and then a longer ending. Even if we didn't have clear evidence from the age of the manuscripts, most people can tell just by reading these endings that they don't fit Mark's famously terse style. Listen to these words from the shorter ending of Mark: "And afterward Jesus himself sent out through them, from east to west, the sacred and imperishable proclamation of eternal salvation." Nowhere in Mark's Gospel when everything seems to happen "immediately" does this kind of language fit. No, in the earliest version of Mark's Gospel we get an empty tomb but no further proof of resurrection.

I love this. In Matthew, Jesus appears to the women at the tomb and says, "Greetings!"; he commissions the disciples on the mountain. In Luke, he crashes a dinner party at Emmaus in the form of an unknown traveler and eats fish with the disciples. And of course, in John he lets Thomas get handsy with his wounds. But in Mark the only thing we get is an empty tomb. This puts the ancient disciples on the same footing with us. Unless Jesus himself shows up during the service, we won't have his physical presence either. We get the empty tomb, we get stories about Jesus—and Mark implies that this is enough.

The most interesting thing to me is the way the text ends. The text literally ends with the Greek word *gar*, a preposition translated as "for." In Greek, as in many English classes still, one does not normally end a sentence with a preposition. In Greek, this is the equivalent of ending the sentence in the middle, as if the text ends with an ellipsis or a question mark. Some have argued a better ending must have been lost either because Mark was prevented from finishing his story or because the text itself was mutilated. But New Testament scholar Joel Marcus notes an open ending is much more in keeping with Mark's style and sensibilities. Marcus points out that Mark alludes to a resurrection appearance in 16:7, and that "allusion can be a more powerful mode of reference than outright description."[3] Indeed, to Marcus the effect is to actually put us, the listening congregation, into the story. He imagines the ending through the lens of a movie: "The women run away, disappear from the screen, and the sound of their rapid footfalls and terrified cries gradually fades away; but viewers are left confronting the awful mystery of the gaping tomb. Its open door confronts them, not with 'evidence that demands a verdict,' but with questions. What does it all mean? Why was all this suffering necessary? Does Jesus' empty tomb point toward a triumph over death, even while it acknowledges death's terrible reality? Does Jesus' absence from the sepulchre mean that he is present somewhere else, perhaps where his story is retold and heard with faith?"[4]

The resurrection story in Mark isn't something we can point to for proof of Jesus' rising from the dead. Rather, it is a story that envelops us in an experience the early church had where they saw an empty tomb and then had to decide how to respond. Hence, the resurrection isn't an argument to me. It's not a doctrine to which you can just check a yes or no belief box and keep moving. It's the great mystery of our faith that's both greater than our comprehension and best seen in everyday life when people say yes to life when they have every reason to give up.

3. Marcus, *Mark*, 1095.
4. Ibid., 1096.

3

Hints of Light

Hebrews 11:1–3

HINTS OF LIGHT

In memory of Verne and Pearl and Dorothy

They saw more clearly
by seeing nothing.
They listened more sharply
for hearing no sound.

If faith is walking into the dark
and trusting the ground not to give way
these saints hailed
from the holiest order.

He was the sign of skin and bone in hand.
She was the weight of warmth and heartbeat beside.
When little ones approached
hands searched hairlines
closed eyes, nose, and cheekbones
until the knowing smile spread
as sun breaks through cloud
"There you are!"

Without faces
without voices
they knew best by knowing nothing
and trusting all.

It is like this with every love.
It is so with each life.
We never possess the full picture
only the traces and hints of light.

THE STORY BEHIND THE POEM

My family hails from the little town of Mars, about an hour outside of Pittsburgh, Pennsylvania. (When people get to know me, it's as if this makes sense of the unusual character I can be. They nod and say, "Oh, of *course* your family is from Mars.")

My mom's dad, Ches (short for Chester) had six siblings with the best early 1900s names: Verne, Frank, Mabel, Dorothy, Ralph, and Bess. Both Verne and Dorothy were born with a genetic disorder called Usher syndrome, which meant they were born deaf and lost their sight due to retinitis pigmentosa in their twenties. The family somehow scraped up enough money to send Verne and Dorothy to this amazing school for the deaf and blind in Pittsburgh where they learned to sign and read Braille. It was there Verne met and later fell in love with and married a deaf woman named Pearl.

As adults, Verne and Pearl and Dorothy all lived in the little house just down the hill from where my mom grew up. My Great-Grandma Cashdollar, Verne and Dorothy's mom, lived with them as long as she was able. Verne kept chickens so there was always an abundance of food: eggs, homemade chicken noodle soup, and freshly-baked bread. Dorothy crocheted beautiful afghans. My mother treasures the memory of running down to visit Verne or Dorothy and standing still as they ran their hands over my mom's face. Then, their faces would brighten into this huge smile when they recognized her. They would say her name and declare how delighted they were to "see" her. There is something so intimate and fundamentally human about a person running their fingers over the features of your face.

My mom also remembers fondly all the deaf and blind friends of Verne and Pearl and Dorothy who came out to visit from Pittsburgh. They may have been blind or deaf, but they were people who really knew how to have fun.

Especially after my Great-Grandma Cashdollar was no longer able to live with them, Ches would check in on Verne and Pearl. Or Pearl would sometimes come up and let him know they were out of some things, and he'd take her in his car to the store and get whatever they needed. Passion for fairness and social justice runs deep in my family. My mom wonders if this personal experience with people who were often overlooked helped to form this passion. She remembers Ches was always proud of what they were able to do and never ashamed of their limitations. She can also remember him reprimanding her and her brothers if they ever called anyone "dumb" or any kind of epithet that had to do with disability. He told them they were fortunate to be smart and able, and they should use these gifts to help others—never to make anyone feel small.

One of the ways I was taught to think of faith is to imagine it as the trust that when you walk into a dark room that the floor will hold you. I was taught that faith presumes doubt and causes us to question. When Anselm described faith, he called it *fides quarens intellectum*: faith seeking understanding. Faith isn't just closing our eyes to reality and wishing everything will be okay, but an active, searching process of hoping and learning. Hoping and learning! Verne and Pearl and Dorothy, especially Verne and Dorothy who were blind *and* deaf, had to live that way every day. Every room they walked into was dark. But they kept walking, living, learning, and loving.

THE SCRIPTURE: HEBREWS 11:1–3

> Now faith is the assurance of things hoped for, the conviction of things not seen. Indeed, by faith our ancestors received approval. By faith we understand that the worlds were prepared by the word of God, so that what is seen was made from things that are not visible.

THE STORY BEHIND THE SCRIPTURE

Words shape our world. In his beautiful travel memoir *Travels with Herodotus*, Polish writer Ryszard Kapuściński writes: "I noticed, too, the relationship between naming and being, because I realized upon my return to the hotel that in town I had seen only that which I was able to name: for example, I remembered the acacia tree, but not the tree standing next to it, whose name I did not know. I understood, in short, that the more words I knew, the richer, fuller, and more variegated would be the world that opened before me, and which I could capture."[1]

For being such a big deal in the Protestant world, it's amazing to me how difficult it is for people to define the word faith. Often, when I ask people to define what faith is, I get a list of beliefs—as if being a person of faith is a kind of a fill-in-the-blank, standardized test. What's faith? Um . . . Believing in the resurrection? Believing in the Bible? Believing Mary was a virgin?

1. Kapuściński, *Travels with Herodotus*, 22.

This sterile, intellectualized version of faith has been with us for a long time. Calvin derides this popular understanding as "mere assent." For Calvin, faith isn't a platform of beliefs with yes or no checkboxes, faith is, and I quote: "A firm and certain knowledge of God's benevolence toward us, founded upon the truth of the freely given promise in Christ, both revealed to our minds and sealed upon our hearts through the Holy Spirit."[2] For Calvin faith isn't about opinions, but a deep, physical sense of God's love for us. Faith isn't something that just happens in our minds; it is something that happens in our hearts as well.

While Calvin's understanding is certainly an improvement on the popular check-the-box version, I do take issue with Calvin's use of the word knowledge. Greek has several words for knowing. The word *gnosis* gives us English words like diagnoses and ignorance. This kind of knowing carries a deeply embodied, even mystical kind of knowing. The Gnostics were an early Christian variant, melding Greek philosophy with Christian faith. They viewed themselves as having a kind of secret knowledge. Another word for knowing in Greek is *oida*. *Oida* is an ancient word coming from an Indo-European root *wid* that refers to seeing. If gnosis is the kind of knowing that happens when we sense or intuit something, *oida* is the kind of knowing that happens when we see or touch something.

Faith, though, is not a species of knowledge in Greek. The word for faith in Greek is *pistis*. The best way to translate *pistis* into English is the word trust. *Pistis* is not an act of knowing but an act of trusting—that sense of walking into a dark room not knowing the floor will hold you but trusting it will.

If it seems as if I'm splitting hairs, this distinction between knowing and trusting could not be more important. This is most evident when you consider the antonyms of these words. What is the opposite of knowledge? Doubt. If faith is treated as a species of knowing, then the opposite of faith is doubt. And if doubting is the opposite of faith, then faithful people shouldn't have questions. If the opposite of faith is doubt, then faithful people must be constantly certain of God and God's goodness all the time no matter what is happening in the world. And I . . . I don't know anyone like this if they are honest. The people I trust the most, the people I admire most for their faith are people who are full of questions.

Faithful people have doubts and questions because faith isn't a species of knowledge. Faith, *pistis*, is a kind of trust. And the opposite of trusting is the kind of rigid certainty of demagogues and fools who pretend to know more than they do. When faith is understood rightly as trust, then

2. Calvin, *Institutes*, 3.2.7.

the opposite of faith isn't doubt—it's certainty. In fact, faith implies doubt if doubt means not knowing everything. As the author of Hebrews says, faith isn't seeing. Faith is the conviction, the hope, of things not seen and unknown.

Leaders in my tradition must affirm a series of questions when they are ordained. Part of what we affirm is a series of statements known as confessions. One of the common questions I'm asked is what if I don't believe or agree with everything in there? I tell them faithfulness doesn't mean agreement. Melissa (I call her Melis), my wife, sees and thinks about the world very differently than I do. We disagree with one another a lot. She doubts some of the things I perceive and think and vice versa. Is this unfaithful? Of course not. Faithfulness means disagreeing with one another openly and honestly and respectfully arguing until we see something in a new way or just agree to disagree. In this sense being faithful to God or to a religious tradition doesn't mean agreeing all the time. It means hanging in there when things aren't making sense or feeling right. Faith always looks like the response of the father who asked Jesus to heal his seizure-stricken son: "I believe; help my unbelief!" (Mark 9:24).

I like Calvin's definition of faith, I do. But for me writer Frederick Buechner's definition is even better: "Faith is better understood as a verb than as a noun, as a process than as a possession. It is on-again-off-again rather than once-and-for-all. Faith is not being sure where you're going but going anyway. A journey without maps. Tillich said that doubt isn't the opposite of faith; it is an element of faith."[3]

---

3. Buechner, *Wishful Thinking*, 25.

4

It's Not About You. It Is About You

Luke 15:11–32

IT'S NOT ABOUT YOU. IT IS ABOUT YOU

This day, this ordination, your ministry.
    It's not. About. You.
It's not about you, but the God who lives, and breathes, and works
    in, around, and through you.
You're going to need to remember this
    on the morning you wake up and can barely crawl out of bed
because your faith, your faith in what you can do, in your gifts, will be dead.

Dead because no matter how many meals you serve
    how much hospitality you show
the hungry will still flow through your doors
    children of God needing more than you could ever have to give.
Dead because every time you preach, some "helpful" soul will say,
      "You're getting better and better. This time was OK!"
        And you'll mumble, "Thanks?"
            scratching your head as you walk away.

Dead because no matter how many times she tells you
    this time she's quit for real
part of you hopes, but another part of you steels for the next time
    she uses, comes down, and quits again.
Dead because you will wonder on that morning what's the point of it all
    if maybe you shouldn't have gone into insurance or law
where yes, you'd have more paperwork, but at least you wouldn't have
    to worry quite so much about where the demons lurk.

You are going to wake up on that morning and think,
    "No. Hell no. Not this. Not any of this. Not today."
You will feel like walking away
    to fantasize about Iona, India, or even Sherwood, Oregon . . .
        (given enough pinot or cabernet).

But on that day, you'll remember this day. This ordination.
    And your ministry.
        It's not about you, or me
but God and this impossible possibility of
    the Father, Son, and the laughter between them.
        The Holy Spirit
dancing in those the world has declared done
    already at work in the darkest places
        in wounds unseen by the sun.

This ordination, this ministry is not about you
    but the God of the prodigal, the father standing on the edge of the land
        head cradled in hand but his eyes never leaving the horizon
            scanning for the one, his broken, dead dog of a son
        who spent it all on wine, women, and song
            and when it ran out decided to move along
to move . . . back home. So he came up with a story, maybe even a poem
    thinking if he worked his words enough, spun them just right
        maybe he'd have some place warm to stay the night.

But before he could cry his fake tears and sing,
  his father's already seen him, already called
    for the fatted calf and the ring.
And when the boy opens his mouth to talk
  his dad just says, "Shut up. Shut up and walk. With me.
    Back to the house.
      Back home. Your home.
Where I have never. Stopped. Loving you."

Because this God, the one you serve, is the God who raises the dead
  and that will mean you, too
    on that morning you can barely roll out of bed.
So this day, remember
  it's not about you—but this Lazarus-hearted God instead.
And . . . yet. It's not about you? It is, a little bit, isn't that true?
  This day. This ordination. Your ministry?
    It is about you.
      All you've been through, and all you'll do.

Because there will come a moment on another day
  when a young kid will enter your office and say
he's confused, he can't remember how it started
  but now he can't make it go away.
He always liked girls, they were always his friends
  but now there's this boy and there's no end
to the places they go together, the time they spend.
  And he's beautiful, this boy—everything about him is beautiful
    his face, the way his lean body moves with grace.

But he knows they can't be right
  these feelings inside of him.
Maybe it's the devil, or some kind of sickness or sin?
Put them all on an island his dad would say
  better off dead than gay
and now that's all this kid can think about night and day.

Knife, gun, bridge, or pills.
Knife, gun, bridge, or pills.
But he can't even pick, and his self-hatred fills
        every minute, every hour.
Something has to give. He doesn't have the power
        to hang on for dear life anymore
                and so he's there at your door.

And you. You. This day. This ordination. Your ministry.
        It is about you. All you have been and all you will do.
And you will look at him with a love in your eyes
        a love stronger than the hate, stronger than the lies
a love born from your own struggle to stand
        and be yourself, your own God-created
                God-blessed gay man.
And that look . . . that's a look only you can give.

And you will rise up before him a lone holy angel
        announcing to him what no one else has before
that there's nothing here to fear—these feelings
        being gay, being queer?
And because of who you are
        what you have known and seen
the sadness you have swallowed
and your soul washed clean ten thousand times over
        ten thousand times again.
Because of your life this young man will trust you
        and grace will wash over him, too.
                And maybe
we will lose one less Tyler Clementi
        say one less prayer for Bobby.

This day. What we are doing here. It is about you . . . and it's not.
    And you will spend the rest of your days
feeling wonderfully caught between the two,
    sometimes not knowing what to do
but on your best days trusting that knowing that you don't know
    is the very best place to be
to follow after the one wild spirit blowing in your ministry.

THE STORY BEHIND THE POEM

When I first started at the church I currently serve, Tualatin Presbyterian Church, I was told I had to meet David Norse. David was a child of the church, having grown up there since the third grade. When I first met him, he was studying religion at Lewis & Clark College in Southwest Portland, ranked as the least religious school in America by The Princeton Review in 2009.

I liked David immediately, and we've been close ever since. He was interested in ministry but not entirely sure he wanted to be a pastor, which I took to be a sign of great wisdom on his part. So, we just started an open-ended conversation about ministry that really has never ended. I watched David serve our congregation as a deacon showing incredible kindness and a maturity beyond his years. He helped lead this wild youth retreat on the coast where we made art, floated candles on a lake one night, and wrote messages to God in bottles we tried to send out to sea. (I don't know if Sting is aware of this, but it's way harder to send a message in a bottle than I would have guessed.) David eventually made his way to Princeton Theological Seminary, struggled with Greek, traveled to the Iona community I don't know how many times, and then did this amazing summer field education program working with farmers in rural Japan. (Who *does* that?)

While all of this was going on, David was also wrestling with something else that not many people knew about: his sexuality. For a time David thought he might be bi-sexual, but ultimately he came to realize his identity as a gay man. And this, at least early on, was a challenge because the church we both serve, the Presbyterian Church (U.S.A.), was itself struggling with how inclusive to be of lesbian, gay, bisexual, transgender, and questioning people. I'm proud to say that today our denomination welcomes openly gay pastors and blesses same-sex marriages; but when David was discerning his call, those decisions all lay in our future. And it was anything but clear in those days that our church would be courageous and faithful enough to make inclusive decisions.

This is an extremely important issue to me personally and to our family because my older brother came out as a gay man in college. We grew up in Texas during the 80s, and needless to say coming out was a courageous act on his part. My mom became active in PFLAG (Parents and Friends of Lesbians and Gays), helping other families in Texas learn to love their gay and lesbian family members. In 1993 the pastor of the church I attended, Emmanuel Presbyterian Church, celebrated my brother's Covenant Ceremony with his partner. In 1993. In Texas! We were legitimately concerned about whether we would be able to safely honor their love with a public ceremony.

This witness shaped my faith in profound ways. I never questioned whether God loved my brother or blessed the lives of gay and lesbian people. That was always evident to me. I struggled more with whether I could serve a denomination that didn't recognize all children as equal in God's eyes. There were times, especially early on in my journey, when I was fairly intolerant of those I considered to be narrow-minded. Over time, while my commitment to LGBTQ inclusion has never wavered, I have mellowed enough to be a good pastor to families who want to love their gay kids but honestly don't know how to do this sometimes. And I was politically astute enough to know that David needed to walk a careful line when he was seeking to be ordained.

So, it was with the most intense joy that I received the news that David was going to be ordained by the Philadelphia Presbytery; he invited me to offer this charge on a cold, January night in 2014. Broad Street Ministry was the perfect place for David to follow his call, serving as Pastoral Associate, also known as minister for hospitality, to hundreds of people experiencing homelessness week in and week out. David's ordination was an incredible night that I will truly never forget.

THE SCRIPTURE: LUKE 15:11-32

Then Jesus said, "There was a man who had two sons. The younger of them said to his father, 'Father, give me the share of the property that will belong to me.' So he divided his property between them. A few days later the younger son gathered all he had and traveled to a distant country, and there he squandered his property in dissolute living. When he had spent everything, a severe famine took place throughout that country, and he began to be in need. So he went and hired himself out to one of the citizens of that country, who sent him to his fields to feed the pigs. He would gladly have filled himself with the pods that the pigs were eating; and no one gave him anything. But when he came to himself he said, 'How many of my father's hired hands have bread enough and to spare, but here I am dying of hunger! I will get up and go to my father, and I will say to him, "Father, I have sinned against heaven and before you; I am no longer worthy to be called your son; treat me like one of your hired hands."' So he set off and went to his father. But while he was still far off, his father saw him and was filled with compassion; he ran and put his arms around him and kissed him. Then the son said to him, 'Father, I have sinned against heaven and before you; I am no longer worthy to be called your son.' But the father said to his slaves, 'Quickly, bring out a robe—the best one—and put it on him; put a ring on his finger and sandals on his feet. And get the fatted calf and kill it, and let us eat and celebrate; for this son of mine was dead and is alive again; he was lost and is found!' And they began to celebrate."

"Now his elder son was in the field; and when he came and approached the house, he heard music and dancing. He called one of the slaves and asked what was going on. He replied, 'Your brother has come, and your father has killed the fatted calf, because he has got him back safe and sound.' Then he became angry and refused to go in. His father came out and began to plead with him. But he answered his father, 'Listen! For all these years I have been working like a slave for you, and I have never disobeyed your command; yet you have never given me even a young goat so that I might celebrate with my friends. But when this son of yours came back, who has devoured your property with prostitutes, you killed the fatted calf for him!' Then the father said to him, 'Son, you are always with me, and all that is mine is yours. But we had to celebrate and rejoice, because this brother of yours was dead and has come to life; he was lost and has been found.'"

THE STORY BEHIND THE SCRIPTURE

The story of the prodigal son carries enormous personal significance for me. My childhood was complicated by a troubled father with a volcanic temper who often terrorized our family and a mom who suffered from thyroid disease that presented as serious depression. In the midst of all this turmoil, my sixteen-year-old brother wrecked the family truck and sustained a life-threatening brain injury. He was in the hospital for weeks, couldn't remember how old he was or who we were for a time, had to relearn how to read and write, and still suffers from epilepsy due to his closed head injury. The older I get the more I realize how much trauma my family experienced when I was growing up.

After my mom and dad divorced and my brother had healed enough to actually enroll in college, I guess I thought everything in our home would settle down. I had assumed much of the emotional turmoil we experienced was due to my father's anger and my brother's medical needs. But when I turned sixteen, my mom and I were fighting a lot; there was as much tension in the house as there ever was. With the arrogance of a teenager, I decided my unhappiness was a clear signal that I was really the only sane one in my family so I decided I needed a change. I grew up watching M.A.S.H. with my mom, and sometimes we talk in what we call M.A.S.H.-speak. At one point Trapper John McIntyre just decides to leave Korea. He says to Hawkeye: "Hey listen, I don't like a movie, I get up and leave. I don't like the war. I'm going." Well, I decided to leave this particular movie.

So, in my sixteenth year, I moved in with the family of a girl I was dating. My mom was less than pleased with this idea, but chose not to fight it as long as I met with her once a week. At first, the move worked out exactly like I thought it would. The family I moved in with was quiet and stable. The dad had a good job with Motorola; the mom stayed at home. But as the days turned into weeks and the weeks turned into months, I noticed a disturbing trend. Some of the dynamics I hadn't liked at home—some of the tension and the fighting—started bubbling up between me and my new family. Even at sixteen I knew that I could keep blaming my frustrations on others, but as the only constant I just might have to think a little harder about my own role in the dynamics.

At the same time I was growing up a bit, my mom was also doing some growth work of her own. She had started to date an amazingly kind man whom she eventually married. My kids don't know my father, Larry, but they sure know "Grandpa John."

Nearly a year after I moved out, I met my mom for our weekly lunch. She told me she had something to say to me. I braced myself for her to tell me how painful my actions were and that I had to come back home. But she didn't. She said something I never imagined I would hear from her. She told me she loved me. She loved me, and that while it was hurtful for me to leave, she was going to choose love. She said if I never needed to come home, she would love me. If I decided at some point that I wanted to come home, that was fine, too. She would love me. It was the single most courageous act of grace I have ever known.

Around this time I was talking with my pastor and he was telling me about the story of the Prodigal Son. He asked me if I noticed that when the son finally gets hungry enough he heads home. On the way, he cooks up a story to try to weasel his way back into his father's good grace. The speech, while fantastic, isn't what does the trick. Before the boy even comes back, before he utters a word, the father is already on the horizon scanning the land looking for his son. Before the boy even tries to ingratiate himself back into his father's love with his rehearsed speech, the father is already loving him and calling for the ring and the fatted calf. I had never noticed the father's generous grace before, but now it's hard for me to hear this story without thinking of my mom and the grace she offered me. That was really the moment I knew whatever I wanted to do in my life, I wanted to do in service of this kind of love. Today I realize this story is quite honestly the reason I do what I do and forms the foundation for the person I have become.

5

The Spacious, Dim Ground
John 14:1–14

THE SPACIOUS, DIM GROUND

"Our situation today shows that beauty demands for itself at least as much courage and decision as do truth and goodness, and she will not allow herself to be separated and banned from her two sisters without taking them along with herself in an act of mysterious vengeance."[1] —Hans Urs von Balthasar

Sometimes truth is stingy.
Ten and ten will always be twenty
(unless you're being crafty).
And squares will be rectangles
but not all rectangles, square.
Even the vaguest relativist must finally find ground after
listing limply through cloud-crowded air.

---

1. von Balthasar, *Glory of the Lord*, Kindle location 186.

There is a diamond-hard beauty
in positivist certainty
but sometimes
sometimes the truth blurs, blends
and bleeds.

Truth can be a never-ending conversation
an afternoon walk of artistic contemplation
like when we sat with Monet's blind lilies
or lay down in love under Le Bonheur de Vivre.
You would never say I don't see what I see
or tolerate the same lack of imagination from me.
No, with art there's always more
there's the surplus of Ricoeur.

And so too it's this way with love
no one perfect person who meets every need
happily ever after a walking fantasy
but hundreds and hundreds of hot-hungry souls
all split, splintered, and marred.
Below the rhythm of our fractures, falling together and coming apart
beats the unceasing, unthinking animal-wild heart.

And with faith, the holy, it's the same.
The Tao that is the true Tao can never be named.
You must kill the Buddha you find on the road
because the path before you is yours alone.
And Jesus, the way, the truth, and the life? The gate?
Better a person the way than some church, creed, or state
for when it's Jesus and not the robes who guard the door
who is welcome but the broken, outsider, unloved
the overlooked, the poor?

Sometimes the truth is stingy
but in what matters most
she brings us to the darkness of Byron's beautiful night
beckoning us onto the spacious, dim ground
where I don't have to be wrong
for you to be right.

THE STORY BEHIND THE POEM

There are eight years and eight days between my older brother Rob's birthday and mine, and he shaped me in many ways. I can attribute my love for 80s music to him blasting Adam Ant and Men at Work in the bathroom next to my bedroom in the morning as he was getting ready for school. He honed my appreciation for practical jokes when he came home from college. One winter break our neighbor had this weird, duck wind sock. One night late my brother told me he thought that duck wanted to escape. For a week we moved that duck all up and down the neighborhood. At the Christmas Eve party our neighbor always threw in his pit BBQ (it was Texas after all), he complained to us that his damn duck had been moving all over the neighborhood. He said he knew we were good kids, but did we know if any of our friends had been up to no good. My brother and I suppressed our smiles and solemnly promised we had absolutely not seen any of our friends moving his duck.

When my brother healed enough from his car accident to start college, he attended the University of North Texas up the road from us in Denton, Texas. He started as a Radio, TV, and Film major but graduated with a degree in philosophy, ultimately earning his PhD. Somehow his undergraduate textbook on philosophy wound up on my shelf, and it blew me away.

I was particularly taken with the chapter on epistemology, the study of how we know what we know. While it seems self-evident to me now, up to that point in my life I had never considered that there were different kinds of truth. Exact, mathematical truth, for instance, is different than poetic truth. When Robert Burns sings that his love is a red, red rose, it makes no sense to evaluate that statement the same way as you would a geometry proof.

When it comes to faith, a healthy appreciation of the many varieties of truth is crucial. Indeed, ignorance of epistemology can be deadly. Religious violence in the world today is not an unchangeable by-product of diversity but the result of unarticulated understandings of truth that have nothing to do with individual faith traditions.

I open this piece with a quote from one of the best theologians no one talks about today: Hans Urs von Balthasar. A Roman Catholic contemporary of his more famous Swiss countryman, Karl Barth, von Balthasar deserves to be better known. One of his most interesting ideas is that religious truth isn't like propositional, mathematical truth at all; rather, religious truth is aesthetic. Religious truth is like visiting an art gallery with a friend. When two people take in a piece of art, each has an individual experience they might share with one another. But the fact that you see something different than your friend doesn't mean one of you is wrong. You would never gaze at Guernica with a friend and then argue with them and tell them how wrong they are if they experience different thoughts and feelings than you do. Rather, you listen to their perspective and come away enriched by their view even if you might not quite see what they are seeing.

It's laughable when you think about it, except, von Balthasar argues, this is precisely what we do with the Scriptures. The Bible itself doesn't come with reading instructions. We make decisions before we come to the Bible about how to read and interpret the stories inside, but most of the time our interpretive frameworks are assumed and unspoken. How many Bible studies have I sat through where people assumed the text had a single, correct meaning? Rather than read a text and offer their own perspective, they want to ask me what the "right answer" is as if such a thing exists. Unlike mathematical truth, when it comes to art and poetry, others don't need to be wrong for you to be right.

Philosopher Paul Ricoeur articulates the same thing when he says that texts, particularly biblical texts, contain a "surplus of meaning." That is to say, the cup of meaning found in texts is forever brimming over with possibilities. No matter how many times you read a particular Scripture passage and think you understand it completely, the text is always capable of surprising us.

THE SCRIPTURE: JOHN 14:1–14

"Do not let your hearts be troubled. Believe in God, believe also in me. In my Father's house there are many dwelling places. If it were not so, would I have told you that I go to prepare a place for you? And if I go and prepare a place for you, I will come again and will take you to myself, so that where I am, there you may be also. And you know the way to the place where I am going." Thomas said to him, "Lord, we do not know where you are going. How can we know the way?" Jesus said to him, "I am the way, and the truth, and the life. No one comes to the Father except through me. If you know me, you will know my Father also. From now on you do know him and have seen him."

Philip said to him, "Lord, show us the Father, and we will be satisfied." Jesus said to him, "Have I been with you all this time, Philip, and you still do not know me? Whoever has seen me has seen the Father. How can you say, 'Show us the Father'? Do you not believe that I am in the Father and the Father is in me? The words that I say to you I do not speak on my own; but the Father who dwells in me does his works. Believe me that I am in the

Father and the Father is in me; but if you do not, then believe me because of the works themselves. Very truly, I tell you, the one who believes in me will also do the works that I do and, in fact, will do greater works than these, because I am going to the Father. I will do whatever you ask in my name, so that the Father may be glorified in the Son. If in my name you ask me for anything, I will do it."

THE STORY BEHIND THE SCRIPTURE

This is one of the most quoted and least understood texts in the entire Bible. When I was growing up, people would quote "I am the way, the truth, and the life" as a short-hand way of saying that Christianity, namely *their* particular version of Christianity, was superior to other beliefs. Indeed, they would quote this as a way of saying Christianity was so superior there isn't even any room for other traditions at all—it's Christianity or nothing.

I get it. I do. If I just read this single verse, I can read the text in a way that makes it sound as if Jesus is making some exclusionary statement. But I can't hear it that way when I read the whole passage. When I hear the popular understanding of "I am the way, the truth, and the life, there's no way to the Father except through me," people seem to assume that the context is like a large stadium filled with the leaders of the world's great religions. There are six-armed Shiva saying Hinduism is the one right way. Then, the Buddha stands up shaking his head arguing that Buddhism is the one right path. Then Muhammad stands up. And so on and so forth until you finally get to Jesus who, with eyes blazing, pounds the table with his sandal saying, "*No*, I am the way, the truth, and the life, there's *no* way to the Father *except through me!*" And hey, maybe it isn't very politically correct for us to interpret it this way, but it certainly seems to be the meaning.

Except, Jesus isn't in a giant stadium full of the heads of the world's great religions. He's not even talking with leaders who didn't always agree with him like the Pharisees and the Sadducees. Who is Jesus addressing? The disciples! He's talking to the people who already believe in him, the people who have left their jobs and families to walk after him. And the disciples aren't saying to him that they are kind of on the fence about him, either. They aren't saying they're thinking of converting to paganism or becoming adherents of Mithras.

No, they are talking about Jesus going away. Jesus is leaving them. Jesus is telling them that he's going away and they know the way to the place where he is going. Except they don't. Thomas says, "Uh, Jesus? We don't know. We don't know where it is you are going, so how in the world can we know the way?" It's a fair point, really. Jesus tells them he's leaving them but that everything is going to be okay, and the disciples are pushing back on him saying they want him to spell this out a bit more.

All of us are like this. When the pastor says major changes need to happen and happen fast, the congregation will rise up and ask her how exactly she plans on this taking place. We like plans. We like feasibility studies.

But Jesus must have missed the day they taught project management because he has no interest in giving them details. He's asking them to trust him. So, when Jesus says, "I am the way, the truth, and the life," he isn't making a claim about Christianity. He's not talking about other faith traditions. He's responding to the anxiety the disciples have about Jesus leaving them. Jesus is responding to their desire for more certainty. And when he emphasizes that *he* is the way, he is tacitly telling them he is not willing to provide them with the details they are wanting. When Jesus claims to be the way, the truth, and the life, then all of our ways, our theologies, our interpretive schemes, are not. When Jesus says he is the way, the truth, and the life, he is telling the disciples (and us) that following him means we must trust him—something none of us like to do. No, it's easier to beat our chests and have jingoistic arguments about having a particular kind of faith. But it isn't what Jesus is talking about.

6

Forts and Fires

Psalm 139

FORTS AND FIRES

Forts and fires can never
be too big
said the dad on Cannon Beach.

He was dragging driftwood
to the delight of his son
grunting, if not gracefully
then gratefully, when he
finally laid its weight
atop his pyre.

Everything seems possible
on the beach
this flat expanse
when time and chance and tide
press without relent.

social

Dream castles drip
two-string kites rip.
Dogs and children run
beneath the gaze
of rocks weathered by wind and sun.

Here on the wings of the morning
at the farthest limits of the sea
over every tiny thing hovers the vastness of grace
love above and below, reaching into the depths of every hidden place.

Forts and fires can't be too big?
Why not something more significant?
What about desires, needs, loves, and pain?
Why so open in this place
only to return to life the same?

The difference between fleeting fantasy
and firm, fixed faith flows from facing
Sheol's inevitable, tidal pull of loss
and living fiercely still, knowing full well the cost.

THE STORY BEHIND THE POEM

In the Pacific Northwest where I live there are mountain people and there are ocean people. Mountain people are drawn to the hills and high deserts of the Cascades and Central Oregon. "Climb the mountains," as John Muir wrote, "and get their good tidings."[1] We wake up at two and three in the morning to get an alpine start to make the summit while the snow and ice are still intact. We climb through low clouds with little visibility until suddenly we break through the cloud line and look out and see Mount Jefferson, Three Fingered Jack, Mount Washington, and the Three Sisters in the distance like islands floating in a white sea. I am a mountain person.

Ocean people are different. Ocean people head over the rolling coastal range until they come to the very edge of the world, the place where Oregon basalt flows into surging Pacific. Ocean people sip Pinot Noir while the burning sun sinks into the western horizon. Ocean people warm themselves by the fire while the winter storm rages against the windows. Ocean people walk along the beaches at dawn, wide open tidal expanses where everything seems possible. My wife Melis is an ocean person. (Although, I will admit I am coming around.)

I wrote this piece during a getaway weekend to Oregon's Cannon Beach. We were coming back from riding these beach bikes with enormous fat tires that enabled us to sail over sand when I overheard a dad building this huge bonfire saying: "Forts and fires can never be too big." I thought, "That's a great line."

It made me think about how the ocean and the beach symbolize expansive, endless possibility. The ocean stretches as far as you can see. The beach is one enormous slate wiped clean every morning. My creativity always comes alive at the beach, and I can feel myself brimming with ideas.

What I wrestle with in the poem is the relationship between place and state. Why am I so creative at the coast, but sometimes have a hard time bringing this creativity back home? Is it the space itself? Are some places just more special than others? While the answer to most of us seems like an obvious yes, I ask this in light of Psalm 139, which emphasizes how God is present everywhere. At the ends of the earth, there God is. In the depths of Sheol, the ancient Hebrew notion of a Hades-like underworld, there God is. When we lie down and rise up, there God is. At one point the church I serve now displayed a poster depicting a scene of hardship and devastation with the caption: "There are no Godforsaken places."

I don't have an answer to this question. I do feel differently in the mountains than I do at the coast. Oklahoma really is different than Oregon.

1. Muir, *Our National Parks*, 53–54.

Paris, France, is an entirely different world than Paris, Texas. And yet, I also believe God is present in each of these places.

David Whyte, someone who knows well the value of travel, wrote a poem called "Leaving the Island," which I read to myself every time I left Invitas, Whyte's Institute for Conversational Leadership, on the ferry from Whidbey Island back to Mukilteo on the Washington state side. In the poem he speaks of becoming a larger, more beautiful version of ourselves when we travel. It's an invitation as well to ask the question: Are we escaping when we experience the privilege of these places, these travel destinations—or released from the ordinary, is our travel self who we are at our best?

Here are David Whyte's thoughts on the value of travel, excerpted from "Leaving the Island":

> Above all, the way afterwards,
> you thought you had left the island
> but hadn't, the way you knew
> you had gone somewhere
> into the shimmering light
> and come out again on the tide
> as you knew you had to
> as someone who would return
> and live in the world again
> someone granted just a glimpse
> someone half a shade braver
> a standing silhouette in the stern
> holding the rail
> riding the long waves back
> ready for the exile we call a home.[2]

THE SCRIPTURE: PSALM 139

> O Lord, you have searched me and known me.
> You know when I sit down and when I rise up;
>   you discern my thoughts from far away.
> You search out my path and my lying down,
>   and are acquainted with all my ways.
> Even before a word is on my tongue,

2. Whyte, "Leaving the Island," Kindle locations 438–43.

O Lord, you know it completely.
You hem me in, behind and before,
    and lay your hand upon me.
Such knowledge is too wonderful for me;
    it is so high that I cannot attain it.

Where can I go from your spirit?
    Or where can I flee from your presence?
If I ascend to heaven, you are there;
    if I make my bed in Sheol, you are there.
If I take the wings of the morning
    and settle at the farthest limits of the sea,
even there your hand shall lead me,
    and your right hand shall hold me fast.
If I say, "Surely the darkness shall cover me,
    and the light around me become night,"
even the darkness is not dark to you;
    the night is as bright as the day,
    for darkness is as light to you.

For it was you who formed my inward parts;
    you knit me together in my mother's womb.
I praise you, for I am fearfully and wonderfully made.
    Wonderful are your works; that I know very well.
My frame was not hidden from you,
    when I was being made in secret,
    intricately woven in the depths of the earth.
Your eyes beheld my unformed substance.
    In your book were written all the days that were formed for me,
    when none of them as yet existed.
How weighty to me are your thoughts, O God!
    How vast is the sum of them!
I try to count them—they are more than the sand;
    I come to the end—I am still with you.

O that you would kill the wicked, O God,
    and that the bloodthirsty would depart from me—
those who speak of you maliciously,
    and lift themselves up against you for evil!
Do I not hate those who hate you, O Lord?
    And do I not loathe those who rise up against you?
I hate them with perfect hatred;
    I count them my enemies.
Search me, O God, and know my heart;
    test me and know my thoughts.

See if there is any wicked way in me,
and lead me in the way everlasting.

THE STORY BEHIND THE SCRIPTURE

There are so many things I love about this psalm. Mainly, I love the pervasive sense of God's presence. On the door to my office rests a plaque modeled after the one Jung hung on his door: *vocatus non vocatus deus aderit* (summoned or not, God is present). Kind of like how *X-Files* Agent Fox Mulder hung an "I Want to Believe" poster in his office to affirm the possibility of UFOs, the best and deepest parts of me believe these "God is present" words wholeheartedly.

In the Pacific Northwest among the mountain people and ocean people, there aren't a whole lot of church people. We are very suspicious of organized religion where I live, and I can understand this distrust. Historically, the church has been responsible for senseless brutality, forced baptisms, sexual abuse, and the hair styles on the Trinity Broadcasting Network. So many people I know say they can visit with God just as well walking along a soft, fir-needle-lined path as they can sitting in a stuffy church building. And there is definitely truth to this sentiment. God can be found in the world. No question. But one of the things I love about congregational life— one of the best kept secrets—is that faith is better as a team sport than a solo adventure. I've told my congregation many times that the reason we say prayers collectively during the liturgy is not to brainwash people or put words in their mouths they neither understand or agree with. We say the prayers together as a way of praying with and for one another when we've lost the ability to believe. When I wake up on Sunday morning and feel as if God is quite dead and all this business about Jesus is just wishful thinking, I need my brothers and sisters to surround me and believe with and for me until I can believe again. And then, when I am full of faith, I can do the same for them. So, God is everywhere, as the psalmist sings, but for me this includes the church as well as the mountains and the coast.

Another thing I love about this psalm is the term Sheol, which is a fairly unfamiliar word to folks for as often as the Scriptures mention it. Sheol represents an ancient Hebrew understanding of the afterlife. One of the amazing misperceptions of Holy Scripture is that they a) agree on everything, and b) tell a consistent story about heaven, hell, and everlasting life.

In fact, I tend to use the term "the Scriptures" rather than "the Bible" to acknowledge that the Bible is really more of a library than a book. The books of the Bible were written over an incredibly long period of time and were shaped by hands too numerous to count. They were written in ancient languages and use arcane words and images, the meaning of some of which are lost to even the brightest scholars today. Ideas such as the afterlife change over time, and the Scriptures reflect this.

Sometimes I think of the Scriptures as an archeological dig: the different layers showing us different glimpses into the past. Sheol shows us an extremely early view of the afterlife. The ancient Hebrews didn't believe in a heaven above with clouds and harps and a fiery hell below with a red devil brandishing a pitchfork. The ancient Hebrews believed you died and that was it. When people died, everyone—the good, the bad, and the ugly—all went to Sheol, or the pit. Perhaps due to the tribulations the Jews endured and the influence of dualistic faiths like Zoroastrianism, in the first century when Jesus was alive some people still believed in Sheol while others articulated a final judgment. Jesus himself uses the Greek term Gehenna for hell. Gehenna is an actual place, a valley outside of Jerusalem where the trash was sent and burned. While some apocalyptic literature started to imagine tours of heaven and hell, the three-tiered notion that still has influence today didn't exist until long after the Scriptures were written. Revelation itself ends not with the destruction of the earth as the *Left Behind* people wrongly think, but with a restoration of the earth. Revelation ends with a vision of heaven coming down adorned like a bride to exist here on earth as the new Jerusalem. Of course, what's more important than anything else about Sheol in Psalm 139 is that even in this place, even in this shadow land, God is present.

Finally, the last thing I want to lift up about the psalm is what is ironically left out in most services of worship. When people read Psalm 139 in worship, nearly everyone cuts out verses 19–22 where the psalmist kind of snaps and talks about hating the enemies of God with a perfect hatred. One of the things I love about the Psalms, and this one in particular, is how we see our full humanity in the psalmist. We see the whole range of human emotion—from the lofty emotions of which we're proud to these dark feelings of rage we'd like to pretend we don't experience. Except we do. In a psalm that sings of God being everywhere, I am grateful that God is present even in the darkest parts of my heart that do, from time to time, feel hatred. I am even more grateful that, as Andy Dearborn at Austin Presbyterian Theological Seminary once said: "Not every verse in Scripture is a go and do likewise." We can read these words and feel these feelings, knowing that we are not to act on them but resting in the assurance that God is still present.

7

The Conspiracy
Psalm 141

THE CONSPIRACY

*For Professor Warren Smith of Duke Divinity School who reminds us
to keep looking beyond the realm of appearances for the Good, for the
Holy One of Israel who abides with us invisibly but not imperceptibly*

↳ how does
God abide
with you?

The web glistens
wet in morning dew
once invisible lines
now heavy, dripping
for all the world to see.

These slender threads
look like nothing
but they are
stronger than steel
strong enough to hold
up life and even
death itself.

Is it like this with prayer?
What weight could these
mere words bring to bear
on a world bent on blood
and hatred?

And what are we doing
lifting these pitiful pleas
into an empty night? Please.
And yet as incense rises, seemingly dissipating
disappearing into nothing
though unseen this smoke still
covers the whole house with
her purple canopy of scent.

And these fragile words weave
into one the broken
pieces of the world
and join together the
fractured shards of your life.
To pray is to join in the conspiracy
against the tyranny of the visible.
To pray is to risk remembering
that you are never alone
even when there is no one
else in sight.

THE STORY BEHIND THE POEM

This poem came to me during Holy Week in 2017. The community I serve generally celebrates Maundy Thursday, Good Friday, and Easter Sunday. Occasionally, we have observed the full Triduum by adding a Holy Saturday service as well, but we've been leaving Jesus alone in the tomb on Saturday the last few years. Holy Friday, and to some degree Easter morning, are all fairly scripted events. My predecessor crafted a beautiful Tenebrae service full of word and action for Good Friday evening that I have been more than pleased to honor. It's a powerful, dramatic service: someone snuffs out the candles and shrouds the communion table; I slam shut the pulpit Bible and cover the lectern; another member drags in a heavy wooden cross, throws it down, and pounds spikes into it; and we hear the cry of dereliction wailed into the darkness. And for Easter we overcompensate for the mystery and darkness of the empty tomb as most congregations do with a boatload of special music and flowers. Don't hear me wrong. I'm not complaining. But there is a part of me that feels as if the joy of Easter morning is a bit forced in comparison to the confusion and shock so evident in the resurrection narratives.

Maundy Thursday, on the other hand, provides space for much more creativity. While I admit that some years planning this service can feel like "one more thing to do," for the most part I love the freedom to experiment. We have celebrated foot washing per Jesus' command. We have walked labyrinths both large and small. One year we rented a labyrinth large enough to fill our sanctuary, but most years now we have three smaller labyrinths painted on canvas large enough for two or three people to walk at a time. I remember the first year we used these small labyrinths in Maundy Thursday worship. My instructions were clear: allow the person in front of you to make it to the center before entering. One older couple, Glenn and Maxine, walked in together, holding on to one another as they slowly made their way around the winding path. What none of us could know at the time is that it would be their last spring together. They didn't do what I asked them to do. They did what felt right instead. They walked that labyrinth as they walked through their lives together: side by side.

For this particular Maundy Thursday, I created a slew of prayer stations. After remembering the last supper and celebrating communion together, people were free to choose among the stations: some walked labyrinths, some lit candles, and some wrote prayers and pinned them up to the wall. Others approached our translucent, Turkish alabaster baptismal font and picked up a dark river rock, a symbol of something heavy in their lives. Then, they placed the dark rock into the waters—along with whatever was heavy on their hearts—and exchanged it for a bright, colorful stone to carry with them the rest of the year. This year one woman told me how thankful she was that we were repeating the river rock ritual because she had misplaced her colorful stone from last year—it had been more meaningful to her than she had expected. Still others approached the station where I waited with a tincture of holy oil I picked up during a pilgrimage to Israel. Making the sign of the cross on their foreheads, I offered these words: "Instead of the ashes of mourning, receive the oils of gladness, and may you know faith, hope, and love."

Standing off to the side at my holy oil station provided me with the gift of just watching the congregation I serve engage in prayer. When people approached, of course, I focused entirely on them; but in the moments in between anointing, I was able to watch people embody their prayers in a way I always find powerful beyond words—even more so this year.

The election of Donald J. Trump in 2016 created challenges for me as a pastor I could never have anticipated at the time. Deeply troubled by Mr. Trump's comments about women and people of color, along with his triumphalist, militarist rhetoric, I grieved personally when he won. Like others I know, I had to turn off NPR for weeks just to give myself space to heal. What I didn't realize, though, is that the most difficult aspect of the election wasn't personal but professional. Since the election of our forty-fifth president, pastors all over the nation have struggled to speak to once peaceful congregations now experiencing fresh lines of division.

The congregation I serve, for example, Tualatin Presbyterian Church? I would say we lean left politically, but we are anything but homogeneous. Ask ten people in my congregation a question, and I guarantee you will get thirty different answers. And before the 2016 election, I absolutely loved this diversity. It's been more painful in the aftermath, however. I would estimate about ten percent of the people I serve probably voted for Mr. Trump. To my knowledge I don't have any uber-Trump people, but these folks voted for him out of historic Republican loyalty or because they saw him as the least worst candidate, which I absolutely honor and respect. These folks did not want to hear me say anything about the election. For them it was done. As one person put it to me: their team won; our team lost; get over it. About forty percent of our congregation, however, was just wrecked after the election. They wondered what would happen to our world and our children's world. They expressed concern about healthcare, the environment, and the list goes on. For these people, if I wasn't addressing the political situation, then I was just mouthing unacceptable, sweet nothings from the pulpit. These folks were hungry for a word that connected with the world. And then, I would say the remaining half of our congregation were deeply unsettled, but they also desired healing for the nation and were greatly concerned by our growing divisions. They really just wanted me to tell them everything was going to be okay.

I know how to preach to each of these separate congregations; I have no idea how to preach to them all together in the same room.

Several years ago we lost a little, three-year old girl in our community; she choked on a meatball at her preschool and emergency personnel could not save her. My younger daughter was in her class. Our congregation hosted a community meeting that created space for fire and rescue workers and the preschool staff and parents to debrief after the tragedy. And a few days later, we celebrated her life—with her heartbreaking, four-foot long, pink casket. My congregation didn't know this family. This family didn't attend our church. They didn't attend any church. But when my congregation heard what happened, people came out of the woodwork to make food and prepare the sanctuary with boxes and boxes of Kleenex. They were amazing. We were grieving, and we were grieving together. Our grief brought us close.

I have realized this year, and I write this as we are marking the first one hundred days of President Trump's leadership, the community I serve is grieving again. Only now, our grief is splitting us apart. The grief isn't as sharp as it was in the beginning. Some healing has occurred. But it's still there.

On that Maundy Thursday early in 2017, one of the things I saw and felt in my body was the power of prayer to connect us with God and connect us with one another. We prayed for the world on Maundy Thursday. That very day our military dropped the largest conventional bomb ever used in combat: the mother of all bombs. We prayed for world leaders. We prayed for allies. We prayed for enemies. We also prayed for our community and for our families. We prayed for the people we loved and for the people that were causing us great pain. I will admit there have been times in my ministry when I have wondered about the point of prayer. I have asked myself what we are accomplishing when we lift these petitions into what can feel like a very empty sky.

But not that night.

That night, these words of prayer—spoken, written, and silent—surrounded us and covered us. I felt myself being re-woven into community with the people I love and serve. And the image of a spider web came to me. Particularly in the fall when I walk my kids down to their bus stop in the morning, spider webs, invisible during the day, become beautifully apparent in the morning dew. I have often stopped and marveled at these creations—so delicate, and yet so powerful and strong. That is what prayer felt like to me on Maundy Thursday 2017. Our words and phrases can sometimes feel so weak, so thin. But that night, when combined together, when woven into a fabric, I was reminded that God is God, and we most certainly are not.

THE SCRIPTURE: PSALM 141

I call upon you, O Lord; come quickly to me;
    give ear to my voice when I call to you.
Let my prayer be counted as incense before you,
    and the lifting up of my hands as an evening sacrifice.

Set a guard over my mouth, O Lord;
    keep watch over the door of my lips.
Do not turn my heart to any evil,
    to busy myself with wicked deeds
    in company with those who work iniquity;
    do not let me eat of their delicacies.

Let the righteous strike me;
    let the faithful correct me.
    Never let the oil of the wicked anoint my head,
    for my prayer is continually against their wicked deeds.
When they are given over to those who shall condemn them,
    then they shall learn that my words were pleasant.
Like a rock that one breaks apart and shatters on the land
    so shall their bones be strewn at the mouth of Sheol.

But my eyes are turned toward you, O God, my Lord;
    in you I seek refuge; do not leave me defenseless.
Keep me from the trap that they have laid for me,
    and from the snares of evildoers.
Let the wicked fall into their own nets, while I alone escape.

THE STORY BEHIND THE SCRIPTURE

I have always been drawn to this metaphor of prayer as incense. In *Seeing the Psalms: A Theology of Metaphor*, Bill Brown writes: "Rife with the language of analogy and anomaly, the Psalter is the schoolhouse of incarnational imagination."[1] This sense of prayer spreading throughout a space and

---

1. Brown, *Seeing the Psalms*, 13.

infusing the room with beauty and a sense of mystery speaks deeply to me. And if I'm honest, at least one time it got me into trouble.

When I was in college I partnered with a friend of mine, Jim Langford, to teach a summer class on centering prayer to the youth of my local church. Jim Langford and I had a relationship forged in adventure. In high school when I realized that just not being like my father wasn't quite the same thing as knowing what kind of man I wanted to be, I stumbled upon an abundance of fathers all hiding in plain sight. Jim was one of these men.

One year Jim posted an advertisement for a mission trip to New Mexico in the church newsletter. The article was short on details: it didn't really say who was going, what we would be doing, or why. It did state the dates and the destination. Well, the dates fell on my spring break. All I needed to know was that it was Jim Langford and spring break, and I was in. In one of those beautiful moments of serendipity, John Martin, the man whom my mom would eventually marry and would really become my father, was the one other person who responded.

So, on a cool, spring Texas Monday morning we loaded up John Martin's Honda station wagon and headed off for New Mexico. The mission, such as it was, was to dig out the floor of a Navaho hogan so that more (and taller) family could move in with the diminutive grandmother who had been living there by herself. Rather than build a new structure with a higher roof, it was just easier to dig out the dirt floor. Talk about an adventure!

One day I went hiking and discovered that mountain distances are deceiving and New Mexico weather is fickle. I was finally headed back through a driving sleet storm only to find my return blocked by a herd of longhorns with massive, life-threatening horns. While I was wandering through my bovine nightmare, Jim and John were helping one of the Navajo guys retrieve his vehicle—a truck in need of serious repair. To compensate for the broken back axle and missing wheels, they lashed logs as skids in place of the back wheels. What could go wrong? John was in the front truck and Jim was in the back one, madly trying to keep the two-wheeled thing steering straight. I could see them coming a mile away, fish-tailing through a cloud of dust.

Then, when we were finished with our mission project and headed back, we stayed at this desolate state park in the Texas panhandle. It looked like a post-apocalyptic wilderness with no trees and seemingly no people, but at one point this man turned up out of nowhere. Like something out of a David Lynch movie, this guy with a crazed look on his face asked us if we had seen his bucket: "Pardon me," he said in a raspy voice, "Have you seen my yellow bucket?" To this day if something seems strange, my family will repeat this phrase with a chuckle.

One of the things Jim brought back from that trip was pinion pine incense, the very smell of New Mexico to us. And the class on centering prayer that Jim and I were leading for the church youth? I taught the kids about the hesychasm tradition in Eastern Christianity, the Jesus Prayer, and centering prayer. At one point we tried centering prayer as a group. Jim lit some of the incense as we all sat together, breathing deeply and keeping silence. The smell of the incense filled the room. Apparently, it filled more than the room. The associate pastor, who had no idea what our curriculum involved, barged in. He looked at Jim and me exclaiming, "Is something on fire?" Jim and I explained calmly—we were meditating after all—about the incense. For some reason we weren't asked to teach the youth class again after that summer.

8

The Table

Matthew 16:21–28

THE TABLE

For Rob and Jennifer

Who are they? These two
huddled together in the pooling
lamplight while darkness
gathers around the table
their evening interrupted
by phone call's cry
interrogated by a question
that would not wait.

As a family they had
made so many plans
carefully accounted for
so many variables.
But there is no calculus
no engineering process
for this opaque, blank wall
this question staring them down
and no way to their future
now except by having
a real conversation.

An hour to decide
that's all they were given.
An hour to decide a lifetime
a lifetime of sidelines, recitals, and mountain tops
and, one day, walking his girl, somehow now
all grown up, down the aisle
sending her into the arms of her new life
just as they both once had walked.

When I saw them slide
their answers, carefully written, face down
across the smooth, wooden grain
I saw who they were.
I recognized them at once.
They were Moses turning
aside to see, choosing to face
the mystery instead of looking away.
They were Abraham and Sarah
leaving everything and everyone
they ever knew, carried along
by the slender thread of a single promise.
They were the bleeding woman
who dared to grasp the master's mantle
her faith the faith that made her well. Her
faith the faith that made her well.

And they are you
every time you step into the unknown
and discover once again
that you are well able
your courage enough
to carry you through this
conversation and the ones to come
again and again and again
around this ancient table.

THE STORY BEHIND THE POEM

In *The Irrational Jesus: Leading the Fully Human Church*, I chronicled an incredible decision members of the church I serve had to make. Rob was born with primary sclerosing cholangitis of the liver, a disorder in which the ducts leading to the organ were too small for proper function. As he grew older, Rob's liver became progressively more damaged. By the time I met Rob, the illness was quite serious, and he was placed on Oregon's organ transplant list.

It was painful to watch Rob's health decline. A prolific hiker and climber, Rob was the first person to really introduce me to the raw beauty of Oregon's wilderness. The first summer I moved here Rob took me and my black lab, Rigby, on the Timberline Trail that circumnavigates the Mount Hood wilderness. Starting out at Timberline Lodge, we passed through old-growth forests sheltering the black basalt of Ramona Falls, hiked through the alpine meadows of Paradise Park, crossed raging rivers swollen from melting glaciers, and traversed the trackless moonscape of the mountain's east side. Rigby received her trail name on the first night. An inside dog, she woke up shivering uncontrollably. Not knowing what else to do I pulled her into my tent and wrapped her in one of those silver emergency blankets. It did the trick. In the morning we woke up to see her little black nose poking out of this thin, silver material and "Jiffy Pup" was born. So, watching anyone grow sicker from an illness is painful, but with Rob it was personal.

One night Rob and his wife Jennifer were sitting together when the phone rang. It was the hospital. They had a liver that was a match for Rob. But there was a problem. Ideally, the best organs for transplant occur as a result of brain death. With brain death the heart continues to function un-interrupted so that organs receive all the oxygen they need to stay healthy. This liver came as a result of a donor experiencing a cardiac event, which means that for at least some period of time the organs were deprived of oxygen—how long, though, no one knew. Moreover, the physicians would not be able tell whether the liver was damaged. It was quite possible, they said, if Rob accepted this liver that it would fail, leaving him weaker than before. Oh, and by the way, they had mere hours to decide, or the hospital would move to the next possible recipient on the list.

I included Rob's story in my first book to highlight the decision process that Rob and Jennifer adopted. They both wanted each other to be honest, but they also both understood how easy it would be to be swayed by the other. If one of them signaled a strong feeling early in the process, it would be difficult not to be moved by that. So, they agreed to write what they thought was the best decision down on a piece of paper. Then, sliding these papers across the table to one another, they were able to discover the other's true thoughts at the same time. In *The Irrational Jesus*, although I acknowledged how personal the decision was, I purposely stepped back and took a more analytical approach. I noted how they intuitively agreed on how much process to use, since too much process can be as harmful as too little. I saw how writing down their thoughts slowed down the process, helping them avoid the harmful effects of loss aversion and affect bias. I also observed that they didn't pull too many other voices into the decision, given that too many opinions can actually make it harder to make a good call. While all of that analysis is good, it doesn't begin to touch the more powerful, emotional, human element of choosing to show up and make a life or death decision in the face of the complete unknown.

Psychologists tell us we make around ten thousand decisions a day, but the vast majority of these decisions are insignificant and ask little of us. What are we going to wear today? What do we want to have for lunch? These small, quotidian decisions provide us with the false sense that we have more control than we really do. The stark reality of life is that we are fragile, radically contingent beings and our lives hang upon innumerable forces beyond our control. There is a practical element to our illusions, of course. If all of a sudden we were to realize all of the ways life could go sideways for us and the people we love, most of us would head to bed, pull the covers up, and never emerge again. But the difficult truth is, for each of us, our lives can come crashing down with a single word or unexpected phone call. When those moments come, and they will for each of us, what's critical then is the ability to accept our fundamental lack of control, show up in the moment, and be present to whatever might occur. Given how much time we spend believing in our own abilities and how little time we practice being present in our vulnerability, it's a wonder to me we're able to face these moments at all.

This is why Rob and Jennifer's story is so compelling to me. With so many ways to shrink from the moment, they not only managed to be present for one another, but they did so with fierceness and ingenuity. While the idea of writing down their ideas and sliding them to one another was clever from a behavioral perspective, it was probably harder from a human point of view. It would have been far easier to jot down a tired pro and con list, or poll friends, or just have a messy conversation with one person taking the lead. To write down their honest thoughts added the risk of real disagreement to an already impossible decision. Their respect for honest conversation come what may is what courage looks like to me. And the good news is their process resulted in a good outcome. Rob is alive and well and, now with his family, continues to climb mountains of the Pacific Northwest.

THE SCRIPTURE: MATTHEW 16:21–28

From that time on, Jesus began to show his disciples that he must go to Jerusalem and undergo great suffering at the hands of the elders and chief priests and scribes, and be killed, and on the third day be raised. And Peter took him aside and began to rebuke him, saying, "God forbid it, Lord! This must never happen to you." But he turned and said to Peter, "Get behind me, Satan! You are a stumbling block to me; for you are setting your mind not on divine things but on human things."

Then Jesus told his disciples, "If any want to become my followers, let them deny themselves and take up their cross and follow me. For those who want to save their life will lose it, and those who lose their life for my sake will find it. For what will it profit them if they gain the whole world but forfeit their life? Or what will they give in return for their life?

"For the Son of Man is to come with his angels in the glory of his Father, and then he will repay everyone for what has been done. Truly I tell you, there are some standing here who will not taste death before they see the Son of Man coming in his kingdom."

THE STORY BEHIND THE SCRIPTURE

Poor Peter. I don't think anyone in history went from the top of the class to donning the dunce cap so fast. Just before this Scripture reading Jesus engages in a real conversation with the disciples: "Who do people say that I am?" They give all kinds of answers: Some say John the Baptist back from the dead. Some say Elijah. "Yeah," Jesus nods, "but who you do you say that I am?" And all of a sudden, an academic conversation gets very real very fast. To the relief of the others, Peter jumps in with the right answer declaring Jesus to be the Messiah, the son of God. Good job, Peter! Gold star. But then, just seconds later, when Jesus describes the suffering nature of his servanthood, Peter can't help himself. Peter tells Jesus to shut his mouth about all this talk of suffering. And Jesus famously calls Peter Satan and tells him to get behind him.

For me, David Whyte's work has been instrumental in understanding what's happening here. And to understand Whyte's work is to begin to grasp what he means when he describes the conversational nature of reality. The conversational nature of reality comes down to the fundamental alterity, or otherness, of the natural world, the people around us, and even our own inner lives. Because these others in our lives are, as Karl Barth would put it, *totaliter aliter*, wholly other, they will not behave exactly as we wish. They will, at some point, disappoint us. As Whyte puts it in his fantastic 2017 TED talk: "But equally, whatever the world desires of us—whatever our partner, our child, our colleague, our industry, our future demands of us, will also not happen. And what actually happens is this frontier between what you think is you and what you think is not you. And this frontier of actual meeting between what we call self and what we call the world is the only place, actually, where things are real. But it's quite astonishing how little time we spend at this conversational frontier, and not abstracted away from it in one strategy or another."[1]

There is a deep resonance between this distinction David Whyte makes between stepping into our lives through real conversations versus distancing ourselves and the contrast the Christian mystical tradition draws between living a vital, engaged, abundant life and merely surviving. In *Mere Christianity*, C. S. Lewis points out that there are two different words in ancient Greek for life: *ho bios* and *he zoe*. To Lewis, these terms correspond to two qualitatively different kinds of living—*ho bios* signifies biological life, a kind of living that is just getting by, as opposed to *he zoe*, which connotes spiritual life: "The Biological sort which come to us through Nature, and which (like everything else in Nature) is always tending to run down and decay so that it can only be kept up by incessant subsidies from Nature in the form of air, water, food, etc., is *Bios*. The Spiritual life which is in God from all eternity, and which made the whole natural universe, is *Zoe*. *Bios* has, to be sure, a certain shadowy or symbolic resemblance to *Zoe*: but only the sort of resemblance there is between a photo and a place, or a statue and a man. A man who changed from having *Bios* to having *Zoe* would have gone through as big a change as a statue which changed from being a carved stone to being a real man."[2]

Because we are made in the image of the living God, the Christian tradition holds that we are fashioned for *he zoe*—this engaged, passionate, real life. But just as David Whyte points out that we spend more time abstracted away than in the conversational frontier between us and the world, we so often settle for less than the *he zoe* life for which we are made. We settle for less because it's risky to step into our lives and live for real. It's risky to engage in real, unpredictable conversations and, critically for understanding Peter, conversations that will lead us into suffering. Sometimes it feels safer to avoid these risks by pulling away rather than by taking chances.

1. Whyte, "Lyrical Bridge," 1:06/20:15 min.
2. Lewis, *Mere Christianity*, 139–40.

Peter, like all of us, wants to avoid suffering. How alarming it must have been for Peter to hear Jesus talk about walking directly into the path of pain. If Jesus himself, the Messiah, is not immune to suffering, who is safe? But true discipleship, according to Jesus, entails suffering. Following Jesus means bearing a cross. And trying to avoid pain—trying to keep our lives, as Jesus puts it—causes us to lose the very lives we're trying to protect.

David Whyte articulates the same thing using different language. Stepping into our lives for real conversations means entering into the unknown where we will be disappointed, heartbroken, and vulnerable, but conversely, where we will also be truly and fully alive. We don't have a choice to suffer loss or be vulnerable, he writes: "The only choice we have as we mature is how we inhabit our vulnerability, how we become larger and more courageous and more compassionate through our intimacy with disappearance, our choice is to inhabit vulnerability as generous citizens of loss, robustly and fully, or conversely, as misers and complainers, reluctant and fearful, always at the gates of existence, but never bravely and completely attempting to enter, never wanting to risk ourselves, never walking fully through the door."[3]

While I was at the church I started in Austin, one of the leaders asked me to lunch at one point. She said she wanted to talk to me about some things and really get to know me. It had been a few months, and I knew she wasn't entirely thrilled with me. But we ate, and we talked. And toward the end she asked me if she could share something, something that she was concerned might be hurtful but felt she needed to say. And I said what I believe is the least self-aware thing I've ever said: "Oh, nothing you can say will hurt my feelings." I suppose I had this illusion that because I was playing the role of pastor, I was somehow immune from being hurt? So, this church leader, with a pained expression, uttered, "Well, it's . . . it's just your preaching. It isn't inspiring to me. It isn't very interesting, and I just don't feel very moved by it." And I nodded and showed her my CPF, my "caring pastor face." But *inside* it was as if the floor had given away.

I started this church right out of seminary and had no idea what I was doing. We were setting up and breaking down worship services in an elementary school cafeteria, and some days hardly anyone would show up. Most of the time the only thing I felt good about was my preaching. But with one real conversation she demolished that tiny little support that was keeping me afloat. It hurt. Badly. But today, while I wouldn't want to sit through that particular conversation again, I find myself more and more grateful for it. The truth is I had a lot to learn about preaching. Often, I was too careful

3. Whyte, "Vulnerability," Kindle location 1090–1102.

and leaned more toward safe than honest. But preaching isn't for the careful. Preaching, at its best, allows your heart to walk around outside of you in front of other people once a week. And learning how to continue to preach in front of her every week, knowing how she felt, meant learning how to feel vulnerable and at the same time keep showing up.

SECTION TWO

David the Beloved

9

Love in David's Life

Predictable irrationality is on full display in David's love life. Nowhere else is David so entirely rational and self-interested on the one hand, and entirely passionate and irrational on the other.

David Wolpe notes the irony that David, whose name means "beloved," was loved by many, and yet the Scriptures rarely describe David as loving anyone himself. It is as if David is passively surrounded by love yet unable to actively love back. You absolutely get the sense that, especially in his marriages, David treats women entirely as a means to an end. Michal, David's first wife, adores him and helps him escape from her father, Saul. The fugitive David repays her love by marrying other women, and then destroys Michal's later marriage to Palti because David values his political security over her needs. In a pathetic scene the emotional Palti follows Michal all the way to David's realm only to be turned away by David's henchman, one gets the feeling, on pain of death.

And what about David's marriage to Abigail? David, on the run at the time, marries a woman who provides him with wealth and powerful political connections. Does David really love Abigail? Who knows? He has more than enough reason to pretend so.

Even instances of love that seem noble, such as the two times David has the opportunity to kill Saul and doesn't, may not be as loving as they appear. David, already anointed as king, surely realized that for him to off royal blood set a bad precedent for anyone dissatisfied with David's rule.

And yet, part of why we love David are the moments he appears to be so moved by love, or at least lust, that he acts in entirely irrational, fully human ways. David's inability to contain his desire for Bathsheba comes to mind. At the time of year when he should have been out leading his men in battle, David was home and entirely at loose ends. Without the stabilizing presence of his closest friends, David's loneliness and sense of entitlement proved devastating to Bathsheba and fatal to the child of their union. This scene is like passing an accident—you know you should look away but some macabre part of us is drawn to rubberneck. We do this, if we are at all honest with ourselves, partially because we realize we are not so different from David and know well how our own brokenness is always with us. Marti J. Steussy, author of *David: Biblical Portraits of Power*, includes one woman's observation: "'What I like about David,' announced a woman in a church Bible study group, 'is that if God can love him, God can surely put up with me.'"[1]

The irrationality of David's love also caused him to be softer on those he should have dealt with more harshly. While David's adventure with Bathsheba captures perhaps the most attention, David's lowest moment for me happens later. In a scene I have difficulty reading, David's son Amnon rapes his half-sister Tamar and then is filled with such loathing for her that he tells her to get out. Tamar protests that Amnon's abandonment is worse than his initial crime of rape and winds up a desolate woman ending her days in her brother Absalom's home. When this dark matter becomes known, David, out of his love for Amnon or perhaps, his inability to punish a crime so similar to his own, does nothing. He does nothing! Tamar's brother, Absalom, enraged, plots revenge: first he kills Amnon in a cold-blooded set up and then rebels against his father. In this case, David's love extended only to the perpetrator of the crime; not to Tamar. It is this strangely impaired capacity to love that destroyed the house of David.

And yet, David's love was not always so disordered. He soared to heights of nobility on occasion. David spared Mephibosheth, Saul's disabled grandson, even when he had the chance to eliminate him with the rest of Saul's family. Because the boy was an heir to Saul's throne, the rational, logical thing to do would have been for David to kill the boy; but whether it was pity for Mephibosheth's disability or some kind of unaccountable fondness for Jonathan's son, David looked after the child as his own.

There is one time in the Scriptures when David speaks openly about his love, and this is when he sings over the deaths of Saul and Jonathan. How the mighty have fallen, David laments, calling both Saul and Jonathan

1. Steussy, *David*, 3.

beloved. Indeed, in regard to Jonathan, David says plainly what his actions have always belied: his love for Jonathan was greater than his love for women. Unable to tell him while he was alive, at least according to the text, David finally expresses his love for this young man who saved his life on more than one occasion. While some today get excited over what could sound like homoerotic overtones, my sense is this titillation has more to do with our impoverished understanding of male love and friendship in that era than it hints at anything sexual between David and Jonathan. David's love for Jonathan is beautiful; that he could only bring himself to express this love after Jonathan's death is tragic.

Tragedy marks the end of David's love life as well. In one of the most pitiable end-of-life accounts, the Scriptures portray David—this roaring lion of irrational, sexual intensity—limping to the end of his life in tired impotence. Frail and cold, David takes a beautiful young girl, Abishag, into his bed. With the embers of David's sexuality finally extinguished, he winds up wearing the girl as a blanket, her body only useful to him for warmth. I've often wondered how David felt about that. Was he ashamed, like Samson shorn of his hair? Was he relieved, finally free from the drive that once so badly derailed him? We will never know, but for once at least, David's love manages not to destroy a woman's life.

It's always risky to venture guesses about why someone is the way they are, but the Rabbinic midrash writes a compelling backstory to David the shepherd boy. Puzzled by why David's father Jesse leaves his youngest son in the field when Samuel comes to anoint a king, the rabbis weave a dark, riveting history about David's mother, Nizevet. (For an accessible, creative retelling of Nizevet's story and its place in the making of King David, read Pulitzer Prize-winning author Geraldine Brooks's novel, *The Secret Chord*.[2])

Here is how the midrash story goes. A highly religious man, Jesse became obsessed with his Moabite grandmother, Ruth, questioning whether he was worthy of being married to a fully Jewish woman. Eventually, his neurotic obsession caused him to cease sleeping with his wife. But when loneliness wore on Jesse, he decided it would be fine to sleep with their Canaanite servant. Now, whether the servant was loyal to Nizevet or terrified of what might happen if Jesse carried out his plans, the girl went to her mistress with the details. Hatching a plan straight out of the Genesis tale of Jacob and Leah, Nizevet and her servant planned a swap on the night the deed was supposed to take place. Now, I have no idea how dark it was supposed to be, or how drunk Jacob or Jesse would have to be, but the plan worked. Jesse wound up unknowingly sleeping with his wife. And all of this

2. Brooks, *The Secret Chord*, 34–54.

would have been fine, albeit weird, except Nizevet became pregnant. When her pregnancy became apparent, Nizevet's own sons wanted to stone her for betrayal. Jesse kept her from death, but then commanded everyone to treat her and her bastard son with the contempt they deserved. This misbegotten pregnancy is why Jesse consigned his youngest son to the fields where the child faced the real possibility of being eaten by a lion. The rabbis believed David's death by lion probably would have been a relief to Jesse. So, David grew up unloved by his father, scorned by his brothers, and this . . . this shapes a person.

It makes all the sense in the world to me that this kind of early life experience would form (malform?) David into someone hungry to be loved but rarely able to reciprocate this love in return. It makes sense to me because it's something of my story as well. Growing up with an erratic, angry, and frightening father and a mom battling both illness and the difficulty of living with an erratic, angry, and frightening husband, I developed protections as a young person. I cultivated an ability to retreat into myself, creating a rich, inner life separate from and cut off from what felt like an unstable and unsafe world.

In college I went through a season of devouring Roberston Davies; the first novel of his Cornish Trilogy, *The Rebel Angels*, gave me the most helpful image for understanding myself. I grew up creating a kind of rebel angel, an internal defense, that protected me from the outside world and created an inner sanctuary where my imagination and creativity flourished. But this rebel angel comes with a downside. While protecting me from threats, it doesn't know the difference between friend and foe. As we might surmise about David, it's difficult for me to feel loved, admired, and cared for, too. While some have lauded me for pastoring a church, caring for a family, and writing on top of it all, there is, at times, more than a tinge of what Brené Brown terms "hustling after grace" in all this striving. The defenses that protected me, in other words, also kept me from being vulnerable enough to fully experience love. For me, part of growing up has been to find ways to lovingly thank the rebel angel part of me that protected me as a child, while also telling this insurgent protector that it is no longer in charge—so that I can embrace the sureness that loving and being loved are risks worth taking.

10

Not Running, but Dancing

Luke 1:39–56

NOT RUNNING, BUT DANCING

She wasn't running away.
She wasn't running away to hide her face.
She wasn't digging a hole a thousand-miles deep with a shovel of shame
       to bury her poor, tender head.
She wasn't throwing up her arms around her body
       like guard rails on 101
             the only thing keeping her from falling into that fir-tossing
                rock crushing
                      blue depression beneath.
She wasn't running away.
She wasn't running at all.

Not running, but dancing.

Dancing to a song only the heart can hear.

Dancing without the help of a husband to lead the way.

Dancing without "a sonogram"[1] in hand

    the black and white hazy little alien

        the sometimes thumb-sucking always certain proof

            that she was not making it up.

Dancing without "an affidavit from the Holy Spirit"[2] stating:

    "To whom it may concern. This child is mine.

    So put down your rocks

    the rocks in your hands

        the worse rocks flying from your mouths

            falling from the loose rocks in your heads.

    Put down your rocks and leave the girl alone.

        She's just scared. And so are you."

She was dancing.

    Dancing across the desert at night.

    Dancing across the moon-drenched sand.

    Dancing across the rules, across the expectations.

    Dancing across "But this isn't how we do it around here."

    Dancing across "Nice girls don't get knocked up.

        And nice girls *definitely*

            don't get knocked up and then lie about it."

        Holy Spirit? Holy cow, girl. You couldn't come up

            with something better than that?

                (Even if you did believe it.)

She was dancing.

    Dancing across "What are they saying about me?"

    Dancing across her own voice saying,

        "There are things you can do to mess up your life

            and you can never, ever fix it."

1. Taylor, "Singing Ahead of Time," 18.
2. Ibid., 18.

She was dancing across.

    Dancing a cross.

        Dying to the girl they wanted her to be

           rising to become a mystery.

And this strange stranger coming to be

    she can't wipe this girl's smile off her face

        get the song out of her mouth

           and she can't keep this strange girl's feet from moving.

Who will they be, she wonders?

    She and this little one hitching a ride, growing inside

whoever they'll be never has been

    and yet somehow always was, is, and ever shall be, she thinks.

        Scattering the proud

           filling the hungry

                and lifting up what has been held down

                  for far, too, long.

She was dancing that night.

    Dancing for herself and all the girls like her.

        Girls who became pregnant when the world said they shouldn't.

        The girls who couldn't or didn't become pregnant

           When the world said they should.

        The girls who gave up their little ones to adoption or abortion

        or lost them and died a little inside as the dream of their baby

           slowly, slipped away.

    For these she danced and dances still.

She danced for the son growing inside her body
    and all the boys like him.
        For the boys who have to look to their father in heaven
            because the one here on earth keeps forgetting to call.
        For the boys who will grow up to care for women
            as they were cared for by them.
        For the boys who will stand up and say, "Don't talk to her like that.
            She's just scared. And so are you."
    For these she danced and dances still.

She danced for Abraham and his children.
    You are one of them. And so am I.
        Synagogue, mosque, and church.
        Synagogue, mosque, and church.
            All Abraham. All the time.
        And what we have in common is so much more
            than the fear that drives us apart.
    For these, the least of these, she danced and dances still.

She wasn't running that night, but dancing.

And if it could happen to her, it could happen to you.
    To me. Do you see?
        Do you see what I see? Do you hear what I hear?
Because there's music in the air, everywhere
a song an angel is singing that only the heart can hear
    and if you hear it
        even a little
    if it gets inside of you
        even a little
then when you leave this place
    you won't be running away.
        You'll be dancing.

THE STORY BEHIND THE POEM

"Not Running, but Dancing" was one of the earliest pieces I wrote. In the span of a few months I encountered two spoken-word poets: TED talks introduced me to Sarah Kay, and my sister-in-law, Lizzy, who is a teacher, showed me the greatness of Taylor Mali. I loved the energy and emotion of these spoken word poets. (Truth be told, for years I watched Taylor Mali's "What Teachers Make" before worship on Sunday mornings as a kind of weird pre-worship psych-up. Some pastors pray before worship . . . I listen to poetry. To each their own.)

"Not Running, but Dancing" is an advent poem. The church I serve has a thriving liturgical arts program, and our leaders generally pull out the stops during Advent and Holy Week. While we normally follow the revised common lectionary, occasionally the Holy Spirit brings us ideas and connections too fun not to follow. That particular year we spent the entire Advent exploring different sides of Mary. In our Protestant anxiety over making it absolutely, crystal clear that we *do not* worship Mary, we sometimes throw the momma of the baby out with the theological bathwater.

At the same time "Not Running, but Dancing" follows the story of the Holy mother, it also brings to mind my own mom as well. As I described earlier, my family experienced a great deal of instability when I was growing up. My father's anger and unwillingness to take direction prevented him from keeping a job, putting all the burden of breadwinning squarely onto my mom's shoulders. My mom suffered from Grave's disease, an autoimmune disorder that impacted her thyroid, which was treated by radioiodine when I was young. And then, of course, there was my brother's car accident. My mom had to figure out how to care for me and a severely head-injured teenager, which was just one more shock to an already strained family system.

Before all these events though, my family already knew difficulty. When my mom was eighteen, she became pregnant with my brother before she and my dad were married. A co-valedictorian of her high school class with a bright future, she left college to have my brother. She carried the marks from this shame throughout my childhood. I remember my mom saying, in some of her more despondent moments, something along the lines of: "You can mess your life up when you're eighteen and there's just nothing you can do to fix it." (She might have used more colorful language.)

Whenever I read Mary's story of a pregnancy that didn't fit well into the world's expectations, I think about what my mom and countless other women have experienced. As a pastor, I've cared for women who have suffered through the loss of a child to stillbirth, abortion, or the inability to conceive despite many attempts. Although each experience is different, difficulties with pregnancy hit us in the deepest places.

And yet, even with this incredibly painful and frightening situation that Mary is facing, she manages to sing—to embrace her complicated future and declare her humble self blessed. She runs to her cousin Elizabeth in the middle of the night and when she arrives, sings one of the most famous songs in all of Scripture, known as the Magnificat from Mary's first line: "My soul magnifies the Lord."

To honor Mary's singing, I used more repetition than I usually include to give the poem more of a song feel. There are fragments of songs included in the piece as well, such as "Do you hear what I hear," which are meant to be sung rather than spoken.

THE SCRIPTURE: LUKE 1:39–56

In those days Mary set out and went with haste to a Judean town in the hill country, where she entered the house of Zechariah and greeted Elizabeth. When Elizabeth heard Mary's greeting, the child leaped in her womb. And Elizabeth was filled with the Holy Spirit and exclaimed with a loud cry, "Blessed are you among women, and blessed is the fruit of your womb. And why has this happened to me, that the mother of my Lord comes to me? For as soon as I heard the sound of your greeting, the child in my womb leaped for joy. And blessed is she who believed that there would be a fulfillment of what was spoken to her by the Lord."
And Mary said,
"My soul magnifies the Lord,
and my spirit rejoices in God my Savior,
for he has looked with favor on the lowliness of his servant.
        Surely, from now on all generations will call me blessed;
for the Mighty One has done great things for me,
        and holy is his name.
His mercy is for those who fear him
        from generation to generation.
He has shown strength with his arm;
        he has scattered the proud in the thoughts of their hearts.
He has brought down the powerful from their thrones,
        and lifted up the lowly;
he has filled the hungry with good things,
        and sent the rich away empty.

He has helped his servant Israel,
    in remembrance of his mercy,
according to the promise he made to our ancestors,
    to Abraham and to his descendants forever."
And Mary remained with her about three months and then
returned to her home.

THE STORY BEHIND THE SCRIPTURE

I'm not sure who said it, but one of the best aphorisms regarding Scripture is all of the stories are true . . . and some of them actually happened. This is probably most apropos when it comes to the Christmas narratives.

Yep. Narratives. Now, it's true that being a pastor for so many years probably has given me a somewhat Grinch-y outlook toward Christmas, but I still decorate for the season: I put up lights, and I help set up one of the many crèches in our family's possession. And you know how it goes. You've got Mary and Joseph and the little baby Jesus. (At least most of the time we have a little baby. Half of the time he goes missing, and one of our kids substitutes a Lego figure in his stead.) And, like a scene out of a crazy musical, flanking the holy family are all the animals, the magi, and the shepherds.

You see this scene so often you could almost begin to believe it's true—except, of course, that it's not. Matthew gives us the magi; Luke gives us the shepherds. Stingy Mark and John give us nothing. (Well, that's not entirely true. John gives us that logos hymn, and that's pretty good stuff. But it's no Jingle Bells.) If this seems picky, it's just the tip of the iceberg.

Have you ever actually read the Christmas stories in Matthew and Luke? They aren't even close. Not by a mile. In Matthew, Jesus' family lives in Bethlehem. They *live* there. Then, they flee Bethlehem because of that whole baby massacre thing, and they head to Egypt. After they're done touring the pyramids, they head back home—only they must have taken a left turn at Albuquerque with Bugs Bunny because they end up in Nazareth.

Luke remembers it . . . kind of differently. In Luke, the holy family starts out in Nazareth. But then, because of that pesky tax deadline, they travel south to Bethlehem where, much to their chagrin, the Motel 6 did not leave the light on for them. (If you ever travel to Israel and have the privilege of taking a side trip to Bethlehem, the funniest place to visit after the Stars & Bucks Café is the Holy Family Hotel. It took everything I had not to stop in and see if they had any rooms.) According to Luke, after Jesus' dedication in the temple, the family returns to Nazareth and we hear nothing more about his childhood except for one Passover trip to Jerusalem when Jesus was twelve.

That's . . . uh . . . pretty different. Kings and shepherds are one thing, but confusing hometowns?

The reality is that the way we were taught to understand differences among Scripture passages as children isn't terribly helpful as adults. When we were kids, kindly Sunday School teachers wielding flannel boards told us the differences among Scripture texts could be explained away the same way eyewitness accounts sometimes vary. If four people witness a car accident, we were told, we would hear four slightly different versions. One person might remember the color of the cars, another one might recall the make, and another who hit whom first. But the important thing, we were told, is that they all agree on the main point, which is there was a car accident. In the same way, well-meaning adults told us the evangelists were four eye-witnesses who may remember things a little bit differently sometimes but agree on the main story: Jesus was born!

But whether Jesus' family lived in Nazareth and traveled to Bethlehem, or whether they lived in Bethlehem, fled to Egypt, and then returned to Nazareth courtesy of witness protection—this geographic confusion seems like a pretty important detail.

To understand scriptural differences as grownups requires tossing out the eyewitness metaphor. According to the best scholarship today, the first gospel, the Gospel of Mark, is written around the year AD 70. This is roughly forty years after Jesus' crucifixion, resurrection, and ascension. Why did it take so long? The first followers of Jesus didn't need a gospel because they knew Jesus, or they had access to someone who did. But then, when Jesus had left the building and the disciples who knew him personally started to die, people needed a way to keep the stories alive. The first version of what would come to be a gospel was probably just a record of Jesus' statements and actions. (This is one of the reasons why many scholars think so highly of the Gospel of Thomas, which is simply a collection of Jesus' sayings.) What Mark did is take the collection of sayings that existed in the oral tradition and arrange them to tell the story of Jesus' Galilean ministry and his crucifixion and resurrection in Jerusalem.

The writers of Matthew and Luke knew Mark's Gospel. They had it on their desk when they were composing their own version. How do we know? We know because there are parts of Matthew and Luke that parallel Mark's Gospel verbatim. It's a little bit like watching the speeches of Melania Trump and Michelle Obama side by side. You can understand two people coming up with similar sounding images; but when they say the exact same thing in multiple locations, you know something is up.

Matthew and Luke draw from Mark and other sources and then shape this material for their own context and purpose. Do you think it's a mistake that Matthew tells a Christmas story where a tyrant puts male babies to death and there is a flight involving Egypt? Um . . . sound familiar? Of course, it does. Matthew lifts imagery from Exodus as part of his project to model Jesus as a new and improved Moses. It is why Matthew takes so many of the sayings that happen in discrete places in Mark, stitches them together, and has Jesus deliver them on a mountain. It is also why, in Matthew, Jesus says he doesn't come to abolish the law but to fulfill it.

Luke also shapes Mark's material, but he does so in a different way than Matthew. Luke shapes the material to show Jesus came for the least, the last, and the lost. The first people to hear about Jesus in Luke, other than Mary, are the shepherds. While we romanticize shepherds today, shepherds were despised in the first century to the point where their word wasn't accepted in a court of law. And speaking of Mary, women lead the way in Luke's Christmas story; they also play a notably prominent role in the rest of Luke's Gospel. And Mary's song, the Magnificat? She also had some help, but not from Mark. Mary's song draws on Hannah's song in the second chapter of First Samuel; justice for the poor and marginal figure prominently in both songs.

I know it can be a little unsettling the first time you realize the complexity behind the Gospels. But honestly, I love and appreciate them more now than I did when I was young. Now the differences aren't embarrassing or examples of faulty human memory: they are the product of intentional, careful artistry. Remember the saying attributed to Picasso: "Good artists borrow; great artists steal."

11

Asking for It

Luke 7:36–50

ASKING FOR IT

Dedicated to "Emily Doe" of Stanford University and survivors of sexual assault everywhere

"I now see how owning our story and loving ourselves through that process is the bravest thing that we will ever do."[1]

—Brené Brown

You didn't ask
for it.
Permission.
You took what you
wanted assuming
it was the price of admission
into the rare air
of your inner circle.

1. Brown, "Preface," xiv.

Late night. Blurry.
I was in a hurry to get
to know you better.
Sighing slightly, you said
you would slip into something
more comfortable.
First shoes, then shirt sloughed
as you coiled, a snake about to strike
while I mumbled on about my past
unaware of my present plight.

You didn't ask
for it.
Permission.
You took what you
wanted assuming
it was the price of admission
into the rare air
of your inner circle.

He didn't ask
for it, either.
Permission.
He just stated what had
already happened.
His own admission
that she had been forgiven.
Her faith
the faith that made
her whole.

Late night. Dinner.
In walks that "sinner"
noticed but never known
seen only as unclean
except to him
the one who saw her
on her knees knowing you cannot forgive
what has already been set free.

She also didn't ask
for it.
Permission.
But just waltzed
right in without admission
tear-streaked hair
lips on toes
as all of them stare
but she is free now
and she does not care.

No one can give us
permission to be
to think our own thoughts
to laugh and live loudly.
No, this can only be claimed
in bravely, courageously rising when
called by your one, true name.

THE STORY BEHIND THE POEM

In January 2015, a young woman went to a party with her sister and woke up in a hospital bed, the victim of Brock Turner's brutal and vicious rape behind a dumpster on the Stanford University campus. To protect her identity, one of the few things Turner wasn't able to take from her, we know her only as "Emily Doe." She did get a chance to confront Turner after the judge handed down his light sentence: directly addressing her rapist, Emily Doe read from a twelve-page victim impact statement, explaining in excruciating detail what she suffered because of his actions.

One of the hardest moments to read occurs after the hospital staff conducts a forensic examination, a necessary but also violating series of actions. Only after that additional indignity was she finally allowed to shower, giving her time to absorb what had happened to her. She writes: "I stood there examining my body beneath the stream of water and decided, I don't want my body anymore. I was terrified of it, I didn't know what had been in it, if it had been contaminated, who had touched it. I wanted to take off my body like a jacket and leave it at the hospital with everything else."[2]

This story triggered my own memory of a man, a trusted friend and mentor, who took advantage of our relationship. When I was in college, I took a short trip to visit him, this man I deeply respected and admired. I wasn't quite sure what I should be doing with my life, and I thought he might be helpful. What I didn't realize is that he thought I might have come for another reason.

I remembered waking up one morning with his hands on my body. He was massaging my back. I felt confused. On the one hand, I suppose it felt good, but on the other hand, I also felt incredibly strange, uncomfortable, and frightened. He had never touched me in this way, and I had been asleep. He had not asked me if I wanted his touch, and I just didn't understand what was happening. Moreover, there was something hungry in the touch of his hands that made me recoil inside. Later, I would be angry with myself for not pushing him away and demanding to know what the hell he was thinking. But I didn't do or say those things. I didn't know what to do except to play dead and wait him out. He eventually lost interest with my lack of response and left the room. But that wasn't the end of his advances.

After breakfast, we stood outside his home looking at the view from the deck. He moved behind me and put his arms around me. I was paralyzed again. Again, part of me wanted to push him away and, this time, make a run for it. But then another part of me worried what he would do if

2. Kadvany, "Stanford Sex-Assault Victim," impact statement, par. 7.

I ran. I was in college. I didn't have much money, and I had no obvious way out of there. I was dependent on him and trapped. And, at least up until this point, I also had deep regard for him. I actually worried about what would happen to him if I said anything. He was putting his entire life and career at risk acting like this.

So, again feeling sick, I just pretended as if nothing was happening and stood there motionless as he continued to embrace me, his hot breath on my neck. I don't honestly know how long he persisted in keeping his arms around me and pressing his body into me. It felt like forever. I can't ever remember feeling more split inside between wanting to honor what my body needed, which was to flee, and what I felt I could do in the moment, which was to just stand there and hope to God he didn't take his advances any further.

He eventually relented, pouting, but for the rest of the trip there was a tension between us that hung in the air the way the smell of a dead animal reeks in a closed room.

I had only shared with a couple of people that this moment ever happened. Even then I never really explained it in detail. I certainly had never written about it or examined it closely. When I read Emily Doe's letter, my experience came flooding back. I felt angry—angry with him for touching me in that way, angry with myself for not doing more in the moment to stand up for myself. Moreover, I was angry that I didn't really feel comfortable talking about it. Even though I knew I had done nothing wrong, I perceived that if I shared my experience, I would risk people wondering if I had done something or said something that might have encouraged him.

Now, I was not raped. I did not experience the magnitude of what Emily Doe did. I know this. But I also realized I knew what it was to be the victim of sexual assault: I was the victim of unwanted physical contact to which I did not consent, which left me angry, confused, and missing a relationship that before had been life-giving and inspiring. Since then, I have learned more men experience sexual assault than I would have ever guessed. I had seen the unacceptable numbers regarding women, but I honestly didn't know anything about male sexual assault. My guess would have been that it really didn't happen that often. However, one study included on the website www.1in6.org shows that one in six men experience some form of sexual assault in their life. One is six. This statistic shocked me. After Linkin Park's lead singer Chester Bennington's death by suicide in 2017, more light is now being shed on the life-long trauma sexual abuse inflicts on survivors. Despite phenomenal success as a musician, Bennington ultimately succumbed to the damage caused by a man who sexually abused Bennington starting when he was just seven years old. Men who experience sexual abuse as children suffer from far higher rates of alcoholism, drug abuse, and, in Bennington's case, suicide than the general population.

When I was watching former FBI director James Comey testify regarding President Trump's attempts to bully him into backing off his investigation into the Trump campaign's ties with Russia, many in the Senate openly wondered why Comey didn't just push back in the moment and tell Trump to stop. In essence, they questioned Comey's account of the incident, suggesting if Trump really threatened the FBI director, then Comey should have reacted differently. Or worse, they were intimating that while Trump's behavior might have been suspect, Comey's failure to step up and confront it was at least as blameworthy. After Comey's experience came to light, I noticed many women on social media immediately recognize and name this classic blame-the-victim mentality; I was grateful for their witness. They knew exactly what Comey had experienced.

And now, because courageous women risked their careers to come forward, the world actually feels as if it's changing because of the Harvey Weinstein scandal. Thousands upon thousands of people have posted their own accounts of sexual harassment and abuse using the hashtag #MeToo. Previously untouchable stars, such as Kevin Spacey, Charlie Rose, and Matt Lauer, now find themselves accountable for their past actions. While it is still early days, it feels as if we might be experiencing real cultural change. Recognizing the significance of this paradigm shift, *TIME* named "The Silence Breakers"—the women and men who spoke out against sexual assault and harassment and launched the #MeToo movement—as person of the year 2017.

THE SCRIPTURE: LUKE 7:36–50

One of the Pharisees asked Jesus to eat with him, and he went into the Pharisee's house and took his place at the table. And a woman in the city, who was a sinner, having learned that he was eating in the Pharisee's house, brought an alabaster jar of ointment. She stood behind him at his feet, weeping, and began to bathe his feet with her tears and to dry them with her hair. Then she continued kissing his feet and anointing them with the ointment. Now when the Pharisee who had invited him saw it, he said to himself, "If this man were a prophet, he would have known who and what kind of woman this is who is touching him—that she is a sinner." Jesus spoke up and said to him, "Simon, I have something to say to you." "Teacher," he replied, "speak." "A certain creditor had two debtors; one owed five hundred denarii, and the other fifty. When they could not pay, he canceled the debts for both of them. Now which of them will love him more?" Simon answered, "I suppose the one for whom he canceled the greater debt." And Jesus said to him, "You have judged rightly." Then turning toward the woman, he said to Simon, "Do you see this woman? I entered your house; you gave me no water for my feet, but she has bathed my feet with her tears and dried them with her hair. You gave me no kiss, but from the time I came in she has not stopped kissing my feet. You did not anoint my head with oil, but she has anointed my feet with ointment. Therefore, I tell you, her sins, which were many, have been forgiven; hence she has shown great love. But the one to whom little is forgiven, loves little." Then he said to her, "Your sins are forgiven." But those who were at the table with him began to say among themselves, "Who is this who even forgives sins?" And he said to the woman, "Your faith has saved you; go in peace."

THE STORY BEHIND THE SCRIPTURE

This text is such a strange passage. Nothing makes sense. First off, Jesus, instead of arguing with the Pharisees, is reclining over a lavish dinner, which isn't where we expect to find him at all. Even more surprising, during the dinner a woman—a known sinner—enters the dinner party, drops to her knees, massages oil and her tears into Jesus' feet, wipes them with her hair, and finally begins to kiss them with her hungry mouth.

I . . . don't remember this story being taught in my Sunday school. You?

Possibly, the most surprising thing of all is that we think we understand what's happening in the story when we really don't. The standard interpretation of the story is that Jesus is having dinner in a prominent man's home when this broken harlot intrudes and inappropriately throws herself at Jesus' feet. Then, in kind of a classic gotcha moment, the leader, Simon, says if Jesus were such a great prophet, he would know what kind of a woman was touching him like that. Then our hero turns the tables on Simon saying at least the woman was offering hospitality, something Simon wasn't; because of her kindness, Jesus pronounces her sins are forgiven. Of course, Jesus' pardon only makes everyone angrier because who in the world does Jesus think he is that he can tell people their sins are forgiven?

This interpretation certainly seems obvious. And it is. In English. In Greek, however, the story is entirely different. One of the cool things about

Greek is writers have the ability to express action with greater sensitivity and accuracy than we can in English. In this case, Luke absolutely has the ability to write that Jesus was forgiving her sins in that present moment. Luke has the ability to express that when Jesus says the woman's faith saves her, that saving, or healing, is happening right at that exact moment. Luke could have written the story using a verbal aspect known as the aorist tense, but he doesn't. No, in a fascinating move Luke uses the perfect tense, which conveys a past action that carries a present effect. Luke's Jesus doesn't say that he forgave the woman's many sins right there on the spot. No. He says the woman's sins had already been forgiven. The forgiveness happened at some point in the past; now, in the present, she was already in a state of forgiveness. So, her faith didn't save her right then and there. Her faith had saved her some time before.

So, this story isn't about a "bad" woman being so kind to Jesus that he decides to reward her generosity with forgiveness. The woman's sins had already been forgiven before she even walked through those doors. She crashed that dinner party not seeking something from Jesus but celebrating a richness of life she may have never thought possible.

Permission is a theme that connects the already-forgiven woman's story with the sexual-assault experiences of Emily Doe and my own. Emily Doe certainly did not give her attacker permission to rape her behind a dumpster. Going back to the first stanza of "Asking for It," I imagine myself in my friend and mentor's shoes. I speculate that this seemingly honorable man didn't ask permission to violate my trust. He was used to getting what he wanted. I wonder if he assumed that sexual acquiescence was the price for the real conversation I craved. The poem then shifts to the Pharisees, upset that Jesus pronounces the woman forgiven. Who gave Jesus the permission to do that? Finally, the poem closes with the woman who doesn't ask permission to infiltrate that dinner party in the first place. She just walks right through the door and loves Jesus' body with a kind of courage that takes my breath away.

Emily Doe didn't have the choice to remove her body like a jacket. She did have the choice to stay silent, though, which would have allowed the shame to drag her down into the nothingness she was feeling. But she didn't. She did something so unbelievably brave and powerful. In the words of Brené Brown, Emily Doe owned her own story in that twelve-page letter she wrote to her attacker. And her own story—her *self*—that is something the privileged Brock Turners of the world can never touch.

12

The Broken Circle
Song of Solomon 6:3, 8:6–7

THE BROKEN CIRCLE

For Melis, on the occasion of her 40th birthday

It was the finger that did it.
Saturday morning soccer field
the Good Dad chasing the stray ball
but being good was not good enough
(it never is) to stop
the fall. My feet
flying out from under me
my hand, stretching back
unable to bear the weight of my body's burden
I heard the snap, the sharp crack of a tired twig.

This was my ring finger broken for us.

I stood on the suffering sideline the rest of the game
one hand cradling the other.
Later, in the clean, white room, after X-ray machine
the gloved hands sheared through
the ring, cutting into the swelling flesh.

Months later, after the healing
the sealing, the closing of the bone
I slipped this broken circle back on, looked down and read
Ani ledodi.
I am my beloved's.
Break.
Vedodi li.
My beloved is mine.
Break.

This symbolic circle once binding, now dividing
a golden chasm cutting us off from one another.
And all the ways I added to this impossible distance fell on me
twenty years of boxers on the floor, biohazard car
that awful week in the San Juans, my pouting silence
and all the words said and all the words left unsaid.

Fear hissed fix it
make this brokenness appear to disappear
make it look unmarred, unmarked, as if it never happened.
But love whispered leave it
love whispered leave it.
Love liked how the ring still fits
how this malleable mark that divides
now provides the chance to touch and come back together again
fall away, and come back together again. And again.
And to do all this in the memory of who we were, are,
and are still coming to be.

Love saw how the broken circle
still sits over the spot, once broken now healed
and love reminded that bones, like people
grow stronger in the broken places.

THE STORY BEHIND THE POEM

Marriage is hard. Marriage with three children can be really hard. Each year I normally celebrate two or three weddings, and watching these couples say their vows to one another always gives me pause. Some of them giggle nervously. Others are emotional, just trying to keep it together. None of them, though, I know, have a clue about what they are saying. Forever? What does that mean? For better or for worse? None of them have a glimmer of how bad "worse" could be.

I wrote this piece after being married for eighteen years. We've packed quite a bit in during this time: three university degrees after college; three cross-country moves; three kids; and a lot of beautiful memories. But it hasn't always been easy. Not by a long shot.

Within a two-year span, both Melis and I managed to break bones for the first time in our lives. Melis was headed down the stairs to exercise early one morning when she tripped on a water bottle thoughtlessly left the night before by one of our kids (who remains nameless, although I do know the culprit's name). She broke her tibia and fibula in several places. One metal plate and several screws later, we realized walking normally is not something to take for granted.

My break was less serious. I was assistant coach on my son's soccer team. One rainy Portland Saturday morning, I ran to snag an errant ball. I slipped on the sidewalk, fell backward, reached out my left hand (of course I'm left-handed) and experienced a pain unlike any I had felt before. Melis was out of town at the time, and I didn't want to take Ches out of the game, so I stood there on the sideline cradling my hand as my broken ring finger began to swell significantly.

When the game was over, and I was finally able to find coverage for the kids and head to urgent care, it was obvious that I had broken my ring finger. What was less obvious was what was going to happen with my wedding band. My ring is gold and inscribed with the Hebrew: *ani ledodi vedodi li* (I am my beloved's and my beloved is mine). It turns out they have a vicious-looking device, sort of a large, motorized knife, which they clamped around my ring. With a whirring noise, a spinning blade sheared through the metal. As you might imagine, it was excruciating, but it needed to be done. Because of the break, the swelling around the ring was a real problem.

Months later when the break had closed and I was able to wear the ring again, I examined it closely. We were all in such a hurry no thought was given to where to cut the metal. They managed to cut right through the middle of the inscription. Now the ring reads "I am my beloved's" with a space where the ring was cut followed by "my beloved is mine." Words intended to symbolize the union between two people are now marked by a division.

I seriously considered having the ring fixed. I'm sure a skilled jeweler could craft it such that you'd never know the difference. But the more I lived with this break the more I have grown to love it. After eighteen years of marriage I think this broken circle reflects my relationship with Melis more accurately than ever. While we do share so many beautiful memories and a deep love, we have had some truly painful and difficult moments at which I hint in the poem.

On the less painful side I'm a fairly messy person. Melis is an engineer. I live in a constant state of papers and books strewn about my office and clothes left on the floor. I'm forever telling myself, "I'll get to that, I'll get to that," but often become distracted. I know my messiness really bothers Melis, and there are times when I do a good job cleaning up, but my natural state seems to be a fairly chaotic one.

Harder to live with is my tendency to "go dark," as we put it. When I'm hurt or angry, I sometimes have a hard time expressing these feelings and can become non-communicative and terse. I didn't have a lot of good models for expressing these darker feelings growing up, and TV and other media aren't exactly brimming with positive examples. One of the least helpful ways I deal with negative feelings is to be obviously upset—as exhibited by my words, actions, and general grumpiness—but not to acknowledge that anything is wrong. To the quite reasonable question "Is everything okay?" my response is nothing or "I'm fine, I'm fine." One of the worst times in my life was a family vacation trip to the San Juan Islands, normally one of my favorite places. But that year I felt trapped by extended family, young children, and work that really needed to be taken care of; I just shut down on everyone around me, especially Melis. It was awful. I could feel it happening, I could feel myself slipping into this dark pit, but I didn't know how to crawl out.

I'm fairly confident when Melis married me for better or worse, she wasn't imagining having to live through a "vacation" like that one. Of course, there may be harder days ahead. Thankfully, I continue to learn along the way. I've connected with others who have helped me find better coping skills. And hopefully, my good points occasionally make up for my rougher edges.

THE SCRIPTURE: SONG OF SOLOMON 6:3, 8:6–7

Song of Solomon 6:3:

I am my beloved's and my beloved is mine;
  he pastures his flock among the lilies.

Song of Solomon 8:6–7:

Set me as a seal upon your heart, as a seal upon your arm;
  for love is strong as death, passion fierce as the grave.
Its flashes are flashes of fire, a raging flame.
Many waters cannot quench love, neither can floods drown it.
  If one offered for love all the wealth of his house,
  it would be utterly scorned.

THE STORY BEHIND THE SCRIPTURE

What is an erotic love poem like you doing in a place like this? The Song of Solomon was one of the last books to be accepted into the canon due, in part, to its racy nature. Today, it suffers more from neglect than concern.

The story in the Song of Solomon entails two unmarried lovers sneaking out and finding one another at night. The work opens with the woman's bold voice singing of what she wants and who she is: "Let him kiss me with the kisses of his mouth!" (1:2) and "I am black and beautiful" (1:5). As lovers do, they dote upon one another. Sometimes she describes his attributes, and other times he goes on and on about her teeth being "like a flock of shorn ewes" (4:2) and her neck being "like the tower of David" (4:4). (I'm guessing that sounded better in person.)

At points the imagery sounds like the intoxicating Sufi poetry of Rumi and Hafiz: "Eat, friends, drink, and be drunk with love" (5:1). At other points the language is frankly sexual: "'Open to me, my sister, my love, my dove, my perfect one; for my head is wet with dew, my locks with the drops of the night.' I had put off my garment; how could I put it on again? I had bathed my feet; how could I soil them? My beloved thrust his hand into the opening, and my inmost being yearned for him. I arose to open to my beloved, and my hands dripped with myrrh, my fingers with liquid myrrh, upon the handles of the bolt" (5:2–5). Say no more! Nudge, nudge. Wink, wink.

In an attempt to contain and perhaps control this evocative language, the synagogue and the church both have tried to explain the erotic imagery away. The poem isn't to be taken literally, they have said. The poem isn't really about two unmarried lovers trying to find one another in the middle of the night. No, no, no—the poem is really an allegory. The lovers symbolize God and God's people, or Christ and his bride, the church.

Perhaps there is some value to these kinds of allegories. As I have argued before, texts contain a surplus of meaning. Rabbis have talked about seventy faces of Scripture. To me there are at least as many ways to read these words as there are individuals reading them. But for me, I'm also entirely comfortable with this story being about two lovers and God working in and through their erotic search. Spirituality and sexuality are twins in the biblical imagination after all. The Hebrew word for knowing God and having sex are the same: *yada*. And no wonder. You can't experience true sexual intimacy without knowing and being known. As sex therapist Esther Perel points out, the solution for most couples experiencing challenges in their sex lives isn't, as she puts it, "toys and lingerie," but greater vulnerability and exploration of our conflicting inner needs.[1]

---

1. Perel, "Secret to Desire," 19:10 min.

13

Punto de Reunión

Acts 15:36–41

PUNTO DE REUNIÓN

What sharp break
precipitated the earthquake
that split them apart?
Like most disagreements
this stemmed from a
past still very much present.

One couldn't get over the loss
the stab-back betrayal when
all hands were needed on deck.
The other wondered
about his Antiochene about-face
the hardened stone now lodged
in heart's place.

But after the dust settled
shaken from feet
they parted ways, vowing
never to meet.
But their small circle's seduction
plunging back-arc subduction
fused them in rock forged together
by the heat and pressure of an
ancient, pitiless, hand.

Breaking up may be hard to do
but it's impossible, when you are
bound together by a few hungry lives
who cannot let you go.

They would meet again.
Would it be as friends?
Or stand side-eyed on
their *punto de reunión*
amidst the rubble of rock strewn,
broken communion?

THE STORY BEHIND THE POEM

This poem came from a few places. One inspiration was a tiny story in the New York Times about the *puntos de reunión*, literally meaning "reunion points," of Mexico City.[1] I had never heard of these before but because Mexico City is highly prone to earthquakes, you can find these large green areas with different kinds of markings on them around the city. They vary in size; some are enormous, designed to be seen from very tall buildings; others are small, created for community neighbors. These *puntos de reunión* are the meeting places for friends and family in the event of a catastrophe. Everyone knows their *punto de reunión*.

A green spot on a sidewalk—this is a striking image to me, a place of reunion and safety in the midst of terrible, tragic destruction. The power of this image only grew for me after the devastating earthquake striking Mexico City on September 19th, 2017.

Here, I've paired the Mexico City *puntos de reunión* with the mysterious story of Paul and Barnabas. (I'll touch on them more in the story behind the Scripture.) To understand the poem, it's enough to say that Paul and Barnabas, once so close, had a "sharp disagreement" over whether to include John Mark on a journey. While there are indications of some level of reconciliation, at least between Paul and John Mark, the break is far more vivid than the reunion. Whatever reconciliation occurred definitely took place among the rubble of a broken alliance.

Throughout the poem I make use of geologic language as a nod both to the sharp break between Paul and Barnabas as well as the Mexico City earthquakes. Ironically, geological terms like back-arc subduction refer not only to the land tearing apart but also to it being crushed together. While the fracture between Paul and Barnabas seems irreconcilable in the Scripture text, later mentions of John Mark in Paul's writing indicate some measure of, if not reconciliation, at least mutual forbearance.

While there's always the temptation to read Paul in a kind of heroic, individualistic fashion, as if he were out there planting churches mostly on his own, the reality is that Paul was part of a thick, well-networked web of relationships.[2] As Joshua Cooper Ramos writes in *The Seventh Sense*: "We are what we are connected to."[3] It makes me think about the people I have served who were once in relationship and then, for a variety of reasons, needed to separate. Because of kids or social media, it just isn't that easy to

1. Semple, "That Green Square," par. 4.
2. Holmberg, *Paul and Power*, 57.
3. Ramo, *The Seventh Sense*, 35.

make a clean break of it these days. For better or worse (no pun intended), we seem to be bound to one another every bit as much as Paul, Barnabas, and John Mark—sometimes even when we wish we weren't.

THE SCRIPTURE: ACTS 15:36–41

After some days Paul said to Barnabas, "Come, let us return and visit the believers in every city where we proclaimed the word of the Lord and see how they are doing." Barnabas wanted to take with them John called Mark. But Paul decided not to take with them one who had deserted them in Pamphylia and had not accompanied them in the work. The disagreement became so sharp that they parted company; Barnabas took Mark with him and sailed away to Cyprus. But Paul chose Silas and set out, the believers commending him to the grace of the Lord. He went through Syria and Cilicia, strengthening the churches.

THE STORY BEHIND THE SCRIPTURE

One time I led an adult class about irrationality and politics at a downtown church in Portland. I signed on to teaching this class months before anyone knew the final candidates would be Hillary Clinton and Donald Trump, about as irrational a political season as any we've seen. I remember at one point talking about division, noting that division happened even within the early church. I cited the sharp break between Paul and Barnabas as a primary example. Paul and Barnabas were able to acknowledge they were heading in fundamentally different directions but still decide to bless each other on their way.

Immediately, a woman responded to me, "Yes, but they reconciled." I was taken aback and tilted my head at her looking somewhat, I imagine, like the RCA dog. She continued, "Paul and Barnabas. They disagreed there, but later they came back together. It's in Paul's letter." I had never heard this, but she stated her argument with a confidence that caused me to accept her at her word and move the class on to a different topic. But it made me curious.

Did Paul and Barnabas reconcile? And why did they break up in the first place?

First, nothing is obvious about the reason for the break between Paul and Barnabas. Luke, the presumed author of Luke-Acts, simply states the

facts of the case without rendering a judgment. They disagree over including John Mark with them on a planned journey to Antioch. But why?

Some people point out that John Mark left Paul and Barnabas when
they were making an earlier journey. Perhaps Paul was miffed that John
Mark didn't stay the course? Maybe Paul questioned John Mark's loyalty?
Maybe Paul, for talking such a good game about grace, didn't really know
how to extend grace to others? All these possibilities are reflected in the
poem.

I'm incredibly grateful for C. K. Robertson's superb book on the topic,
Barnabas vs. Paul: To Encourage or Confront, which offers not only fantastic
wisdom on church leadership but also a really intriguing interpretation on
their break-up.

Digging deeply into first-century culture, Robertson points out that
Paul's society was every bit as diverse as our own world is today. Five sub-
groups are extremely important: faithful Jews (including Pharisees, Sadducees, Essenes, and others); Palestinian Jewish Christians (including Jesus,
Peter, and the original inner circle); Greek Jewish Christians (Jews in the
first century who lived outside of Palestine as part of the Jewish diaspora.
Stephen and Barnabas are excellent examples of this group—fully Jewish
but raised in other lands.); the "God-fearers" (gentiles who worshipped the
Jewish God and followed most of the law except for adult circumcision);
and finally, Greek pagans.

The huge issue facing the first-century church was how Jewish you had
to be to be a Christian. To Jesus and the first disciples the answer was clear:
Christianity was a sectarian movement within Judaism. But by and large the
Jews of the first century weren't buying it. And who can blame them? Jesus
was the messiah, representing the return of the king, but he was crucified?
And they were already living out the messianic new age even though Roman
boots still marched through Jerusalem? None of this made a lot of sense to
people who expected a redeemer in the image of David, the conquering
king.

Enter Paul and Barnabas. Paul, a zealous Jew, went from persecut-
ing Christians to becoming an apostle radically open to anyone following
Jesus—whether they became Jewish or not. Barnabas, already successful
at converting gentiles in Antioch, the place where Christianity was first
named, vouched for Paul in Jerusalem and took him under his wing. The
problem between Paul and Barnabas occurred, according to Robertson, not
primarily because of John Mark, but because of Barnabas. Even after the
Jerusalem council agreed that gentiles could receive Christ without needing
to be circumcised, Paul confronts the churches in Galatia for reverting to
circumcision and food law requirements for the gentiles. Paul cites a time

when Peter and even Barnabas backed away from table fellowship after ultra-orthodox Jewish Christians criticized them. You can hear the pain in Paul's letter when he writes that "even Barnabas" threw them under the bus.

But Paul could forgive Barnabas. The problem was John Mark. But it isn't because John Mark deserted them at Pamphylia, Robertson argues. It's because of John Mark's close connection to Peter.[4] When Peter is freed from prison, he stays at John Mark's house. And although the letter of First Peter probably wasn't written by Peter, the author mentions John Mark with affection as a dear son in faith. Thus, Robertson argues that Paul isn't being petulant when he doesn't agree to John Mark traveling with him and Barnabas: he is pushing back on including a potential Jewish Christian mole.[5] Paul was so dedicated to the project Barnabas began—full inclusion for gentile Christians—that he couldn't allow someone who might report back to the Jewish Christian holdouts.

It's a fascinating conjecture and makes a great deal of sense. And it's incredibly relevant today; the church isn't arguing now about whether to include uncircumcised gentiles but is still fighting over the full inclusion of lesbian, gay, bisexual, transgender, and queer people—as well as figuring out how to live in an increasingly diverse theological and cultural world. The groups have changed, but the fundamental questions about Christian identity remain very much alive.

Sometimes, I hear good church people lament that the church is so divided today. Why can't it be like the good old days when everyone was of the same mind? Of course, there was no such time. The church, and every vital human institution, was and always will be a dynamic, roiling cauldron. As we put it in my Presbyterian tradition: the church is reformed and ever in need of reforming.

---

4. Robertson, *Barnabas vs. Paul*, Kindle location 1631.
5. Ibid.

14

The Romans Fish

Romans 7:19–25

THE ROMANS FISH

In he cast his line again
the white rubber grub
with hook concealed
the arcing rod
bow bending
revealing the catch.

From the depths emerged
the ancient creature
unblinking eyes, gasping gills
strong body straining in hand
but the mouth, the mutilated
mouth, a hundred holes
marring the mauled, jagged jaws.

How many times
had he lost himself to the lure?
Surely a part of his piscine
presence had to suspect
he was falling prey
to deceit's menace?

But for the chance, just the chance
that this meal could be real
he gave into the pull to risk the reel.

And with another tearing
the man rent his frail flesh
flinging that fish flailing
back down to water below

As he watched the fall he thought
about Paul: "The good I want
to do I don't do. The evil
I don't want to do. That's the
thing I do. Wretched man
that I am."

But before that line
could really sink in
he cast the other line again
and he didn't know
how he could ever stop.

THE STORY BEHIND THE POEM

I mentioned earlier that I took up fly fishing when I moved to Oregon. That doesn't mean that I've had much success. One of the first things you learn when you fly fish is there is a distinct difference between fishing and catching. I will say when I caught my first rainbow trout on the fly, it made up for all the waiting. I was on the Salmon River and cast a dry fly into a little riffle upstream. Suddenly, it was as if my five-weight trout rod exploded in my hands. I couldn't believe how powerful that relatively small rainbow felt.

But most of the time when I fish it's a lot of casting. Once, my father-in-law, Mark, and I were up at Detroit Lake casting from the bank when two old duffers walked by and asked if we were practicing. Mark and I looked at one another with chagrin. "No," Mark said, "we're fishing." The two old guys smiled, shook their heads sadly, and kept on walking.

Naturally, fly fishing isn't the sort of fun you could expect a normal child to embrace. I will always remember the summer our family was rained out of our normal summer camping spot by Wallowa Lake; we found refuge at the Prineville Reservoir in Central Oregon. Prineville Reservoir turned out to be an amazing place to fish, in part because it's such a lousy place to sleep. The abundant California quail, among the noisiest birds I have ever heard, woke us every morning earlier than morning should ever come. So, there was plenty of opportunity for early morning fishing.

There's a dock near the campground where we stayed, and one morning my son and two daughters joined me with their rods. A kind and unexpected friend named Jonathan came to lend his expertise. I was wearing my Duke hat, and it turns out Jonathan earned his PhD in biomedical engineering from Duke. And he loved kids. So, we became fast friends, and he helped me in the never-ending tasks of untangling the kids' lines, and, surprisingly, reeling in an absurd amount of fish.

Apparently, there was a Black Crappie convention going on underneath that dock. If you had the right lure, and Jonathan knew exactly what to use, you no sooner threw your line in than a fish would attack it. My kids were elated. My two daughters caught their first fish that morning, and my youngest even worked her courage up to grab the fish, remove the lure, and throw it back. (This is no small thing given the extremely sharp spines along the back of the Black Crappie.)

I caught one fish that inspired this poem. I threw my grub in, pulled it up, and it was one of the larger crappie I had caught that morning. But when I held the fish to remove the lure, I almost didn't know what to think. There was barely a mouth left. This fish had been caught so many times and had so many lures and hooks yanked from his jaws that he was just a wreck.

What immediately came to mind were my own challenges with moderation and all the people under my care who struggle with addiction. I have known seasons in my life where I have failed to maintain a healthy relationship with God's good gift of the vine. And I have cared for some who have been sober for years and others who were just trying to get through their first week. I continue to hear people ask obvious questions: Why don't they just stop? Why don't they just make better choices? All I can tell you is I've never known anyone who woke up in the morning wanting to make their own or anyone else's life miserable. The truth is life can be unbearably hard at times. And even when we know we're on the wrong path, it's awfully hard to turn back once we've started down the road.

To me, the one really hopeful thing about this poem is the ending. While it could sound futile, as if the fisher hasn't let Paul's words sink in and is just casting in again on autopilot, the character in the poem does acknowledge something new about himself. He acknowledges that he *doesn't know* when he's going to stop.

Once, when I was beating myself up quite thoroughly in a counseling session, I remember the therapist sharing these words: "Ken, I wonder what it would be like if, instead of having to fix yourself or be perfect, you might allow room just to observe yourself? You're so good at extending grace to others, but with yourself, there is so little room for just watching yourself and your patterns." My entire world changed in that moment. I had always thought of counseling (and probably most things in life) as mastering myself and becoming the best I can possibly be. And while I'm incredibly understanding of others, I have held myself to impossible standards and bear the marks from that. But to allow myself to see myself, *my self*, as a stranger? As someone to be observed rather than someone I must fix? It was an entirely new way of thinking for me. And I think the fisherman at the end of this poem at least begins to see himself from a little distance. He begins to see himself as a mystery—a mystery he isn't sure how to predict or perfect. And that . . . that is no small thing.

THE SCRIPTURE: ROMANS 7:19–25

For I do not do the good I want, but the evil I do not want is what I do. Now if I do what I do not want, it is no longer I that do it, but sin that dwells within me.

So I find it to be a law that when I want to do what is good, evil lies close at hand. For I delight in the law of God in my inmost self, but I see in my members another law at war with the law of my mind, making me captive to the law of sin that dwells in my members. Wretched man that I am! Who will rescue me from this body of death? Thanks be to God through Jesus Christ our Lord!

So then, with my mind I am a slave to the law of God, but with my flesh I am a slave to the law of sin.

THE STORY BEHIND THE SCRIPTURE

I remember sitting in a doctoral seminar led by Ed Sanders at Duke that completely blew my mind. I thought of myself as a pretty smart guy. I had studied Paul. I had my MDiv from Princeton. When Paul wrote these words about the good he wanted to do that he didn't do and the evil he didn't want to do that he did do, it was self-evident to me that he was talking about himself. He uses present tense verbs. He uses the first-person pronoun. To me, Paul was experiencing an unusually vulnerable moment here describing himself and his own struggles. So, given my tendency to arrogance, boasting, and sarcasm, these words from Paul became one of my favorite passages.

Indeed, for being a long-term Presbyterian, I read the passage as a through and through Lutheran. Martin Luther loved this divided, tortured side of Paul, too, and he summed up the existential crisis Paul seems to be describing as one of being at the same time sinful and justified. In *Luther: Man Between God and the Devil*, Late Medieval and Reformation scholar Heiko A. Oberman sets forth Luther's description of this state of dual existence: "Through Christ's exchange the faithful Christian is 'simultaneously sinner and just'—'simul peccator et iustus.' He is a sinner because self-love and inner resistance against God remains unconquered; he is just because he has been given the righteousness of Christ, which is valid before God."[1]

Luther's interpretation made so much sense to me both as a believer and as a pastor. Whoever is the worst person in our lives, no matter how much pain they have caused us, they are still children of God. Even when I can't see the image of Christ in someone, my inability to see it doesn't mean it isn't there. Despite the temptation to play a kind of theological duck, duck, goose with the world (good guy, good guy, good guy, jack wagon), the reality is every person is a mixed bag.

But then I encountered Sanders. Ed Sanders, or E. P. Sanders as he goes by on his many book covers, started a revolution in Pauline studies now known as the New Perspectives on Paul movement. Restoring Paul to his

1. Oberman, *Luther*, 184.

Jewish foundation and rescuing him from the death grip of classical Protestant theology, Ed argues this passage isn't autobiographical at all. Rather,
Ed argues that Paul isn't describing himself but what people experience who
don't live in Christ. Ed writes:

> In general, we may say that Paul wanted to depict life without
> Christ as being bad at best, eventually becoming horrific. Help-
> lessness to do what one wants and being bound to doing what
> one does not want is a terrible condition.
>
> The result is to make life in Christ stand out all the more. In
> view of what follows in chapter 8, this explanation of the pro-
> gression of Paul's descriptions of the human condition seems
> overwhelmingly likely. Thus, Paul is describing neither himself,
> nor Christians in general; he is describing the worst state that he
> can imagine and imputing it to people who have not died with
> Christ. The "I" is generalizing: not all people as represented by
> Adam, but all people who are not in Christ.[2]

Part of Ed's argument rests on how utterly confident Paul sounds regarding his relationship in Christ in every other passage. Paul talks about
himself as a new creation: the old is gone; in baptism, he has risen anew with
Jesus. He says nothing can separate us from God in Christ Jesus—nothing.
Paul makes extreme moral demands that, in Ed's view, he actually expects
Christians to be able to follow. To Ed, Paul is an amazing, driven, revolutionary figure, but he's not a man who would have felt so torn and certainly
wouldn't have shared about it.

Ed writes: "But, seriously, the reader should recognize that if Rom. 7:
14–25 is Paul's autobiography, someone else wrote the rest of the material
that is attributed to him. If this had been Paul's state, he would have been
too depressed to conduct evangelical missions and to write letters to his
churches, since he knew that he could do only harm, not good."[3] In other
words, to Ed, if Paul wrote these helpless, hopeless words, then it had to be
someone else who wrote everything else.

I remember feeling agitated sitting through this seminar with Ed. It
had taken me a long time to become comfortable with Paul in the first place.
Like many, I initially had a popular view of Paul: while grateful for his work
as a church planter, I viewed him as sexist, moralistic, and deeply problematic. I liked Jesus, but I felt as if I was living in a church that had been
hijacked by Paul.

2. Sanders, *Paul: The Apostle's Life*, Kindle location 10090–96.
3. Ibid., Kindle location 10078–81.

Actually reading Paul helped. Far from a sexist, if you bother to really read his letters, Paul smashes glass ceilings not splintered again until
modern feminism. In Galatians, probably his first and definitely most extreme letter, Paul effaces the differences between men and women entirely:
in Christ, "there is no longer male and female" (Gal 3:28). Upon a closer
read, Paul's behavior was consistent with this egalitarian view. Paul names
many women as co-partners in ministry. He thanks Prisca before her husband Aquila in every mention. (This is as jarring in classical literature as
it is in modern English.) My predecessor at the church I currently serve
insisted upon naming the women before the men in the church directory.
While I consider myself a feminist, I will admit that this small, but meaningful, change took some getting used to. In Romans, Paul names Junia as
an apostle, and the feminine ending of her name indicates her gender. This
was so disconcerting to the early church (a woman apostle??!!) that anxious
scribes later changed the ending of her name to Junius, probably the first instance of a sex change! And of course, there is Phoebe. Phoebe was a leader
in the church of Cenchreae, the port city just south of Corinth. Paul must
have been incredibly impressed with Phoebe's leadership because at the end
of his letter to the Romans he basically writes a job reference for Phoebe:
he commends her to the Christians as their deacon, a title he claimed for
himself, to lead, preach, and teach them.

Sometimes the ancient language helps us with some of the more
problematic verses, such as when Paul says that women should be silent.
Paul uses the aorist tense in that moment, which has the effect of saying
the women in that particular church should be silent at that time—not that
women everywhere for all time should be silent. Given that we don't know
the context and Paul was simply writing a letter meant for one community
at one moment in time, it seems clear we can't universalize this saying as an
oppressive stick to preclude half of the population from church leadership.

So, I turned from being extremely distrustful of Paul to being a champion. For me, Paul morphed from Mussolini into Che Guevara. And now,
here comes Ed Sanders to destroy my newfound hero?

Honestly, at this point, I still don't quite know what to think. After
reading E. P. Sanders, I am more respectful of the vast differences between
my culture and language and Paul's—enough to be suspicious of attempts
to fit Paul into a mold with which I'm comfortable. However, I still like to
think of Paul as capable of showing vulnerability and giving us a window
into his personal experience. As much as I respect E. P. Sanders, Paul is
hardly known for his consistency. He wrote to different communities at different times and never made any pretense of being a systematic theologian.
Moreover, there are times when all of us say one thing when we're being

aspirational and another when we're being confessional. In this sense, we aren't being inconsistent so much as acknowledging different sides of our whole selves when it's appropriate.

So, while Ed may be entirely right about Paul—and it's worth serious consideration—I also continue to value Luther's understanding and resonate with a view of humanity that holds none of us are perfect. We're all saints and sinners, trying our best to navigate a complicated, challenging world.

15

Grace

Matthew 26:20–35

GRACE

The man who kissed him held the common purse.
At the final table, next to him he sat.
Today his name is spat out as a curse
the one who would betray, the hellish rat.
The fisherman who left became the rock
in protest said that he would ne'er disown
but later shamed by midnight crowing cock
three times his cowardice to all was shown.
Along the way some argued who was best.
They doubted, jabbing hands and feet and side
denied the children coming to be blessed.
From Golgotha they fled from death to hide.
If these were worthy, welcome to receive
then who should be held back, whatever they believe?

THE STORY BEHIND THE POEM

When I was coming to faith (or maybe I should say when faith was coming to me) during high school, one of the most important books for me was Alan Jones's *Passion for Pilgrimage*. In *Passion*, Jones discussed grace in a way that I had never heard and found deeply compelling. Grace, of course, is the freely given love of God. No matter what. When nearly every cultural message proclaims that we are as worthy as our bank account, our waist size, and work ethic, there is nothing more revolutionary and countercultural in the Bible than grace.

Ironically, though, the very church in which I first learned about grace, the Presbyterian Church (U.S.A.), manifested a deep ambiguity about grace when it came to the practice of the Lord's table. For most of my life the Presbyterian understanding of communion held that only baptized people were welcome at the table. Indeed, in the earliest days of our church in America the table was even fenced, a physical barrier that prevented anyone who wasn't in good standing from receiving this means of grace.

An argument erupted between the great theologian Jonathan Edwards (yes, of the sermon "Sinners in the Hands of an Angry God" fame) and his elder John Stoddard. Edwards held that people needed to have a personal awakening in order to receive the Lord's Supper. Stoddard argued that the Lord's Supper could be an "evangelical ordinance": the table could be a place where people actually came to know God's grace.

To be sure, the Presbyterians aren't the only ones who have attempted to limit God's grace. The Roman Catholic Church, of course, welcomes Roman Catholics who have confessed to receive communion. The Lutheran Church Missouri Synod restricts the table not only to LCMS adherents but to local members of the specific LCMS church. Receiving the Lord's Supper is so dangerous, apparently, they wouldn't want to mistakenly cause someone to experience God's wrath by partaking unworthily.

I sort of get the liturgical logic of wanting people to be baptized before receiving communion. There's this historic sense in which baptism is the entrance rite into the church and should precede the Lord's Supper. But I think that made much more sense during Christendom, the long season when the church dominated the West, than it does in this new post-Christendom age in which fewer and fewer people are raised in the church. And, at least to my mind, this attempt to limit God's grace makes no sense when we actually read the story.

Whom does Jesus welcome to the table? Well, Judas, for one, the man who betrays Jesus with a kiss. If welcoming Judas isn't bad enough, Jesus serves Peter as well, the one who would publically deny Jesus not once but three times—some stalwart rock Peter turned out to be. And the other disciples? When they weren't arguing about who was the greatest disciple, they were trying to keep the children from gaining access to Jesus. They were hardly the A-Team by any stretch of the imagination. And yet these disciples—these were whom Jesus welcomed to the table.

For my ministry, I reject my church's traditional language regarding restricting the table to the baptized. I have always extended a welcome using words such as: "Come, whether you are full of belief this morning or riddled with doubt. Come, if you believe in Jesus already, or if you want to come to trust in his grace and love. Come, not because I welcome you, but because Jesus himself does." I'm pleased to say that at our 2016 General Assembly, held in my own backyard of Portland, Oregon, The Presbyterian Church (U.S.A.) voted to open the Lord's table to anyone. We now trust that it's probably a good idea to allow God to decide whom to bless and not to bless.

THE SCRIPTURE: MATTHEW 26:20–35

When it was evening, he took his place with the twelve; and while they were eating, he said, "Truly I tell you, one of you will betray me." And they became greatly distressed and began to say to him one after another, "Surely not I, Lord?" He answered, "The one who has dipped his hand into the bowl with me will betray me. The Son of Man goes as it is written of him, but woe to that one by whom the Son of Man is betrayed! It would have been better for that one not to have been born." Judas, who betrayed him, said, "Surely not I, Rabbi?" He replied, "You have said so."

While they were eating, Jesus took a loaf of bread, and after blessing it he broke it, gave it to the disciples, and said, "Take, eat; this is my body." Then he took a cup, and after giving thanks he gave it to them, saying, "Drink from it, all of you; for this is my blood of the covenant, which is poured out for many for the forgiveness of sins. I tell you, I will never again drink of this fruit of the vine until that day when I drink it new with you in my Father's kingdom."

When they had sung the hymn, they went out to the Mount of Olives.

Then Jesus said to them, "You will all become deserters because of me this night; for it is written, 'I will strike the shepherd, and the sheep of the flock will be scattered.' But after I am raised up, I will go ahead of you to Galilee." Peter said to him,

"Though all become deserters because of you, I will never desert you." Jesus said to him, "Truly I tell you, this very night, before the cock crows, you will deny me three times." Peter said to him, "Even though I must die with you, I will not deny you." And so said all the disciples.

THE STORY BEHIND THE SCRIPTURE

Judas is a particularly fascinating figure in the Scriptures. What I might call the legend of Judas grows progressively in the Gospels over time from the fairly spare, neutral treatment of him in Mark to the image of Judas as an evil Satanic agent of darkness in John.

As I pointed out in the story and Scripture related to the first poem in this book, "Resurrection Isn't an Argument," the Gospel of Mark is the earliest gospel. And in the conversation around "Not Running, but Dancing" (the first poem in section two), I discussed the adult version of how the Gospels were composed: Matthew and Luke built from Mark and other early sources but added their own creative artistry, which is why I say the legend of Judas grows and develops over time.

Mark simply describes Judas as betraying Jesus. No reason is given. No Satanic or devil language is used. Mark tells us nothing about what happens to Judas after the betrayal. Mark offers us a "just-the-facts, ma'am" account, leaving open the possibility of all kinds of interpretations. One of my favorite interpretations comes from Nikos Kazantzakis who actually sees Judas as the real leader of the disciples. In *The Last Temptation of Christ*, when Judas realizes that Jesus isn't going to bring about a military coup, Judas betrays Jesus out of a kind of hurt anger. Kazantzakis's Judas isn't evil but a leader who betrays someone he believes has let the group down.

In Matthew's narrative, the story of Judas gets a little darker. The way Matthew tells the tale, Judas himself seeks out the chief priests and promises to betray Jesus for money. While this is clearly not good, Matthew softens the portrayal of Judas by lifting up Judas's regret: Judas goes back to the chief priests and tries to return their thirty pieces of silver. The chief priests refuse to take the silver back into the treasury because it is blood money. Instead they use the money to buy the potter's field as a place to bury foreigners, which came to be known as the Field of Blood. Judas, acknowledging the sin of his betrayal, then hangs himself.

Judas in Luke-Acts becomes darker still. In Luke-Acts, Luke says that Satan enters into Judas. Moreover, Judas makes no attempt to return the money to the chief priests. Rather, in an interesting twist in Acts, we learn that it was Judas himself who bought the field with the money given to him for betraying Jesus. And then, in a scene reminiscent of Ananias and Sapphira who were struck dead for not giving everything they had to the community, Judas falls headlong, his stomach somehow bursts open, and his bowels gush out over the ground. In Luke's treatment, it is that horrific, gushing-bowels "accident" that gives the field the name, Field of Blood.

In John, the last gospel written, Judas becomes evil personified. John tells us it is Judas who criticizes the woman for anointing Jesus because he holds the common purse and has been stealing from it. John says both that the devil puts the idea to betray Jesus into Judas and that Satan enters into him at the table. Evocatively, John closes the scene when Judas leaves the last supper to betray Jesus with these words: "And it was night."

Whether Mark is right that Judas's motives are unclear or the pitch-black depictions of Luke-Acts and John are more accurate, to me it's still striking that Jesus welcomed Judas to the table and served him. And . . . if Judas is worthy, then who could be unworthy potentially? My favorite story about Judas comes from Alan Jones. (Remember, I mentioned earlier that I gained my sense of grace from reading his book *Passion for Pilgrimage*.) Jones relates that after Judas died, he fell into a deep, dark pit. For thousands and thousands of years Judas fell and fell into this pit, until he found himself at the very bottom. Too tired to breathe or move for thousands of years more, Judas just lay there. Finally, Judas looked up to see a tiny pin prick of light shining like the faintest star on a foggy night. But still, it was a pinprick of light in the darkest of places. Finally able to summon enough strength to move, Judas begins to crawl up the walls of the pit. Year after year, Judas struggles to crawl up those walls, and as he climbs higher the light grows brighter, filling him with more and more strength and resolve. Finally, when he reaches the light, Judas enters into it and finds himself inside a small upper room filled with friends. The rabbi Jesus smiles at the newcomer and says, "Judas! Welcome! We've been waiting for you. We couldn't continue the supper without you."[1] That is the Jesus I know.

---

1. Jones, *Passion for Pilgrimage*, Kindle location 1471.

David the Beautiful Mess

16

The Beautiful, Painful Mess
of David's Full Humanity

One of the stranger things I notice about contemporary Christianity is our tendency to boil down religion to morality—and a narrow, Victorian morality at that. Parents who don't really know what to think of church readily send their children to Vacation Bible School hoping they will learn right from wrong as if by osmosis. Even in the unchurched/de-churched Pacific Northwest, I still occasionally hear people worry about declining morals and link this decline to the erosion of biblical literacy and church attendance. Whenever I hear such comments I always think to myself, "Seriously? Have you even *read* this book?" I can't think of one person in the entirety of the Scriptures I would want my children to look to as a model for behavior. And before you say Jesus, he talked back to his parents, was rude to his elders, and wound up getting himself killed. Yes, he's the Son of God and all that, but if you are seriously okay with your child getting crucified, I'm going to suggest you may want to rethink your bid for father or mother of the year.

No, to me the most striking, unexpected, and compelling characteristic of the Bible is that in story after story it offers less of a model for human behavior than a mirror. The Scriptures do not tell us what to do as much as they show us who we are in all our grandeur and depravity.

Abraham and Sarah are pieces of work. When apparently unbelievably desperate warlords have their eye on Sarah, the luscious octogenarian,

Abraham attempts to pawn her off as his sister not once but twice. He sends his first son Ishmael to a certain death in the wilderness and binds Isaac up as a sacrifice only to have God save both the kids' bacon. Sarah, for her part, acted like the worst dance mother in history by nagging Abraham to send Ishmael away after her precious Isaac came along. (No one was doubting her commitment to Sparkle Motion, thank you very much!) Moses was a murderer who tried to get out of his call a gazillion times until God finally had enough. The Israelites, for their part, were the least happy campers in history on their forty-year hike. My favorite moment is when they ask Moses if it was because there weren't any graves in Egypt that he had to take them out to die in the desert. Classic! Jonah was a racist. Mordecai, in the Book of Esther, responds to genocide with genocide. (I know, I know; Haman started it.) Ruth bags Boaz as a husband because she sexually assaults him after he's passed out drunk in the barn after work. John the Baptist eats locusts and yells at people. Peter denies Jesus not once but three times. Judas goes from BFF to betrayer for thirty pieces of silver, and the rest of the petulant, argumentative disciples are about as useful as an ejection seat on a helicopter most days. The Apostle Paul? While I tend to defend him, he has caused at least as many challenges for the church as he has solved. (Slaves, obey your masters, anyone?)

But the award for most fully human character in the Scriptures has to go to David.

We've already looked at David's horrific treatment of his first wife Michal: he forcibly removes her from her second husband Palti when David doesn't even want her any longer. We've touched on Bathsheba, David's murder of Uriah, and his unconscionable unwillingness to deal with Amnon's rape of Tamar. Any of these incidents would be enough to mark one of our Presidents for impeachment and removal from office. Sure, the Chronicler cleans the First and Second Samuel version up a bit; but given the place David has in the tradition, it is phenomenal to me that we have any record at all of David's brokenness, much less the twisting, sordid tale that was left in the Bible. As Joel Baden puts it: "David was a successful monarch, but he was a vile human being."[1]

As painful as David's story is, there is a strange, terrible beauty in it as well. There is a raw beauty in seeing someone's life so openly and honestly explored. Moreover, there is a riveting quality to a life lived at the extremes, a beautiful spaciousness created by David existing at such heights and depths. It is in David's poetry, however, that we see David's honor alongside his ignominy—that we see the beauty in the mess begin to shine.

1. Baden, *Historical David*, 259.

As I noted earlier, attributing the entirety of the Psalms to David is a tricky enterprise. Clearly, the late setting of some of the psalms precludes Davidic authorship. It's hard to write about times hundreds of years after your death. But at the same time, I don't share the hyper-suspicious attitude of modern historical-critical scholarship that assumes all tradition is bunk until proven otherwise. Like the little friends who told Virginia there was no Santa Claus, it's easy for us to adopt a superior overconfidence in our modern literary tools and forget that there may be much in heaven and earth of which we have not, as of yet, dreamed. Given none of us were actually there when the psalms were written, I'm willing to extend some trust that at least some meaningful relationship existed between David and the Book of Psalms. The fact that he didn't write all of them does not indicate he did not write any of them. And the fact that David sings throughout First and Second Samuel and many of the psalms themselves mention his authorship are enough for me.

My relationship with the psalms started slowly. When I was in middle school, I headed south to a church camp on a bus with kids who were mostly strangers to me. One older girl, awkward and shy with her peers but more comfortable with me, was reading something in the seat ahead of me. Her brown hair was woven into a single, long braid. Her brown eyes were intent on what she was reading. She must have felt me noticing her because she looked up as I turned away. She explained she was reading the Bible and asked me if I loved it in a way that told me she was a fan. With some embarrassment, I acknowledged I didn't really know the Bible well. The truth was I didn't know it at all at that point in my life. Her eyes grew wide and she told me that I should absolutely start with the Psalms because they were the most beautiful poems in the Bible; you could just read them over and over and hear something new every time. I don't remember my response, but today I would have said something like, "Yeah . . . don't oversell it."

My expectations were so high that my first impressions of the Psalms were not great. The language is rough and strange from the very beginning. In Psalm 1 we hear about "the wicked" and "sinners" who will, like chaff, be blown away. Yikes! Church people may be totally comfortable with this kind of language; but for a suburban kid raised on The Brady Bunch and M.A.S.H., let's just say this language did not grab me. Moreover, there's a militancy in some of the psalms I found extremely unattractive. In the very next psalm, Psalm 2, we hear that if we ask God, we will possess the whole world and break other nations like an iron rod shatters a clay pot. Double yikes! (Or, yikes-a-roni as my sister-in-law, Liz, would put it.) What I would come to understand in time is that, like the work of poet Mary Karr, the psalms are not always pretty, but they are always powerful.

But there is a reason why the Psalms are rightly considered a Bible within the Bible. All this strangeness, all this difficulty? When matched with the sublime beauty of other parts of the Psalms, these difficult moments are precisely what make this book so replete. Hailing from the Reformed tradition, I would be remiss if I didn't mention Calvin's deep love for the Psalms; he found in them the full range of human experience and emotion: "I have been accustomed to call this book, I think not inappropriately, 'An Anatomy of all the Parts of the Soul'; for there is not an emotion of which any one can be conscious that is not here represented as in a mirror."[2]

The Psalms express confidence in the midst of hard times. The psalm everyone knows, if they know anything from the Bible, is Psalm 23: The Lord is my shepherd. Whether it is because this psalm is so connected with loss or because of the depth of the imagery, if David didn't actually write it, he could have. It's not hard to imagine David during the period he was on the run from Saul writing this song to comfort himself during a frightening and vulnerable time. This psalm regularly makes it into my own prayer language; I pray for people to discover surprising still waters and unexpected places of green pastures ahead. The range of translations regarding the valley allows interpreters to hear both the shadow lands of depression and loss as well as the harder, more bitter landscape of death itself.

The Psalms also sing of the exhilaration of freedom. In memory of the Exodus in which the Egyptian army was destroyed in a flood of water, Psalm 124 imagines what the Israelites must have felt like. They thought they were trapped, but then they realized they had escaped. The psalmist imagines the Israelites felt like a trapped bird who found her freedom: "We have escaped like a bird from the snare of the fowlers; the snare is broken, and we have escaped" (124:7).

The Psalms explore the beauty and heights of creation itself: "When I look at your heavens, the work of your fingers, the moon and the stars that you have established; what are human beings that you are mindful of them, mortals that you care for them? Yet you have made them a little lower than God, and crowned them with glory and honor" (8:3–5). We don't hear language like this again until Shakespeare, writing in *Hamlet*: "What a piece of work is man! How noble in reason, how infinite in faculties! in form and moving, how express and admirable! in action how like an angel! in apprehension, how like a god!"[3]

And, those who know the entirety of Hamlet's soliloquy offered to Rosencrantz and Guildenstern understand that Hamlet was only establishing

2. Calvin, "Preface," 1.xxxvi–xxxvii.
3. Shakespeare, *Hamlet*, act 2: scene 2, 1141.

the greatness of humanity to express his disappointment: "The beauty of
the world! The paragon of animals! And yet to me, what is this quintessence
of dust? Man delights not me; no, nor woman neither."[4] David is equally
capable of switching moods in the Psalms. Claiming to be just fine after
Nathan renders judgment on David for sleeping with Bathsheba and killing
Uriah, we hear the depth of David's lament in Psalm 51: "For I know my
transgressions, and my sin is ever before me. Against you, you alone, have I
sinned, and done what is evil in your sight, so that you are justified in your
sentence and blameless when you pass judgment. Indeed, I was born guilty,
a sinner when my mother conceived me" (51: 3–5).

And quintessence of dust? How about the lowliness of a worm? In
Psalm 22, we hear: "But I am a worm, and not human; scorned by others,
and despised by the people. All who see me mock at me; they make mouths
at me, they shake their heads" (22:6–7).

Harder to hear than even this worm language, however, is the murderous rage emanating from what scholars call the psalms of imprecation.
To this day I have yet to see anyone cross-stitch the final verses of Psalm
137: "O daughter Babylon, you devastator! Happy shall they be who pay
you back what you have done to us! Happy shall they be who take your little
ones and dash them against the rock!" (137:8–9). These lines from Psalm
137 are far from unique; the Psalms are full of these dark, violent fantasies.
Psalms 57–59, all attributed to David, describe the period when Saul was
trying to kill him while David was hiding in the hills. These psalms are filled
with harsh moments: "O God, break the teeth in their mouths; tear out the
fangs of the young lions, O Lord! Let them vanish like water that runs away;
like grass let them be trodden down and wither. Let them be like the snail
that dissolves into slime; like the untimely birth that never sees the sun"
(58:6–8). Wow!

Notre Dame's Gary A. Anderson offers the most helpful way of understanding this vicious language: "The imprecatory psalms give witness to that
deep abyss of personal hatred that David, through divine grace, was able to
overcome."[5]

Anderson takes the Davidic authorship seriously and notes the setting.
These psalms were written when Saul was hunting David, and David was
given the chance, not once but twice, to take Saul's life. The first time, David
finds Saul indisposed in a cave and tears a piece of his cloak; the second
time, David sneaks into Saul's camp under the cover of darkness and steals
Saul's spear. In both instances it would be entirely understandable for David

4. Ibid.
5. Anderson, "King David Psalms of Imprecation," 272; italics removed.

to kill Saul and put an end to his fugitive nightmare. Yet, Anderson notes the important line setting up each psalm: "Destroy not." Anderson notes this is precisely the language David uses with Abishai during the night mission to steal Saul's spear. When the young warrior wants to pin Saul to the ground with his spear, David tells Abishai: "Do not destroy him" (1 Sam 26:9). Anderson argues these psalms were a way for David to work through the emotions teeming within him in order to keep him from physically acting upon them. Anderson, drawing upon the wisdom of the Jewish tradition, writes: "The conclusion the Rabbis drew was as simple as it was inevitable: David composed these two prayers while attempting to flee the hostile attacks of King Saul. He entertained thoughts of doing Saul in himself—indeed according to the words of the psalm David burned with a desire to have his vengeance—but at the fated opportunity David managed to hold these feelings in check."[6] By allowing himself to feel his feelings and give them air, David didn't give in to murderous rage; by using song as something akin to a live vaccine, David sang his rage in order to immunize himself from it.

Given the mirror of the Psalms, it's fair to say that David was a mess inside. But, when we consider the difference between all that David felt and all that he did, in addition to the incredible heights and sheer grandeur of imagery in the Psalms, David is, at least, a beautiful mess.

6. Ibid., 274.

17

Ziklag

1 Samuel 22:1–3, 27:1–7

ZIKLAG

"Later the Philistine king, Achish, became David's protector and gave him the village of Ziklag as a base to work from. It became his 'church,' if you will, for his family and his soldiers. The congregation was made up of 'every one who was in distress, and every one who was in debt and every one who was discontented'—the sociological model of David's congregation: people whose lives were characterized by debt, distress, and discontent—a congregation of runaways and renegades. It isn't what I would call the cream of the crop of Israelite society. More like dregs from the barrel. Misfits all, it appears."[1]

—Eugene Peterson

It was a mixed bag, Ziklag
slippery David escaping Saul's insanity
sliding into a second base, sleeping with Philistine enemy.

---

1. Peterson, *The Pastor: A Memoir*, 106.

He was not alone
soon six hundred showed
ragtag runaways, renegades, and strays, misfits all
no place to lay their mutinous heads.

They weren't the ones you'd pick
this mess unlikely to stick, but the Shepherd's
still waters surrounding, rising rocks enfolding
flocked them into one.

Of course, you may not stumble upon Ziklag's zoo
in a wilderness outpost or downtown glass building.
Your Ziklag might be within.

A whole host of angels and demons, nobility and sin
all bleating for blessing, pressing
unfit prodigals yearning for the ring, welcoming
them back in to the fold.

The ugly desire, the shameful smallness
grazing green pasture next to your deepest hope
highest intention, and purest love.
You cannot make sense of this.
Your only choice to bring in these black sheep along with the rest
and see how the discarded shards of today
draw into the strongest hand tomorrow
how hollowing depression
is carving you out for a creativity
you could never have conjured.

Or you can sustain the assault
against yourself playing the small, controlling Saul
to the lion of David's roaring hospitality.
You can. You can. For a long time you can. But not forever.

See, we are mysteries, you and I
the passing thought, the untoward look, and absurd fantasy.
The deepest faith silences not these unruly souls
but sings a new song spacious enough to weave together the whole.

THE STORY BEHIND THE POEM

When I was in high school, I became enthralled with the psychology of Carl Jung. (Like most high schoolers, right?) Jung, a young colleague of Freud, was enamored with the great psychoanalyst but eventually broke with him over their differing views of sexuality. While Freud's contention that infantile sexuality represented the primary determining cause of all adult behavior, Jung eventually abandoned this position. In the preface to *The Psychology of Dementia Praecox*, Jung writes:

> Fairness to Freud does not signify, as many fear, a condition-less submission to a dogma; indeed independent judgment can very well be retained beside it. If I, for instance, recognize the complex mechanisms of dreams and hysteria, it does not at all mean that I ascribe to sexual trauma in youth an exclusive significance, as Freud apparently does; still less does it mean that I place sexuality so preponderantly in the foreground, or that I even ascribe to it the psychological universality which Freud postulates under the impression of the very powerful role which sexuality plays in the psyche. As for Freud's therapy, it is at best a possible one, and perhaps does not always come up to expectations.[2]

For Jung, our drive for what he calls individuation is where the real action is. In place of Freud's orthodox tripartite self, composed of the super ego, the ego, and the id, Jung posits a conscious ego floating on a massive, unconscious Self. Individuation is the process in which our small egos integrate more and more of our larger Self. Dream analysis offers one of the most powerful ways to become more aware of this process. Things aren't always what they appear in dreams. Jung counseled dreamers to pay particular attention to menacing, frightening figures. Such seemingly negative images might actually indicate what he referred to as the ego's shadow. Given the ego is a much smaller expression of ourselves than our full Self, the shadow represents aspects of ourselves we don't feel comfortable owning or have been taught to suppress. A quiet, gentle man might dream of a powerful, violent figure, calling him to honor stronger parts of himself with which he is less comfortable. A woman taught to be a "proper lady" might dream of a hedonistic, sexual figure, reminding her of her own animal sexuality.

When I was a senior in high school, once a week I would drive into South Dallas to join a Jungian dream group led by analyst Marshall Voris. Less than half the age of everyone else in the group, I was greeted with a

2. Jung, "Preface," xx.

mix of bemusement and curiosity. Marshall, a charismatic, boyish man who looked much younger than he actually was, would open the group by asking if anyone had a dream to share. It was one of the strangest groups I had ever been a part of at that time in my life. Adults shared intimate dreams, exposing some of the most vulnerable places in their lives. A favorite technique of Marshall's was to ask the dreamer to enlist others in the group to act out the different characters in a dream. I remember being asked to stand up and become part of a tableau vivant for this woman who was bored with her husband and tired of her seemingly perfect life. Along with a few other men, I was playing the role of one of her ex-lovers. As I stood there she got up and prowled around the room sniffing and pawing at us like the jaguar in her dream. I remember feeling deeply uncomfortable but also amused at the same time—as if I didn't know whether to bolt from the room or to laugh at this bizarre performance.

Unable to avoid the hot seat forever, one week I had one of the most vivid dreams I have ever had in my life. I was inside a large white house that, in the dream, I knew to be mine. Outside sprawled a lush green yard, and around the yard circled a picturesque white fence. Everything looked perfect except I noticed the gate was open, the wind banging it against the fence. I was filled with dread, and I didn't know why until I looked down the street. Running toward my open gate were three massive figures that looked as if they came straight out of *Where the Wild Things Are*. Somehow in my dream I knew the figures were named Meshach, Shadrach, and Abednego, the three men in the fiery furnace with the prophet Daniel.

At that time, I was still very much on the fence about how I felt about the church. Religion was something of a no-holds-barred affair in the Texas of my childhood. When I was in kindergarten, one girl was going around to all the kids on the playground during recess asking them if they believed in God: "Do you believe in God?" She asked in question form, but it was really more of a demand. Now, I had no idea at the age of six what I believed or didn't believe, but I knew for sure I didn't like this girl going around and getting in everyone's face. So when she came to me, I told her no. Her eyes narrowed into angry little slits. She hissed the question at me again. Slowly. Again, I gave her the same answer. Then, with something approaching glee, she told me I was going to hell. To this day I can't understand how people believe that God is loving *unless* you don't say or believe the right things, and then this "loving" God will throw you into a fiery pit of suffering without end.

Of course, it would take me many, many more years to discover a Christianity that didn't think of God in this retributive and bloodthirsty way. So, for most of my young life, it felt as if choosing Christianity meant choosing a thoughtless, narrow, and base path. By the time I got to high school, my appreciation of the faith was deepening and growing. I loved everything about the church we attended—the preaching, the openness, the willingness to make room for my questions and doubts, but love for the church was still very much part of my shadow.

In my dream I ran out of the house in a mad dash to close the gate. I felt as if my life depended on it. And that was true in a way, as I look back. The life I had known—the free-thinking, anti-church identity I had constructed—depended on it. The creatures and I made it to the gate at nearly the same time, but the creature in the lead had the edge on me. I wound up sprawled on the lawn as the creatures entered, but instead of devouring me they picked me up. Taking hands, we danced around the lawn. They weren't there to terrorize me; they were there to celebrate with me. When I shared this dream with the group, Marshall asked me how I felt about it. I reported a deep ambivalence. On the one hand the feeling I had in the dream was deeply joyful. But at the same time this invitation to draw closer to Christian faith filled me with anxiety. Marshall seemed thrilled, saying this kind of anxiety often accompanied healthy growth. Great, I thought. But with the clarity of hindsight Marshall turned out to be right.

Individuation—this process of becoming human—means integrating the disparate parts of ourselves. It means seeing and honoring all the many voices crying out in our innermost being—especially the voices we were taught to suppress, control, and, if at all possible, to banish. Similar to David singing his rage in the psalms of imprecation as a way of taking the wind out of the sails of those dark fantasies, owning the shadow is a way of acknowledging our darkness in order to keep it from taking us over. This integration of the shadow goes against our popular cultural wisdom of accentuating the positive and eliminating the negative (as the song goes), but I have found that ignoring the darkness rarely, if ever, pretends it away. In my case learning to embrace the shadow meant learning to own my faith in Jesus Christ, something that was difficult and personally embarrassing to me for years. But now, I can't imagine who I would be if those monsters hadn't crashed my gate.

THE SCRIPTURE: 1 SAMUEL 22:1–3, 27:1–7

1 Samuel 22:1–3:

David left there and escaped to the cave of Adullam; when his brothers and all his father's house heard of it, they went down there to him. Everyone who was in distress, and everyone who was in debt, and everyone who was discontented gathered to him; and he became captain over them. Those who were with him numbered about four hundred.

David went from there to Mizpeh of Moab. He said to the king of Moab, "Please let my father and mother come to you, until I know what God will do for me."

1 Samuel 27:1–7:

David said in his heart, "I shall now perish one day by the hand of Saul; there is nothing better for me than to escape to the land of the Philistines; then Saul will despair of seeking me any longer within the borders of Israel, and I shall escape out of his hand." So David set out and went over, he and the six hundred men who were with him, to King Achish son of Maoch of Gath. David stayed with Achish at Gath, he and his troops, every man with his household, and David with his two wives, Ahinoam of Jezreel, and Abigail of Carmel, Nabal's widow. When Saul was told that David had fled to Gath, he no longer sought for him.

Then David said to Achish, "If I have found favor in your sight, let a place be given me in one of the country towns, so that I may live there; for why should your servant live in the royal city with you?" So that day Achish gave him Ziklag; therefore Ziklag has belonged to the kings of Judah to this day. The length of time that David lived in the country of the Philistines was one year and four months.

THE STORY BEHIND THE SCRIPTURE

One of the more mind-bending moments of seminary, for me, came when I learned that Exodus—rather than Genesis—should be viewed as the beginning of Israel's story.[3] Genesis certainly seems as if it is the place the story begins. After all, it's the first book, and its first words are: "In the beginning." However, scholars view Genesis as something more akin to a prequel. The story of Israel really begins with the epic escape of the people from the clutches of an oppressive Pharaoh. And as it turns out even that story is highly shaped.

The story is well known. After Joseph reunites with his brothers at the end of Genesis and magnanimously forgives them saying what they meant for evil God intended for good, a concerning development occurs:

3. Anderson, *Understanding the Old Testament*, 9.

a Pharaoh arises who does not know Joseph. Cue the ominous music. And indeed, the position of the Israelites in Egyptian society plummets. Pharaoh enslaves the people and puts them to the hard labor of pyramid building. In spite of the backbreaking work, the Israelites flourish much to the concern of Pharaoh who apparently knew very little about either decent human behavior or practical population control; Pharaoh ordered all the male babies put to death.

Of course, Shiprah and Puah, two of the most important women in the Scriptures everyone should know but hardly anyone talks about, refuse to comply and allow some of the male babies to escape. The most famous of these, of course, is Moses. One of the most hilarious moments in my pastoral experience came when a new member, Stephanie, was reading the Sunday morning Scripture text for the story of Moses' escape. Stephanie was supposed to read that his basket was covered in bitumen and pitch. Reading in a clear, loud, and authoritative voice, this strong, professional, brilliant young woman transposed the letters and declared that Moses' basket was coated with "pitumen and bitch." Her response was the best part. She heard herself. She stopped reading. She looked up, and then she just laughed. And the whole congregation erupted in holy hilarity.

As the story goes, Pharaoh's daughter winds up raising Moses, and the boy might have risen to power like Joseph, except that Moses runs across a taskmaster beating a Hebrew slave and goes all *Breaking Bad*. He kills the taskmaster, buries him in the sand, and flees into the wilderness. Then, although Moses tries to start over, God isn't having it and sends Moses and his brother Aaron back to lead a revolt against Pharaoh to free the Israelite slaves. After a series of plagues and Pharaoh going back and forth about losing his labor force, the moment finally comes after the death of the Egyptian first-borns for Moses to lead the Israelites out *en masse*. However, Pharaoh changes his mind again and sends his army after the Israelites. Then, cue the triumphal music, the waters part, the people pass on dry land, and the Egyptian soldiers, their chariot wheels clogged in the mire, are destroyed.

So, the story I was told, the story I just re-told, of the Israelite people? The tribe whose identity was traceable through the patriarchs and matriarchs, the people who wind up in Egypt, escape, and then go on a forty-year journey to the promised land? Well . . . sigh. The more likely historical scenario is that the Israelites actually came to be Israelites through the Exodus experience itself. The word Hebrew is actually our best clue. The term Hebrew probably stems from the word *habiru*; in the ancient Near East, the *habiru* were less an ethnic group of people than a class of wandering bandits and mercenaries who worked for the highest bidder. So, historically, what likely happened is that Moses, Aaron, and Miriam led a *habiru* rebellion. The *habiru* did not have a shared story or ethnic heritage. They didn't yet think of themselves as Israelites. Only through the Exodus experience and the wandering in the wilderness was the identity of the Israelite people forged. Only through that prism did the *habiru* become known as the Hebrews. Then naturally, over time, as the people began to ask where they came from, storytellers emerged who imposed order and transformed a messy, tangled reality into a seamless, epic narrative.

Many scholars see this *habiru* heritage rear its head in the story of David. When David was on the run, he gathered a group of stragglers around him; David's band ended up eventually working for, of all people, the Philistine king Achish. David who, as the song goes, killed his ten thousands while Saul was merely killing his thousands, was now working for the same people he was only so recently slaying? The text bends over backward to assert that while David made an alliance with Achish, this alliance was purely practical and that David only used his newfound position to attack enemies of Israel, particularly the Amalekites. But many scholars believe the text protests too much, that David most likely was raiding the residents of Judah along with everyone else.[4] David, noble David, the man after God's own heart, was also capable of high treason in his *habiru* heart.

For at least one scholar, Joel Baden, the connections between Israel's *habiru* past and David's mercenary Ziklag rabble are too close to ignore:

> These mentions from across the Near East make it possible for us to draw a fairly good picture of the *habiru*. They were not an ethnic group—indeed, they seem to have come from a wide variety of ethnic backgrounds. Instead, the term *habiru* is descriptive of a social class more than anything else: they were people who were forced out of normal social structures for whatever reasons and who were compelled to make their livings however they could, wherever possible. They acted as bandits operating independently and as mercenaries available for hire to either side of a conflict. The parallels with David, both generally and, in some cases, with almost uncanny specificity, are obvious. David—forced out of Israelite society, raiding and murdering across the wilderness of Judah, and eventually becoming a mercenary for the Philistines—participated recognizably in a centuries-old pattern.[5]

For Eugene Peterson, this *habiru* side of David's community at Ziklag provided the perfect metaphor for what he experienced starting a new

4. Baden, *Historical David*, 101.
5. Ibid., 103.

congregation. While he was hoping for these amazing, super-Christians who were on fire for Jesus and wanted to roll up their sleeves and do anything to support their fledging church, the reality is the people who formed Peterson's new church were imperfect, flawed, and disconcertingly human. As a pastor, Peterson had to learn to work with people as they were rather than people as he wished them to be. Peterson realized he was working in Ziklag—not Jerusalem.[6]

Recently, Peterson's own flaws have been on display. In 2017 Peterson gave an interview to Jonathan Merritt for *Religion News Service* in which Peterson indicated his previous views on homosexuality and same-sex marriage have changed and grown more accepting over the years. When asked directly if he would officiate at a same-sex wedding for a gay couple who were Christians in good faith, Peterson said yes.[7] Upon reflection, and perhaps influenced by a bullying threat from LifeWay publishers to pull Peterson's books from their shelves, Peterson later retracted his statement about officiating at a gay wedding.[8] While I share the anger and pain of many of my friends and colleagues, I would also gently suggest that Peterson's moral failure here should not negate his entire life's work. Peterson himself is as much a Ziklag as the rest of us, full of good, bad, and ugly. It is possible for Peterson to be dead wrong and cowardly in this instance about same-sex marriage but still offer many lessons worth hearing.

---

6. Peterson, *The Pastor*, 106.
7. Merritt, "Eugene Peterson Changing Mind," par. 7–9.
8. Merritt, "Eugene Peterson Backtracks," par. 10.

18

To Forgive Another
Matthew 18:21–35

TO FORGIVE ANOTHER

To forgive another
first start with yourself
your sin the seed
of understanding and empathy
which you will need
to travel this
long and difficult path.

Remember black Moses
who struggled in his cell
willing to forgive four thieves
who broke in to attack
but unable to let go of a
past he could not change.

Listen to Saint Isidore
who taught him to sit
and pray and to stay
in the pain:
"Only slowly do
the sun's rays
dispel the darkness
of night
only by staring
your demons in the face
do they begin
to take flight."

When the brothers
called him to
convict another
he took his time
walking slowly, the sack
of sand weighing
down his broad back
the hole he cut
spilling grains onto the
ground behind him.

When pressed he explained:
"The sand is my sin
always following
behind me even as I
come to judge another."
And one by one
they walked away
until there were
none left
to accuse their brother.

To forgive another
first start with yourself
your sins the seed
of understanding and empathy
which you will need
to travel this long and difficult path.

THE STORY BEHIND THE POEM

There is nothing people schedule time to speak with me about more than forgiveness. We struggle with forgiving the people in our lives—especially the people close to us. The closer someone is the more they know about us—and the more they know exactly how and where to plunge the knife in and twist it. And we struggle with forgiving them for the painful words we can't stop hearing, for the awful things done that cannot be undone. Or, sometimes we struggle with forgiving ourselves. Even if no one else knows what we've said and done, God does. And we do. People of integrity, people who won't accept cheap grace, struggle with forgiving ourselves for a past that we cannot change, no matter how much we would like to.

I am convinced there is nothing more important in life than forgiveness because it's what allows us to step into our present lives fully and wholly. Forgiveness in Greek is *luo*; it literally means a loosening, an untying. When we experience the gift of forgiveness, and so often it comes to us as a gift, it is as if we have been untethered from the hurts and the pains of the past. It is as if those hurts and pains no longer have power over us. But when we can't forgive all that pain? It's as if those hurtful words and actions are all still happening to us all over again, no matter how many years it's been. When we can't forgive, we experience Faulkner's truth: "The past is never dead; it's not even past."[1]

The key to forgiveness—the key to forgiveness is to start with yourself. The key to forgiveness is to examine yourself honestly and acknowledge where you have made mistakes, and especially, where you have been shown mercy. Especially, when this mercy wasn't deserved.

We are always tempted to focus on the person who wronged us. It feels good to think about them and how awful they are. But as long as our eyes are on our oppressor, as long we keep the focus on the terrible thing they did to us, we're at the same time allowing the offender and all of that past pain to continue torturing us. And we're also not being honest with ourselves. When we're focused on the person who wronged us and how bad they are, we are also setting ourselves up as if we are oh-so-superior, as if we've never made a mistake and haven't stood in serious need of mercy ourselves.

No, if you are stuck and trying to figure out how to forgive someone, the first thing you must do—the hard thing you must do—is to look inward. The hard thing is to go inward and be honest with yourself before God, acknowledge your own past mistakes, and see and be grateful for the number of times you've been shown forgiveness yourself. There is a reason why Jesus

---

1. Faulkner, *Requiem for a Nun*, act 1, scene 3, 73.

says in the Lord's Prayer: "Forgive us our debts as we forgive our debtors." Our ability to forgive others hinges on our awareness and acknowledgment of our own need for forgiveness.

Forgiveness is, quite simply, the process by which we move on and free ourselves in such a way that the painful past no longer has power over our present and future. *Do you want to be free?*

Moses the Black, the subject of the poem, is among the most famous of the Desert Fathers and Mothers. Moses the Black was not someone you would pick to become a holy man; he was a man with a vicious, violent past. As a slave, he stole from his master and used his great size to bully others. After murdering a man, he ran away. Moses wound up forming a band of thieves that terrorized the Nile Valley, taking whatever they wanted and killing anyone who stood in their way. Moses led these men until one day he came upon some of the Desert Fathers and Mothers. After threatening them, he noticed the most curious thing. They weren't afraid. He told them he could kill them, taking their lives away just like that. And they nodded and said he could do as he wished. They feared no man—only God. And they would pray for him. They had this incredible sense of peace—a peace Moses himself had been searching for his entire life. He quit his gang on the spot and joined the monks in the desert.

But contemplative life proved incredibly difficult for Moses the Black. The more he learned about the love of God in Jesus Christ, the more he felt tortured by the violence in his past: the people he had killed and violated and the other awful things he had done. Fortunately, his teacher, Saint Isidore, was exceptionally wise. Isidore taught Moses how to sit in his cell and stay with this pain; he told him to trust that a day was coming when he would be free from this torture. But there were days Moses wondered if such peace would ever come. There were times he stayed awake praying all night, feeling the weight of his past heavier than ever.

There's an old saying among therapists and pastors: however long it took you to get into a certain situation it's going to take at least that long to get out of it. There's often a lot of truth to this expression. And it proved true for Moses the Black. It took decades for him to finally feel the gift of forgiveness for all the pain he had caused. But when this forgiveness came, Moses became one of the most trusted and sought after spiritual advisors in the monastery. He was someone who could listen to anything without judgment—any pain, any failing. He always told people what he honestly thought in truth and in love; his authentic compassion was a gift to the whole community.

Once, one of the brothers committed some kind of sin—it's unknown what the sin was. But it was serious. And some of the angry, younger brothers called for a gathering. They wanted this man put out; they wanted him gone. They called for Moses the Black. They needed everyone to participate, but they especially needed the stature and wisdom of Moses. At first he wouldn't come to their gathering, but they pressed. When Moses finally decided to attend, he walked in slowly—on his back he carried an enormous sack, an enormous sack with a hole cut in it. Behind him as he walked, sand poured out behind him. He entered the circle of accusers and accused and sat down without a word. They stared at him. Moses explained, "This sack? This sand? This sand pouring out behind me reminds me of my sins, which you know to be grievous. They remind me of my sins, sins that follow me even as I have been summoned to come and sit in judgment over another." And he said no more, but looked every man there in the eye. And, one by one, perhaps thinking of their own past mistakes, each man left until it was only Moses and the accused brother left together sitting in silence one with the other.

Forgiveness is life. If you are struggling with forgiving someone, start with yourself; bring your honest self before God.

THE SCRIPTURE: MATTHEW 18:21–35

Then Peter came and said to him, "Lord, if another member of the church sins against me, how often should I forgive? As many as seven times?" Jesus said to him, "Not seven times, but, I tell you, seventy-seven times.

"For this reason the kingdom of heaven may be compared to a king who wished to settle accounts with his slaves. When he began the reckoning, one who owed him ten thousand talents was brought to him; and, as he could not pay, his lord ordered him to be sold, together with his wife and children and all his possessions, and payment to be made. So the slave fell on his knees before him, saying, 'Have patience with me, and I will pay you everything.' And out of pity for him, the lord of that slave released him and forgave him the debt. But that same slave, as he went out, came upon one of his fellow slaves who owed him a hundred denarii; and seizing him by the throat, he said, 'Pay what you owe.' Then his fellow slave fell down and pleaded with him, 'Have patience with me, and I will pay you.' But he refused; then he went and threw him into prison until he would pay the debt. When his fellow slaves saw what had happened, they were greatly distressed, and they went and reported to their lord all that had taken place. Then his lord summoned him and said to him, 'You wicked slave! I forgave you all that debt because you pleaded with me. Should you not have had mercy on your fellow slave, as I had mercy on you?' And in anger his lord handed him over to be tortured until he would pay his entire debt. So my heavenly Father will also do to every one of you, if you do not forgive your brother or sister from your heart.'

THE STORY BEHIND THE SCRIPTURE

The questions we ask about forgiveness, how we frame forgiveness, make all the difference. And sometimes, we ask the wrong questions, which is what's happening with Peter in the text. Poor Peter. I feel as if I'm always singling him out, but in my defense, he's always doing boneheaded things. It's like Frank Burns on M.A.S.H. when Hawkeye says, "You invite abuse, Frank, it would be impolite not to accept it." That's kind of how I feel about Peter.

Peter is following up with Jesus on a conversation they were just having on forgiveness. They were talking about discipline and the community. And Jesus was saying, "Hey, if someone hurts you, well, go to them directly and have a conversation with them." You know that's the last thing any of us want to do. When somebody hurts our feelings, what we like to do is go to one of our friends and whine about it: "Can you believe she said that thing to me? Can you believe he told me this and that? Ugh. Awful, isn't it? I mean how do people like that sleep at night? How do their spouses put up with them—I mean they're the ones I feel bad for, right? That's probably why their spouses are gone so much; I would be, too." That's the kind of thing we like to do when we're hurt; we like to whine about it. But Jesus says, "Nope. Don't do that. Go to the person and have a real conversation with them. And, if that doesn't work, find someone who's impartial, someone who doesn't have a dog in the hunt, and bring them along." What Jesus suggests is brilliant—sometimes just bringing another person into a conflict can be enough to change the game. So, anyway, Jesus goes on and on about how to forgive people in the community, but then Peter has a question: "Yeah, yeah, yeah, Lord. I get all that. But what I wanna know is how many times do we have to forgive? Would six be enough? Or seven? That's better. How about seven? If we forgive someone seven times, then can we stop?"

And it's so the wrong question. Peter wants to turn forgiveness into something he can understand—a rule, a pattern: "Tell me how many times I have to forgive to seem like a decent person, Jesus, and then tell me when I can stop." But what Peter misses is that rules and patterns aren't how forgiveness works. Forgiveness is part of the grammar of being in relationship with one another, which means as long as we're in relationship, we're going to bump up against one another. Forgiveness is a continual process, which is why Jesus says, "Oh Peter. Not seven times, seventy times seven." Which, scholars tell us, is another way of saying forever.

Imagine if Peter were talking about love instead of forgiveness. Peter's question would sound bizarre: "How many times do I have to tell my daughter that I love her, Jesus? Six times? Seven? But then can I stop?" Of course not. You tell the people you care about that you love them, and you show your love to them in a thousand different ways because this is what it means to be in relationship. Telling and showing love is what relationship is.

The real question Peter needed to ask, and maybe he wanted to but was afraid, wasn't how many times must we forgive—but how do we forgive. How do we forgive? That is a much harder question. Seriously, how on earth are we supposed to forgive the people who have hurt us? Or who have hurt the people we care about? How are we supposed to forgive ourselves when the visions of what we have done haunt us and nothing we do seems to make the memories go away? How? Now that's a question!

How do we forgive, then, is the question that Jesus addresses in the story he tells about the wicked slave. After Jesus instructs Peter to forgive not seven but seventy times seven, Jesus recounts a story about forgiveness. He says the kingdom of God is like this. Once upon a time there was a king. And one of the slaves owed the king ten thousand talents. Ten thousand talents? A talent is equal to a year's wage. Thus, ten thousand talents is an absurd amount. The slave wouldn't be able to pay this debt off if he had several lifetimes of service to offer, but the king demands what he owes and threatens to sell the man and his family. So, the slave begs. The slave begs and pleads for his life. And the king? Somehow, the king is moved by the slave's pleas, and grants the slave mercy. The king, somehow, forgives the slave's debt and allows him to walk away. Can you imagine how you would feel if you were forgiven such a huge debt?

However, a few days later the slave remembers that a buddy of his owes him a hundred denarii. It's a bit of money, but nothing compared to the ten thousand talents. But the forgiven slave tells his friend, "Hey, you better get me what you owe me." Alas, his friend doesn't have the money so this man, this man who was forgiven so much, has no pity and throws his friend in prison. Now, all the slaves, the whole community, are enraged and go and tell the king about the first slave's hypocrisy. The king is beside himself. After this man was forgiven an impossible debt, the same man somehow goes and makes a demand of his friend? Thus, the king responds, "Shouldn't you have had mercy because mercy was shown to you?" At that point, the king is done with him; he hands the wicked slave over to be tortured.

Just as in the story of Moses the Black, the same is true here in Matthew. The key to forgiveness, the key to forgiveness is to start with our own messy selves. The key to forgiveness is to examine when you have made mistakes and, even more so, when you have been shown mercy—especially when mercy wasn't deserved.

19

Asterion Burning

Judges 13:1–7, 16:1–6, 16:18–22

ASTERION BURNING

"Don't fly too high," he said.
"But don't go too low."
Any other don'ts, dear Daedalus?

Advice. That subtle, killing
control of those who would be kind.

What was I thinking? These
wings of wax I wore soaring
up past cloud, past birdcall, past survival?

This wasn't the first time I've been burned.
Seven years old. Family movie. Dark room.
Popcorn in the ball of boiling oil
small hand sneaking into searing pain
the scarring made worse by secret keeping.

Or flying down that logging road from
Middle Santiam, two tires blown
fender flayed, and that crystalline meditation
the awakened realization that:
This.
Is.
Really.
Happening.
And there are no extra lives left.

And then that deeper line
flying so high, so fast
your sun filling me with a flame unknown
my wings melting, feathers fraying
even before I fell, crashing back to sea.

But as I crossed over, transgressed the depths
I saw in the swirl the whirling abundance of life
where the edges kiss and felt
the great mistake was not the flight.

No, the great mistake, the original error
was Minos minus-ing his inner wilderness in the first place
binding his bull child within the tender
animal monster with star-hot heart: Asterion.

It is Manoah making the purity promise for Samson
the Nazirite vow: no wine would touch his lips
no razor his brow, but his menagerie would still escape
to his charred Timnah wife and his final Delilah fate.

No, the hidden light always burns brightest
and will not be put out without
a fight to be seen
a tribute everyone
everyone
must pay.

THE STORY BEHIND THE POEM

I really didn't want forty to be a significant year. It's just a number. But forty turned out to be very hard indeed, although in some of the best ways.

For a year I had been meeting with a very special circle of friends with the absurd title: The Convocation of Christian Leaders. Four times we converged on the Duke Divinity School's campus and heard from leaders doing incredible, innovative work at every level of the church.

At our last meeting we decided we wanted to hear from one another. For me, the most significant lecture occurred at the Nasher Museum of Art. There, in a beautiful board room, my friend Theresa Latini talked about her work with Nonviolent Communication. To be perfectly honest, I wasn't expecting to learn much. I had read Theresa's book and believed I probably already knew everything she was going to talk about.

Then, she handed out a couple of sheets of paper. One of them was a feelings indicator: emotions such as fear and joy and anger. Yawn. I get feelings. I've always had a keen sense of what I'm feeling and what others around me are feeling. But the second handout baffled me; it was a needs barometer: human requirements such as the need for love, the need for food, the need for safety, the need for sexual expression, and so on. Needs? This may sound odd, but I had never, ever in my life thought about needs—and certainly not my own needs.

And then Theresa made the most fascinating distinction. She said sometimes it's possible to meet a need, and that's wonderful; but other times, when you can't meet a need, it is enough to greet it. My head was spinning. She gave this example from her own life: Theresa was working at the time at an extremely homogenous college that said they wanted to increase student diversity; however, the college was sending one message with their words but sending mixed signals with their actions. Theresa places a deep value on diversity and respect for all people. In faculty meetings when she heard a micro (which sometimes sounded more like a macro) aggression against a minority population, she said she immediately felt angry and frustrated. Sometimes, it was appropriate in a meeting for her to act on her feelings and confront the aggression, which met her personal need for justice. But sometimes immediate action was not politically the wisest course. Lines of power mark every organization, and prudent leaders know that sometimes you have to hold 'em and sometimes you have to fold 'em. However, even when she chose to remain silent and not meet her deep need for justice, Theresa said it was still possible for her to privately greet that need. She could, in her own head and heart, acknowledge her feelings and frustration, but also embody those deeper longings for equity, fairness, and love. Greeting needs when it isn't possible to meet them can help keep us from becoming bitter, hopeless, and depressed.

I realized in a deep part of myself that for a long, long time if I couldn't meet a need, then my strategy was to just pretend not to have it. Growing up, it wasn't always possible in my crisis-burdened family to have my needs met so from a very early age I would just put my head down and pretend to be fine. I worked extra hard in school or in music or theater. It was never enough for me just to be "OK" at something; I had to be excellent. Some of this drive is good. But some of it is driven by the vain hope that I might soothe unmet needs by overachieving in other areas.

Sometimes, this sense of achievement has given me an unrealistic sense of limits. The short version of the Middle Santiam reference relates to my somewhat infamous experiences in the Oregon wilderness. (Let's just say I've had a few close calls.) After losing a battle with a late spring snowstorm, I had to abandon some gear in the Middle Santiam wilderness. Unfortunately, when I went back to retrieve it, the road was so bad that I ended up blowing out both front tires. I always carry one full-size spare, but I didn't have two. I couldn't decide whether it was better to leave the car and walk back down the twelve miles to the infrequently traveled highway where I *might* flag down help; change one tire, leave the other flat, and limp down; or leave them both flat and try to make it. Gambling that balanced was the best bet, I left both tires flat and headed back down the road. My right tire completely shredded and the car steered like a boat down the gravel logging road. In the middle of that harrowing downhill run, I had the stark realization that this was really happening and there would be consequences. I wouldn't be able to argue or achieve my way out of it. I was, in the language of poet David Whyte, coming to ground in the most profound way.

The rest of the poem is really about unmet needs. Most people know the story of Icarus, the boy who flew too close to the sun and fell into the sea because he melted the wax holding his wings together, but few know the whole story. The story started decades before when Queen Pasiphae of Crete had sex with Zeus in the form of a bull. The child conceived was half bull and half man, the minotaur. King Minos and Queen Pasiphae named him Asterion, which means star in Greek, and exiled Asterion to a labyrinth built by Icarus's father, Daedalus. The labyrinth wasn't enough, however. To appease this creature, youths from Athens were sent into the labyrinth every year to be consumed. My main point here is that everyone blames Icarus for being foolish when it was really Minos exiling his shame in the first place that set the wheels in motion for the story.

Similarly, the Samson story in Judges shows us what happens when needs are buried deeply rather than faced. It wasn't Samson's fault his parents dedicated him as a Nazirite, which meant he must drink no alcohol, remain chaste, and never cut his hair. Samson managed within the Nazirite restrictions pretty well and grew extremely powerful. Unfortunately, he also developed a hunger for the wrong women. (Huge shock, right?) He first married a Philistine woman from Timnah, which was a huge no-no for a champion of Israel. In a twisted tale of revenge and counter-revenge, Samson's first wife ended up burned to death. Samson then fell in love with Delilah, another woman from the enemy Philistines. Samson's unmet sexual needs found an outlet in Delilah who ultimately used her sexual wiles to destroy him. To this day Delilah gets the blame, but I can't help but wonder what would have happened if Samson's parents hadn't committed him without his consent to such a rigid and inhuman vow.

For me, the point of this poem is whether we meet our needs or greet them, pretending not to have them really isn't an option.

THE SCRIPTURE: JUDGES 13:1–7, 16:1–6, 16:18–22

Judges 13:1–7:

The Israelites again did what was evil in the sight of the Lord, and the Lord gave them into the hand of the Philistines forty years.

There was a certain man of Zorah, of the tribe of the Danites, whose name was Manoah. His wife was barren, having borne no children. And the angel of the Lord appeared to the woman and said to her, "Although you are barren, having borne no children, you shall conceive and bear a son. Now be careful not to drink wine or strong drink, or to eat anything unclean, for you shall conceive and bear a son. No razor is to come on his head, for the boy shall be a Nazirite to God from birth. It is he who shall begin to deliver Israel from the hand of the Philistines." Then the woman came and told her husband, "A man of God came to me, and his appearance was like that of an angel of God, most awe-inspiring; I did not ask him where he came from, and he did not tell me his name; but he said to me, 'You shall conceive and bear a son. So then drink no wine or strong drink, and eat nothing unclean, for the boy shall be a nazirite to God from birth to the day of his death.'"

Judges 16:1–6:

Once Samson went to Gaza, where he saw a prostitute and went in to her. The Gazites were told, "Samson has come here." So they circled around and lay in wait for him all night at the city gate. They kept quiet all night, thinking, "Let us wait until the light of the morning; then we will kill him." But Samson lay only until midnight. Then at midnight he rose up, took hold of the doors of the city gate and the two posts, pulled them up, bar and all, put them on his shoulders, and carried them to the top of the hill that is in front of Hebron.

After this he fell in love with a woman in the valley of Sorek, whose name was Delilah. The lords of the Philistines came to her and said to her, "Coax him, and find out what makes his strength so great, and how we may overpower him, so that we may bind him in order to subdue him; and we will each give you eleven hundred pieces of silver." So Delilah said to Samson, "Please tell me what makes your strength so great, and how you could be bound, so that one could subdue you."

Judges 16:18–22:

When Delilah realized that he had told her his whole secret, she sent and called the lords of the Philistines, saying, "This time come up, for he has told his whole secret to me." Then the lords of the Philistines came up to her, and brought the money in their hands. She let him fall asleep on her lap; and she called a man, and had him shave off the seven locks of his head. He began to weaken, and his strength left him. Then she said, "The Philistines are upon you, Samson!" When he awoke from his sleep, he thought, "I will go out as at other times, and shake myself free." But he did not know that the Lord had left him. So the Philistines seized him and gouged out his eyes. They brought him down to Gaza and bound him with bronze shackles; and he ground at the mill in the prison. But the hair of his head began to grow again after it had been shaved.

THE STORY BEHIND THE SCRIPTURE

Judges is a book about cycles. A judge is a unique Hebrew office of leadership that's kind of a mix between a war leader, a religious authority, and someone who occasionally settles disputes among the people. Scholars refer to judges as charismatic leaders because it isn't a regular office but one that comes into being now and again when the people need it. In Judges, you know it's time for God to raise up a judge when you hear the phrase: "Then the Israelites did what was evil in the sight of the Lord" (Judges 2:11; 3:7; 3:12; 4:1; 6:1; 10:6; 13:1). It happens again and again. The people are doing great; then they begin to slip. When the Israelites "do what was evil again in the sight of the Lord," then God, as God is portrayed in the Book of Judges, allows an enemy to attack the people and at the same time raises up a judge. It's a cycle. Ultimately, it's part of the reason why the people clamor for a king later in the book. This cycle of virtue and vice wears thin.

Ordinarily, the cycle of virtue and vice plays out in the Israelite people, and the role of the judge is to rebuke their evil. Samson stands unique among the judges since this cycle of virtue and vice plays out in the life of Samson himself. As I noted before, Samson's parents dedicated him to God as a Nazirite, an extreme form of religious dedication. One of the themes in the Scriptures is a kind of bargaining. Parents who are unable to conceive children—think Abram and Sarai in Genesis, Elkanah and Hannah in First Samuel, or Elizabeth and Zechariah in Luke—often dedicate their longed-for child to God's service. Hence, Isaac becomes the child of promise; Samuel becomes the great prophet who anoints Saul and David; and John becomes known as the Baptist, the one who points to the coming of Jesus. But this kind of quid pro quo doesn't always work out so well in the lives of the one over whom promises are made.

Samson here is something like Graham Greene's Whiskey Priest in his amazing novel *The Power and the Glory*. The Whiskey Priest serves the church at a time in Mexico when the church is banned and priests are ordered to take wives on pain of death. All the priests in the book capitulate except for the Whiskey Priest who risks his life traveling from village to village to celebrate the sacraments. The problem is he's a raging alcoholic who must choose between salving his wounds with the communion wine or using it to salve the people. Worse, this arrogant, proud man fathered a child out of wedlock, a child portrayed as a kind of cruel monster in the book. The Whiskey Priest is the ultimate irony: he's the only one faithful to his call; yet, he's entirely unworthy of it in every way.

Raised up with a Nazirite vow, Samson becomes a kind of Israelite superhero and an incredibly powerful judge. Remember, though, he has a great weakness for Philistine women. He marries one unnamed Philistine woman from Timnah. When the men of her village persuade her to divulge a secret of Samson's to shame him, he hands her off to his best man; subsequently, Samson burns the Philistines' fields and, in retribution, the villagers burn to death Samson's wife and her father. Samson avenges their deaths, but it doesn't put a dent into his appetites. After a quick stopover with a Philistine prostitute, Samson falls in love with Delilah. The Philistine men pay Delilah to discover Samson's secrets, specifically the secret to his strength. Of course, the secret turns out to be his beautiful long hair which she ultimately cuts. The Philistine men gouge out his eyes and bind him to columns in order to put him to death. In a dramatic last gasp, Samson cries out to God for one last burst of strength and brings down the columns, killing everyone.

While this makes for a great scene, Samson is hardly the model you want to follow as a leader. He had great strength, yes, but at a terrible price. Samson is a warning to leaders not to rely on their outward success but to always, always be digging in the dirt of their own story, their own past, in order to discover what gifts we received from our past that are worth carrying into the future and what are old stories we need to stop telling ourselves.

The first foundation in David Whyte's understanding of conversational leadership poses the beautiful and disturbing question: What is the story we need to stop telling? In order to change, in order to grow, we have to have room and space to do so. But so often we are filled inside with old, tired stories—narratives about what we've been told we can do and can't do. Whyte talks about the point when we become sick of ourselves as actually a good sign. When we've become tired of the old stories that limit us, when we've become sick of who we are, this is precisely the time when we become open to heeding David Whyte's call to:

> Start close in
> don't take the second step
> or the third
> start with the first
> thing
> close in
> the step
> you don't want to take.[1]

---

1. Whyte, "Start Close In," 360.

20

Catching Fish

Jonah 1:1–3

CATCHING FISH

The high desert lake
surface still as glass
now more mirror than window
marrying blue sky above to dark depths below.

On the alder branch a mayfly
too summer drunk to fly, falls
without grace to the trout's waiting mouth
merging burning sex above with hunger's ache below.

Into this elemental drama I cast
my fly, a question snaking over water
as I float, face at the surface
my head above, my body below.

This, this watery symmetry:
this is poetry present
to the conversation between
the ripples above moved by the mysteries beneath.

And when we want to flee and
escape to the shallows of Tarshish
may God appoint some other greater fish
to catch us and drag us down until
we are hungry enough for light
to be driven up by our dark souls below.

THE STORY BEHIND THE POEM

As you might have guessed from my late interest in fly fishing, as a boy I didn't do a whole lot of fishing. My best early memories of the sport were fishing with my Grandpa Hood, my father's dad. Grandpa Hood was an electrical wholesaler who lived and retired on 110 acres of rolling hills in Western Pennsylvania. A thin ribbon of water ran through the property. Now, I don't know what you call such things—in Texas we called them creeks, but in Pennsylvania this stream was a crick. My Grandpa would take me down to a pool that formed around a bend; we'd put worms on hooks and toss them in. On a good day it didn't take long to pull out the chub he hated and the spiky, flat sunfish I loved.

When I finally made it to Oregon, I would learn there are two kinds of people in the world: there are decent upstanding people who fly fish, and then there are awful, no-good bait fishers. (Well, how was I supposed to know?)

Always wanting to be a good person, I decided to learn the fine art of fly fishing. The thing about fly fishing—not only is learning to cast a dry fly an art all in and of itself—it isn't enough to lay the fly in just the right way in just the right spot. No. You must also have just the right fly, just the right pattern, that will fool these fish into taking a bite.

For me, knowing the right fly to use is really the coolest thing about fly fishing. A good fly fisher is an entomologist, alert to what kind of insects are buzzing around the river or lake; a meteorologist, aware of the temperature of the water and the phase of the moon; and a hydrologist, mindful of the water levels and a thousand other variables.

One of my favorite ways to fly fish is in a float tube. With full waders and flippers, a float tube is something like water wings for an adult. You climb into an inflatable chair such that your body is half in the water and half out. It's the perfect place to look for flying insects and see if the fish are striking.

It's also, for me, the best metaphor for poetry I know.

One of the things David Whyte writes and speaks about is the conversational nature of reality. There's a conversation, a back and forth, between the natural world and what's happening inside of us; between the people we encounter and our selves; and even between what we're presenting on the surface and what's lurking deep within our souls. For me, poetry is the nexus—the bridge between these various worlds where the real conversations take place.

Throughout the poem two opposites are juxtaposed in relationship. One summer our family was camping at Wallowa Lake. The water was so calm, the wind so still, that the water itself became a reflecting mirror from one angle and a clear window from another. I could shift my head to see clouds passing over head one moment and the depths below in the next.

The mayfly imagery comes from one of my favorite trips to the Deschutes River, this amazing river slicing a canyon through the heart of Central Oregon. We hit it just right. Mayflies are these huge, awkward bugs that flutter and fly over the water, looking for mating opportunities. However, they are so clumsy they often dip too close and fall into the water. These bugs are so large they hit the river with a splash. The trout below just burst up from underneath and devour the mayflies in a ravenous explosion. There is something so elemental about this drama—the sex of the mating mayflies meeting the hunger of the fish.

But this conversation between the shallows and the depths takes courage. Sometimes we want to flee into shallower water. And sometimes it is necessary to take a break from the depths. But personally, my sense is few of us suffer from spending too much time in the deep water. Our collective suffering seems to stem more from a culture only too willing to skim the surface of life—to appease itself with the bread and circuses of professional sports, reality TV, and a political discourse long on division but short on service.

THE SCRIPTURE: JONAH 1:1–3

> Now the word of the Lord came to Jonah son of Amittai, saying, "Go at once to Nineveh, that great city, and cry out against it; for their wickedness has come up before me." But Jonah set out to flee to Tarshish from the presence of the Lord. He went down to Joppa and found a ship going to Tarshish; so he paid his fare and went on board, to go with them to Tarshish, away from the presence of the Lord.

THE STORY BEHIND THE SCRIPTURE

Jonah is yet another wildly popular and at the same time wildly misunderstood book of the Bible. When I started seminary, one of the favorite things for people to say, especially second-career folks, was that Jonah was their story. They meant, of course, that they tried resisting their internal sense of call until they just gave up fighting it, a decision that felt something like being swallowed into the belly of a whale.

I understand this sense of relenting after an initial period of struggle, but giving in to God isn't actually the story of Jonah. Jonah's story is not one of uncertainty over whether he wanted to serve God and kind of pushing against the call until a giant fish took him down, forcing him to see the light in the midst of the darkness. Jonah was anything but uncertain—Jonah was defiant. And it's not clear Jonah ever fully embraced God's call upon his life.

For one thing, Jonah wasn't resisting God's call because he wasn't sure he wanted to give up a cushy job, move into seminary housing, and then survive on a pastor's salary. Jonah was resisting God's call because he knew exactly what God was asking him to do and he didn't want to do it—he didn't want to extend love and hospitality to the enemy.

Whenever you read the post-exilic books, books written during the time the Jews are returning to their land after the Babylonian exile, one of the striking features is how divisive they are. Nehemiah and Ezra are so concerned with the restoration of the people that they draw boundaries around the community as starkly as possible: there is a clear line between Jew and non-Jew. Marriages with non-Jews are forbidden. Rigid cleanliness laws make it impossible for table fellowship between Jews and outsiders. Many, including me, find this kind of black and white/us versus them thinking, although understandable, painful and difficult to read.

However, at the same time Nehemiah and Ezra wrote about stark divisions, Jonah penned a very different message. Outsiders are the only ones behaving well in the Book of Jonah. When Jonah takes that ship to escape from extending grace to the Ninevites, the sailors on board are the ones who fear the Lord. Even though Jonah tells them to throw him into the sea to calm the storm, they refuse and try to return to shore. By the time Jonah finally heads to Nineveh, the Ninevites not only listen to Jonah, but they also repent, tearing their clothes and sitting in sackcloth and ashes. My favorite detail: even the animals fast, wear sackcloth, and repent!

It is Jonah, the Hebrew prophet, the one you expect to be the good guy—he is the one who is resistant, disobedient, ungracious, and grumpy to the end. When the Ninevites hear Jonah's message and actually repent (seriously, what prophet in the Bible ever had so much success?), is Jonah happy? Does he pat himself on the back for preaching such good sermons? Nope. He's angry. *He's angry!* He tells God the success of his mission is why he wanted to run away in the first place because he knew that God is gracious and these non-Jews might repent and be saved.

Jonah is the part of us that doesn't want to meditate, to pray, to practice spiritual disciplines—not because we're afraid they won't work but because we are afraid they will. Jonah is the part of us that wants to escape to Tarshish, a kind of fantasy land, rather than do the deep work of attending to life's beautiful, disturbing questions that invite us into courageous conversations.

21

There Once Was a Book from Nantucket

2 Kings 2:23–25, Ruth 3, Acts 2:14–21

THERE ONCE WAS A BOOK FROM NANTUCKET

There once was a book far too serious
filled with visions profound and mysterious
from "Let there be light!"
to Michael's last fight
it's revered by those devout and just curious.

But would it be such a terrible disaster
were the Scriptures themselves to cause laughter?
If they made a smile to spread
hilarious tears to be shed
would this cost halos in the sweet hereafter?

Some children once jeered Elisha's skin head.
"Hey baldy, hey baldy, hey baldy" they said.
The old man called two bears
who rose from their lairs
now the animals are full and the kids are quite dead.

Once Ruth went down to the threshing house floor
getting Boaz dead drunk then undoing him more.
Does it come as a shock
in Hebrew *raglayim* don't wear socks?
And now they must marry for sure.

Or on Easter and all the dead bolts they did lock
and in tongues of flame they did talk.
These men aren't drunk . . . yet
but they aren't Baptists, I bet.
Just wait until Peter calls five o'clock.

There was once a book far too serious
filled with visions mysterious
but while it may not be tasteful
it might be more faithful
for the hearer to laugh, cry, or be furious.

THE STORY BEHIND THE POEM

While I am as silly and light hearted as dads of three kids can sometimes be, so much of my poetry tends to be serious. After posting yet another poem to my Facebook page, one of our church members whom I love dearly and with whom I have a great relationship, posted a comment wondering if I was capable of writing anything a bit lighter?

When I told my twelve-year-old son I was writing a poem about the Bible while we were on vacation, he rolled his eyes as only a pre-teen can. I was like, what? And he told me that while he knew I worked hard on my poetry, it was always so epically serious. With a glimmer in my eye I told him, yeah, but what if I told you I was writing a poem about how funny the Bible can be? While still dubious, his smile told me he loved the idea. So, using a limerick form, I picked three of the funnier passages in the Scriptures to shed some light on the lighter side of the Bible. I'm not saying this verse is high art or that it could inspire anyone to change their life, but sometimes I think it's a good thing to lighten up a bit. I think this is especially true when it comes to faith.

I cannot tell you how frustrating it is as a pastor for people to read Scripture passages week in and week out as if the Bible is this impossibly *serious* book with nothing funny in it. Once I remember reading to the congregation the story of the call of Samuel. Little Samuel is sleeping and the voice of God comes to him. He gets up and wakes Eli, the priest. A sleepy Eli barks at the boy: "What?" Samuel asks, "You called for me?" Disgusted, Eli tells him to go back to sleep. Then, it happens again—and even a third time. Finally, Eli realizes something more serious might be going on, but up to this point this scene is pure comedy. An old man is sleeping and keeps being awakened by a kid who doesn't know what's happening? This is early slapstick, people. Alas, whenever this passage is read in church, no one cracks a smile much less sees the hilarity in it.

It isn't just us. The church has a long history of a seriousness bordering on the deadly. Ambrose, Bishop of Milan, held a particularly low view of humor: "Joking should be avoided even in small talk, so that some more serious topic is not made light of. 'Woe upon you who laugh now; you shall mourn and weep.'"[1] In one of the greatest interpretive overreaches in church history, the influential church father John Chrysostom put a dent in the case for God's playfulness when he claimed that Jesus never, ever laughed.[2] These views led to monasteries creating rules against laughter and fashion-

1. Rahner, *Man at Play*, 96.
2. Darden, *Jesus Laughed*, 66.

ing churches into some of the darkest, dullest, and most lifeless places in the world.

Thankfully, in spite of the predominance of seriousness in the history of the church, a minority tradition did develop a small theology of play movement in the 1960s and 1970s. Reaching back to Johan Huizinga's classic *Homo Ludens* or *The Playing Person*, German Jesuit and noted theologian Hugo Rahner seeks to bring play into a more explicit theological framework in *Man at Play*. Rahner lifts up the words of Gregory of Nazianzus describing this mortal life as like a children's game played on the earth to argue that the proper view of life is a playful one.[3] To Rahner, Christians are the true *homo ludens*, the playing humans, for we are called, as the Gospel of John puts it, to be in the world but not of it. The strength of Rahner's work is articulating the surprising number of times the mystics give voice to a positive view of playfulness.

Biblical scholar Elton Trueblood joined the discussion with his 1975 book *The Humor of Christ*. Trueblood took on Chrysostom's oft-quoted line that Jesus never laughed, a claim only a theologicon could ever take seriously. Trueblood's epiphany came after reading through the Gospel of Matthew with his four-year-old son. (What else would a four-year-old want for a bedtime story?) At the time Trueblood was as serious-minded as anyone else in the church. Important matters are meant to be taken seriously, and what could be more important, hence more serious, than the Holy Scriptures? But as he was reading Jesus' words on judgment, that anyone who judges is able to see the speck in his neighbor's eye while missing the two by four in his own, his son started to laugh. Troubled, Trueblood asked his son just what he thought was so funny. But, of course, good humor like a four-year-old picturing a board sticking out of an eye really can't be explained. And Trueblood realized that while he had read this passage hundreds of times, he had never really heard it. He certainly wasn't hearing it as well as his four-year-old, to whom the kingdom of understanding certainly belonged.[4]

This led Trueblood to look into the character of Jesus more deeply and change his entire view. Trueblood reminds us Jesus was known for table fellowship, for eating and drinking. Strange indeed would be the table fellowship that didn't include generous amounts of laugher. Children sought out Jesus to such an extent that the disciples tried to fend them off. Children are drawn to people who know how to play and hold life gently. And along with the log in the eye there are other sayings of Jesus that are obviously funny when heard without the stained-glass filters of the church. When the

3. Rahner, *Man at Play*, 41.
4. Trueblood, *Humor of Christ*, 9.

rich, young ruler visited Jesus and went away in tears, Jesus joked with his disciples that it would be easier for a rich man to enter heaven than a camel to slip through the eye of a needle. I can barely get a thread through a needle much less a camel. This kind of exaggeration is meant to make us smile if not laugh outright. While it is true that the Scriptures don't explicitly state that Jesus laughs, they don't explicitly state he doesn't. Jesus was a fully human being, presumably complete with a sense of humor; I'm with Trueblood in saying the evidence clearly weighs in on the side of laughter.

David Leroy Miller and Robert E. Neale also published on the theology of play, but the efficient reader need only pick up German Reformed theologian Jürgen Moltmann's *Theology of Play*, which includes essays by all three of them, to get the sense of the conversation. Moltmann responds sharply against Rahner's belief that games mainly function to entertain us while we pass through what he viewed as a lovely but evil world. Moltmann states: "Games become hopeless and witless if they serve only to help us forget for a while what we cannot change."[5] Further, Moltmann anticipates the Alternate Reality Games, about which I wrote in *The Irrational Jesus*, when he sees in games the space to creatively dream up a different world that might result in real world changes: "In that case the significance of games is identical with that of the arts, namely to construct 'anti-environments' and 'counter-environments' to ordinary and everyday human environments and through the conscious confrontation of these to open up creative freedom and future alternatives. We are then no longer playing merely with the past in order to escape it for a while, but we are increasingly playing with the future in order to get to know it."[6]

Moltmann makes a strong argument for how play and faith are similar, both having value without any clear utility. He sees this freedom come to fruition in the resurrection of Jesus. Tapping into the early view of the *risus paschalis*, the Easter laughter, Moltmann sees Easter as a time to dance and play: "Easter is an altogether different matter. Here indeed begins the laughing of the redeemed, the dancing of the liberated, and the creative game of new, concrete concomitants of the liberty which has been opened for us, even if we still live under conditions with little cause for rejoicing."[7] But unfortunately, Moltmann loses his nerve when it comes to the crucifixion. Seeing games as only light and fun, Moltmann believes the crucifixion must be left out of any theology of play.

5. Moltmann, *Theology of Play*, 12.

6. Ibid., 12–13.

7. Ibid., 29.

Thankfully, Robert E. Neale takes Moltmann to task on the crucifixion point. Believing that Moltmann has too low a view of play, Neale argues play isn't only fun and trivial. Play can be deadly serious. Linking the
concepts of play and adventure, Neale argues that in the crucifixion God
suffers the consequence of embarking on an incarnational adventure: "The
spirit of play becomes concrete in an adventure, an event which occurs by
chance, involves risk and is striking in nature. The crucifixion was such an
adventure."[8]

In Harvey Cox, retired Harvard Divinity School professor, we encounter the most robust and daring theology of play. Cox reminds us in *The Feast
of Fools* that medieval Christianity had an appreciation of festivity, fantasy,
dance, and humor, which has since been lost in the tragic seriousness marking so much of North American and European Christianity today. In a particularly striking chapter, Cox plays with the image of Christ as harlequin,
or clown. Cox cites the earliest image of Christ—a figure of a crucified man
with a donkey's head. While he admits no one is entirely sure of the meaning of this image, Cox wonders if perhaps the ancient church, not yet the
powerful institution it came to be, had a greater sense that not only were
they fools for Christ but Christ himself was a fool. As a fool, a jester, Christ
played a unique role, moving between spheres of influence and criticizing
the powers: "Like the jester, Christ defies custom and scorns crowned heads.
Like a wandering troubadour, he has no place to lay his head. Like the clown
in the circus parade, he satirizes existing authority by riding into town replete with regal pageantry when he has no earthly power. Like a minstrel, he
frequents dinners and parties. At the end he is costumed by his enemies in
a mocking caricature of royal paraphernalia. He is crucified amidst snickers
and taunts with a sign over his head that lampoons his laughable claim."[9]

The point here isn't just that we should have more fun in the church.
(Although we probably should.) The point is that losing our sense of humor
actually impairs our ability to faithfully interpret the Scriptures. This is a
collection of books inspired by the Holy Spirit, yes, but written by people.
And it is a collection of books written by people who were, from time to
time, pretty funny. If we miss the humor, we may take ourselves too seriously, but more importantly, we will fail to take the honest meaning of the
Scriptures seriously enough.

8. Neale, "The Crucifixion as Play," 85.

9. Cox, *Feast of Fools*, 169.

THE SCRIPTURE: 2 KINGS 2:23–25, RUTH 3, ACTS 2:14–21

2 Kings 2:23–25:

[Elisha] went up from there to Bethel; and while he was going up on the way, some small boys came out of the city and jeered at him, saying, "Go away, baldhead! Go away, baldhead!" When he turned around and saw them, he cursed them in the name of the Lord. Then two she-bears came out of the woods and mauled forty-two of the boys. From there he went on to Mount Carmel, and then returned to Samaria.

Ruth 3:

Naomi her mother-in-law said to her, "My daughter, I need to seek some security for you, so that it may be well with you. Now here is our kinsman Boaz, with whose young women you have been working. See, he is winnowing barley tonight at the threshing floor. Now wash and anoint yourself, and put on your best clothes and go down to the threshing floor; but do not make yourself known to the man until he has finished eating and drinking. When he lies down, observe the place where he lies; then, go and uncover his feet and lie down; and he will tell you what to do." She said to her, "All that you tell me I will do."

So she went down to the threshing floor and did just as her mother-in-law had instructed her. When Boaz had eaten and drunk, and he was in a contented mood, he went to lie down at the end of the heap of grain. Then she came stealthily and uncovered his feet, and lay down. At midnight the man was startled, and turned over, and there, lying at his feet, was a woman! He said, "Who are you?" And she answered, "I am Ruth, your servant; spread your cloak over your servant, for you are next-of-kin." He said, "May you be blessed by the Lord, my daughter; this last instance of your loyalty is better than the first; you have not gone after young men, whether poor or rich. And now, my daughter, do not be afraid, I will do for you all that you ask, for all the assembly of my people know that you are a worthy woman. But now, though it is true that I am a near kinsman, there is another kinsman more closely related than I. Remain this night, and in the morning, if he will act as next-of-kin for you, good; let him do it. If he is not willing to act as next-of-kin for you, then, as the Lord lives, I will act as next-of-kin for you. Lie down until the morning."

So she lay at his feet until morning, but got up before one person could recognize another; for he said, "It must not be known that the woman came to the threshing floor." Then he said, "Bring the cloak you are wearing and hold it out." So she held it, and he measured out six measures of barley, and put it on her back; then he went into the city. She came to her mother-in-law, who said, "How did things go with you, my daughter?" Then she told her all that the man had done for her, saying, "He gave me these six measures of barley, for he said, 'Do not go back to your mother-in-law empty-handed.'" She replied, "Wait, my daughter, until you learn how the matter turns out, for the man will not rest, but will settle the matter today."

Acts 2:14–21:

But Peter, standing with the eleven, raised his voice and addressed them, "Men of Judea and all who live in Jerusalem, let this be known to you, and listen to what I say. Indeed, these are not drunk, as you suppose, for it is only nine o'clock in the morning. No, this is what was spoken through the prophet Joel: 'In the last days it will be, God declares, that I will pour out my Spirit upon all flesh, and your sons and your daughters shall prophesy, and your young men shall see visions, and your old men shall dream dreams. Even upon my slaves, both men and women, in those days I will pour out my Spirit; and they shall prophesy. And I will show portents in the heaven above and signs on the earth below, blood, and fire, and smoky mist. The sun shall be turned to darkness and the moon to blood, before the coming of the Lord's great and glorious day. Then everyone who calls on the name of the Lord shall be saved.'"

THE STORY BEHIND THE SCRIPTURE

To me, the Elisha passage is kind of funny, but for many it's been horrifying—especially for people raised to believe the Bible is literally true in a historical way in the same manner we expect newspapers to be factual (or at least we used to). This story poses a terrifying question: Would God really send she-bears to attack and kill children for mocking a prophet? A cursory scan of the internet Bible discussions of this text shows you the level of anxiety that still surrounds this question: some try to find a way to blame the apostasy of the northern kingdom while others just flat out say God will not be mocked.

Serious attempts to justify God's actions in the Second Kings text rely on fear. Folks defending this interpretive maneuver often invoke the slippery slope argument. If you get rid of one crazy story or ignore one part of the Scriptures, they say, then you're picking and choosing, and when we read selectively, we'll just wind up making the Bible say only what we want it to say. My response: "Of course, I'm picking and choosing." I pick and choose because everyone picks and chooses. Liberals pick and choose when they lift up Jesus' boundary-crossing love as the defining interpretive lens rather than his harsh stance on divorce, for instance. Conservatives pick and choose when they decide that the Old Testament laws against seafood aren't that big of a deal, but the laws against homosexuality are sacrosanct. The Bible is a library of competing, intentionally inconsistent, divergent voices gathered over thousands of years. We all pick and choose. The important thing is that we be honest about our picking and choosing, aware of what drives our interpretation, and open to the text pushing against us in a way that helps us grow.

In the case of Elisha and the she-bears, I'm personally content to just let it be one of those weird moments that just doesn't make a whole lot of sense. You may totally get the Nephilim having sex with the women in Genesis or the bizarre tale of Zipporah saving Moses from God—you know, when God tries to kill Moses and Zipporah saves him by cutting off their son's foreskin and flinging it at Moses' "feet." Well, good on ya! I don't. I'm content to allow the Bible to be what Karl Barth once described thusly: a strange, new world.

Since I mentioned Zipporah's apotropaic (think defense against the dark arts) act of touching Moses' "feet" with the bloody foreskin, I should probably say a word on why I put feet in quotes as a segue to talking about Ruth.

Sometimes feet . . . aren't really feet in Old Testament Hebrew. One of the best things about learning Hebrew in seminary is that you come across weird facts: in Hebrew "feet" often serve as a euphemism for genitalia. For example, when David sleeps with Bathsheba and impregnates her, he orders her husband Uriah to come back from the war. He then tells Uriah to go to his house and "wash his feet." Uriah honorably, if fatally, responds that he can't go and sleep with his wife while his men are suffering in the field. David never tells Uriah directly to have sex with his wife, although that's obviously what he wants Uriah to do to cover up David's act.

And it's the same with Ruth. I'm not sure why Americans believe so strongly that the Bible forbids sex before marriage. Not only is it not a theme in the Scriptures, but books like Ruth actively disprove it.

Ruth and Naomi have come back to Israel after all the men in their lives have died, which leaves them with no protection—an extremely vulnerable time for them. But Naomi sees the way Boaz, the cock of the walk as it were, eyes Ruth and gives her daughter-in-law some advice: "Go down to the threshing floor after Boaz has worked all day. Get him drunk. Then, uncover his 'feet.' And then (cue the dramatic music) he'll *have* to marry you."

Now, if you know nothing about Hebrew, you are probably scratching your head and wondering: What on earth does uncovering Boaz's feet have to do with getting married? When you understand the euphemism, however, it all becomes so obvious. Naomi implored Ruth to get Boaz drunk and take sexual advantage of him in order to force him into marriage. I realize this story raises serious concerns, given the current conversation surrounding the chasm between sexual assault and mutually respectful, consensual sex between equals. I definitely wouldn't find this passage funny if the tables were turned. Still, in the case of Ruth and Boaz, I always smile when I read this story, probably because of the old humor adage: punch up, never down. Punching down on people with less status is boorish cruelty. Punching up at the powerful is sure to get a laugh every time.

And finally, we come to the Pentecost story. I heard Will Willimon preach a sermon on Pentecost at the Festival of Homiletics once. I've since told Will in person that now when I read this Pentecost passage, I can't get his South Carolina drawl out of my head. Paraphrasing Peter, Will said, "These men ain't drunk . . . *yet!*" There's just no other way to read this passage. Considering the crazy events of Pentecost when something like tongues of fire land on the disciples and they speak in the languages of the Jewish diaspora, some mock the disciples saying these men are drunk on new wine. To which Peter responds, "These men aren't drunk as you suppose, for it's only 9 o'clock in the morning." You can imagine internally he was thinking, "But yeah, just wait until five and then watch out. It's been a rough time lately."

I have no idea if Peter was implying that the disciples were as famous as Jesus for being drunks and gluttons. But the way Luke describes that moment is just funny. It is. And it's okay.

22

The Salt of the Good Earth
Genesis 19:15–26

THE SALT OF THE GOOD EARTH

It was a salt assault
her head craning back
her rigid body become basalt.

The burning angels told them to run
to flee and not to stop
but she paused caught between
a brokenness she knew and a world she knew not.

As bad as Sodom was it can always get worse.
And known pain being safer than uncertain gain
she looked back, committed now
only by her curse.

Some lucky few of course escape the gravity
of their own total depravity
like young Jonathan Edwards turning
from his inner dog returning to his own vomit.

But unlike the best of us the rest of us
struggle to move into wholeness
without looking back.
For there's something more frightening to thriving
than there is to surviving what you have always known.

Why doesn't she leave? They murmur
wondering how many more "accidents" it will take.
What was he thinking stepping into that ring?
The whiskey gorilla unleashing blow
after blow on his thick-slurred, blurred head?

We stay in the shadows with Louis and his rats,
whimper with Seligman's learned helplessness pets
and stand frozen with Lot's wife
it being easier to do nothing
than to risk stepping forward into life.

But when we're finally exhausted by the lies of half-lives
hungry finally for joy and for mirth
our hardened hearts can melt again into
Idit: the salt of the good earth.

THE SALT OF THE GOOD EARTH

THE STORY BEHIND THE POEM

This particular poem stems from my own fear and timidity when it comes to taking risks and what I've learned from others. This particular poem employs more obscure imagery that may require explanation to be accessible. The woman in question in this piece is Lot's wife. Although unnamed in the text, later rabbis call her *Idit*, a word which means good soil in Hebrew. I like this hopeful underpinning.

Idit's story is a tragic one with parallels to the Orpheus myth. Remember, Orpheus is allowed to rescue his beloved Eurydice from Hades as long as he doesn't look back—only he can't help himself and loses her right at the end. Similarly, *Idit* looks back as they are leaving the city of Sodom. I'll go into more detail about the terribly misunderstood "sin of Sodom" in the story behind the Scripture. Suffice it to say, while understandable, *Idit* embodies the fear that paralyzes all of us at times when we consider taking major risks. The examples in the poem either point toward people stepping into or away from the fullness of their lives.

Little Jonathan in the fourth stanza refers to the great American theologian Jonathan Edwards. Edwards gets a bad rap. An amazing man who melded science and religion with a deftness the church is still struggling to emulate, Edwards is still most well-known for his dark sermon, "Sinners in the Hands of an Angry God." While I agree this sermon is not one I would ever want to hear aimed in my direction, it's not fair to judge his entire ministry on one work. Indeed, Jonathan Edwards lived an incredible life, due, according to him, to a conversion experience he had when just a boy.

Growing up, Edwards created a "booth" out in the woods behind his home so he could pray and read Scripture. (I'm pretty sure that's unusual even for the Puritans.) As a young man, he kept a journal and recorded the ups and downs of his spiritual life. At one point, he became so disgusted with what he considered his backsliding that he used an image from Proverbs to describe himself: he wrote that he was like a dog returning to his vomit. Today if we read that journal, we'd probably put him on medication. Fortunately, if we are to believe Edwards, he had a conversion experience and left behind whatever was troubling him for good. Edwards became a person who somehow managed to engage life fully, but most of us have a harder time.

The whisky gorilla image comes from a church member I once served who is a long-time member of Alcoholics Anonymous. One day I sat down with him over coffee and asked him this question: "I don't get the first step of AA. It's like admitting you're powerless over the addiction, right? I don't get that. If you are powerless, then what hope do you have? It makes it sound as if you're defeated even before you begin."

An unusually wise and quiet man, he took that in for a moment and thought about it. Then he told me how he understood the first step. In his drinking days, he said, he would start the night out thinking he could control himself. But he said that was like stepping into the ring with a thousand-pound gorilla. Night after night, he'd take a drink and step into that ring. And, for him, one drink led to another after another with that metaphorical gorilla pounding him until he woke up the next day feeling like death. By the next afternoon, he'd start thinking that maybe *this* night would be different. He'd think maybe this night he could step into the ring and win. Maybe this night he could drink and not wind up with the gorilla bashing his head into the ground. But that night would always end in the same way. For him, he said, the only way to beat the gorilla was to never enter the ring in the first place. As long as he didn't have that first drink, he was fine. But if he even dipped a toe into that damn ring, it was game over. He said his understanding of the first step was not that he was entirely powerless, but that his power was limited. He had the power not to enter the ring. But as soon as he stepped in, that's when he became powerless. Of course, he grinned, it took him a lot longer than made any sense for him to figure this out. And there had been too many nights when he walked by the ring, decided to take his chances, and then wound up waking up with that gorilla on top of him.

In stanza seven, Louis refers to Louis de Point du Lac from Anne Rice's *Interview with the Vampire*. Louis is just a normal person living in New Orleans in the eighteenth century when he is bitten by the vampire Lestat, which turns Louis into a vampire as well. Now, there's no turning back for Louis. There's no un-vampiring himself, except at first he is unable to dive in and feed on people. He subsists on rats and other vermin, which keep him alive—but barely. When I think of what it is to live a half-life, to want to risk but not quite be able to dive in, I think of Louis surviving on rats.

The image of Seligman's pets comes from the work of psychologist Martin Seligman who coined the term "learned helplessness." He conditioned (some would say tortured) selected dogs by penning them in an enclosure from which they could not escape and subjecting them to painful shocks. Then, he compared normal dogs and the conditioned dogs by shocking them in pens with an obvious escape route. The normal dogs leapt out of the cage as fast as they could, but sadly, the conditioned dogs just whimpered and endured the pain.

I end the poem with a creative hope. There's no textual evidence that Lot's wife ever returned her focus to life after looking away from her present and future. But the name the rabbis give her, *Idit*, or good soil, is so evocative. Soil is seasonal. If soil isn't conditioned, it must be left fallow for a time before it can produce life again. Whenever I pass a field lying dormant, I see both the present death and the future life. Although we'll never know if *Idit* still stands there locked in a pillar of salt, it is always possible for us to stop turning away from our lives and begin to step into them more fully.

THE SCRIPTURE: GENESIS 19:15–26

When morning dawned, the angels urged Lot, saying, "Get up, take your wife and your two daughters who are here, or else you will be consumed in the punishment of the city." But he lingered; so the men seized him and his wife and his two daughters by the hand, the Lord being merciful to him, and they brought him out and left him outside the city. When they had brought them outside, they said, "Flee for your life; do not look back or stop anywhere in the Plain; flee to the hills, or else you will be consumed." And Lot said to them, "Oh, no, my lords; your servant has found favor with you, and you have shown me great kindness in saving my life; but I cannot flee to the hills, for fear the disaster will overtake me and I die. Look, that city is near enough to flee to, and it is a little one. Let me escape there—is it not a little one? —and my life will be saved!" He said to him, "Very well, I grant you this favor too, and will not overthrow the city of which you have spoken. Hurry, escape there, for I can do nothing until you arrive there." Therefore the city was called Zoar. The sun had risen on the earth when Lot came to Zoar.

Then the Lord rained on Sodom and Gomorrah sulfur and fire from the Lord out of heaven; and he overthrew those cities, and all the Plain, and all the inhabitants of the cities, and what grew on the ground. But Lot's wife, behind him, looked back, and she became a pillar of salt.

THE STORY BEHIND THE SCRIPTURE

Sodom is the Nickelback of the ancient world. Nobody likes Sodom. Even Jesus hates on Sodom. It's because of the sin of Sodom, right? And even if we don't talk about it in polite company, we all understand what that sin is, right? According to Webster, sodomy is "anal or oral copulation with a member of the same or opposite sex." Sodomite, in contemporary parlance, is a slur for a gay man. But Webster wasn't a biblical scholar. Truly, if ever there were a case for *Princess Bride's* Inigo Montoya to say, "You keep using that word. I do not think it means what you think it means," it would be about the term sodomy.

Let's check it out. Here's the backstory to the pillar of salt conclusion. In verses I have yet to see anyone cross stitch and frame on their wall, we hear the story of Lot, Abraham's kinsman, who is hanging out in the city of Sodom when angels appearing as men come to visit. Now, Abraham and Lot both offer these strangers hospitality. The men of Sodom? Not so much. The men of the city show up that night with torches and pitch forks yelling at Lot to send the strangers out into the street so that the crowd can "know" them. And, as previously noted about "feet," know in this context is probably another Hebrew slang for sex. So far, so good for the popular understanding of sodomy in English. We might make an important distinction between violent gang rape and a loving, consensual same-sex relationship, but at this point I can understand how people might equate the sin of Sodom with homosexuality.

But wait! What happens next? It's as if no one ever reads the next part. After the crowd makes this terrible demand to have their way with the strangers, Lot tells them how awful they are behaving. But then, Lot has an idea. Instead of sending the strangers out to be raped, this father of the year tells the men he has two young, virgin daughters. Why don't they take these girls instead and "do with them as they please?"

Um . . . what?

Yep, because of the enormous value Lot placed on hospitality for the stranger, he actually offers his daughters to be raped instead of the men. And just like that, the popular conclusion that Sodom's sin, and hence sodomy, relates to homosexuality unravels. Lot isn't concerned with sex. He isn't even concerned with rape. Lot's only focus is on maintaining hospitality for the strangers he is hosting. The sin of Sodom isn't anal sex, and it has nothing to do with contemporary, loving, lesbian, gay, bisexual, transgender, and queer relationships. The sin of Sodom is inhospitality—at least this is the view of ancient interpreters in other parts of the Bible and other writings of the time.

According to Ezekiel, the problem with Sodom is they "had pride, excess of food, and prosperous ease, but did not aid the poor and needy. They were haughty" (Ezek 16:49–50). The rabbis agree. The rabbis say the real sin of Sodom is that they decided to put their quality of life above the demand to let the poor and homeless reside in their city; there was no place for foreigners in Sodom. In one rabbinical story a woman of Sodom offered a starving stranger a loaf of bread and some water. When the men of the city discovered it, they threw her over the walls of the city to her death. In another story the men of Sodom tortured strangers who wanted to reside in their city by offering them a version of Procrustes's bed. If the strangers were too long to fit the bed, the men of Sodom would cut their feet off; if the foreigners were too short, they would stretch them out. Now, these are stories and probably exaggerations, but the point is that the earliest authorities agreed the sin of Sodom was their lack of hospitality and welcome for the other.

Moreover, I think the context helps us understand why Lot's wife might be looking back. If we read the text through her eyes, there might be several reasons that she wavered. She might have looked back thinking about the horror that might have been theirs. She might have been remembering friends she will never see again. She also, and I think this is serious indeed, might not be so sure about moving into the future with a husband who was actually willing to send her daughters to be gang raped by a crowd of men.

Can you blame her for looking back? I, for one, cannot.

23

The Devil in the Details

Numbers 22:22–34, Job 1:6–12,
Mark 1:12–13

THE DEVIL IN THE DETAILS

"We don't need a wall to keep the enemy out; we need a mirror."
—Unknown

His first appearance came not in serpentine interference
but a Balaam-stopping angel with flaming sword, the adversary, the satan.

He pops up again in conversation with a friend
who boasts, "Have you considered my servant, Job?"
    This time the adversary, the satan

says take everything away, and he'll curse your face today.
And while Job is restored, why was God so friendly with
    the adversary, the satan?

It's not until the apocalyptic that the text goes apoplectic
turning him into the great Evil One, the father of lies, the adversary, Satan.

Then from Dante's frozen worm, Faust's fully human form
and Milton's falling angel, in our own image we make the adversary, Satan.

Or don't we project with the Other's face; always their sex, their faith, their race?
Yes, them not us who just feel more like the adversary, Satan.

The way he keeps changing over time and re-arranging in rhyme
he is but a blank cipher, for us to project or decipher our own adversary:
    the Satan within.

THE STORY BEHIND THE POEM

I used a loose ghazal form for this poem, a Middle Eastern form often used for exploring deeper, philosophical questions. Rumi and Hafiz, for example, both made use of the ghazal form. Ghazals include a series of couplets in which the last word of the second line is always the same. In this case, I used the convention except for the capitalization of the word "Satan" to reflect the change in time as "the satan" turns into Satan. I'll write more about the satan to Satan progression in the story behind the Scripture section. Along with the changing nature of satan throughout the Scriptures, I also explored the way that we use satan and the concept of evil as a way of identifying, but not identifying with, the other—whoever it is we experience as being different from ourselves.

I will be forever grateful to Stacy Johnson, my theological mentor at Princeton and instigator of all manner of shenanigans. Stacy gave me one of the best gifts one person can ever bestow on another: he changed the way I think. He challenged me, deepened me, cracked me open in some ways, and then put me back together more able to welcome the other and thus, to be a better pastor. In particular, the torturous reading he assigned from Jacques Derrida and Emmanuel Levinas led to my master's thesis on the presence and absence of God in the Other. Derrida and Levinas, both marginalized French Jews, shared an argument that changed my understanding of everything. Levinas challenges a Western understanding of the world, which he believes is fundamentally violent and leads to violence. In the West, he posits, we have been taught to think of being largely in terms of sameness. Odysseus sailed away and returned home. We understand an unfamiliar person, Levinas believes, entirely based on our own self-concept; we latch onto what is the same. So when we meet a stranger, we look for things in common; once we find something that's the same, then we can see they are a human like we are. Only then can we welcome them. Until we can see commonalities, the otherness of the other frightens and repels us.

In opposition to this more recent Western mindset, Levinas proposes the story of Abram and Sarai instead: they leave their land, their family, and their home behind and travel never to return. They become strangers in a strange land. Levinas argues that biblical hospitality has nothing to do with sameness. When the angels in the guise of strange men visited Abram under the oaks at Mamre, he didn't have a conversation with them to find out if they had something in common. Rather, Abram leapt about and provided them with lavish hospitality, even a calf.

Levinas believes it is of crucial importance that we remember and honor the fundamental alterity, or otherness, of everyone and everything.

We cannot and should not try to hide or reduce this otherness by only lifting up and focusing on what we have in common or what is similar to ourselves. And ethically, we actually feel this on a deep, visceral level. One of the ideas for which Levinas is most famous is the idea of *le visage*, or the face. He believes the face of the other calls us into a radical sense of duty to care and honor them. This call to care is why it may be easier when we encounter someone experiencing a painful life situation either to give them what they want and get out of there fast or simply stare straight ahead and pretend they aren't there. Whether we give the stranger anything or not, Levinas would probably say the most important gift we could give would be to see them—to see their face, and to acknowledge the humanity in their otherness.

Jacques Derrida, a friend of Levinas, believed Levinas went too far in the demands laid upon us by the face of the other. Playful Derrida turns practical when he pushes on his friend and points out the impossibility of actually living this out. To care for one other, one must sacrifice caring for all of the rest. "I cannot respond to the call, the request, the obligation, or even the love of another without sacrificing the other other, the other others. *Every other (one) is every (bit) other [tout autre est tout autre]*, every one else is completely or wholly other."[1] To live under this duty to serve the other is too onerous a burden to bear in Derrida's eyes.

Well, I certainly didn't solve this argument between two of the deepest minds in continental philosophy. But I was changed by it. Growing up the way I did in Texas with a gay brother, without even thinking about it, I quickly divided the world into two categories: loving, liberal open-minded people whom I saw as good; and hateful, conservative, closed-minded people whom I didn't want anything to do with. Because of my background, I completely bought into the politics of inclusion. Inclusive people are good because they are willing to open their circle and let you come inside. Exclusive people seemed awful to me because their judgment seemed like a kind of violence.

Thing is, have you ever noticed that "inclusive" people pretty much all look, think, and act the same way? And inclusive groups will absolutely welcome you—as long as in some crucial way you agree with them on the importance of inclusivity itself.

At Princeton during my middler year no one volunteered to stand for president of BiGLASS, the Bisexual, Gay, Lesbian, and Supportive Student organization on campus. As a straight, white, married ally, I certainly didn't think it was a good idea for me to put my name in the hat. As the deadline

1. Derrida, *Gift of Death*, 68.

approached, though, I realized if no one ran, the group stood to lose their funding. So, with reluctance, I became the president of that organization. That fall a conservative group was planning to host a forum for reparative therapists, people who believe it's possible to pray away the gay. A friend gave me a heads up about the forum, but I believed Princeton was an educational campus, a place of higher learning. If people didn't like the views of the reparative therapists, I thought they should show up to refute them. As it turned out, most of the people who identified with BiGLASS thought my response was quite inadequate. Many wished I would make a big stink about these people coming to campus and lead a movement to say they weren't welcome. (And just to remind us, "we" were supposed to be the inclusive ones, here. Ahem.)

The Friday night before the event, my inbox was flooded with emails calling me a traitor and a wolf in sheep's clothing. Some of the senders I knew. Some of them I didn't. Although I know that many of them had been the victims of bigotry and intolerance, I was still unprepared that night for the intensity of the anger they directed toward me. At the time, it was one of the most painful experiences of my life. I resigned that night, and for a time I just kind of kept my head down and licked my wounds. But after I emerged, I learned something.

What I learned is that the way I had divided the world into good guys who thought like I did and bad guys who didn't was *way* too simple. What I learned that night is that while there are open-minded liberals, there are a lot of closed-minded liberals, too. And while there are intolerant conservatives, I encountered many friends who considered themselves conservative but who would also listen, appreciate, and seek out other perspectives.

What happened is that I moved from lifting up the importance of inclusion to celebrating hospitality. The difference is crucial. Some inclusive communities can tolerate others only so long as the others act enough like those on the inside. Communities marked by hospitality, on the other hand, extend welcome to the stranger as a stranger. Like Abram, they offer a welcome regardless of whether they have anything in common.

THE SCRIPTURE: NUMBERS 22:22–34, JOB 1:6–12, AND MARK 1:12–13

Numbers 22:22–34:
God's anger was kindled because [Balaam] was going, and the angel of the Lord took his stand in the road as his adversary.

Now he was riding on the donkey, and his two servants were with him. The donkey saw the angel of the Lord standing in the road, with a drawn sword in his hand; so the donkey turned off the road, and went into the field; and Balaam struck the donkey, to turn it back onto the road. Then the angel of the Lord stood in a narrow path between the vineyards, with a wall on either side. When the donkey saw the angel of the Lord, it scraped against the wall, and scraped Balaam's foot against the wall; so he struck it again. Then the angel of the Lord went ahead, and stood in a narrow place, where there was no way to turn either to the right or to the left. When the donkey saw the angel of the Lord, it lay down under Balaam; and Balaam's anger was kindled, and he struck the donkey with his staff. Then the Lord opened the mouth of the donkey, and it said to Balaam, "What have I done to you, that you have struck me these three times?" Balaam said to the donkey, "Because you have made a fool of me! I wish I had a sword in my hand! I would kill you right now!" But the donkey said to Balaam, "Am I not your donkey, which you have ridden all your life to this day? Have I been in the habit of treating you this way?" And he said, "No."

Then the Lord opened the eyes of Balaam, and he saw the angel of the Lord standing in the road, with his drawn sword in his hand; and he bowed down, falling on his face. The angel of the Lord said to him, "Why have you struck your donkey these three times? I have come out as an adversary, because your way is perverse before me. The donkey saw me, and turned away from me these three times. If it had not turned away from me, surely just now I would have killed you and let it live." Then Balaam said to the angel of the Lord, "I have sinned, for I did not know that you were standing in the road to oppose me. Now therefore, if it is displeasing to you, I will return home."

Job 1:6–12:

One day the heavenly beings came to present themselves before the Lord, and Satan also came among them. The Lord said to Satan, "Where have you come from?" Satan answered the Lord, "From going to and fro on the earth, and from walking up and down on it." The Lord said to Satan, "Have you considered my servant Job? There is no one like him on the earth, a blameless and upright man who fears God and turns away from evil." Then Satan answered the Lord, "Does Job fear God for nothing? Have you not put a fence around him and his house and all that he has, on every side? You have blessed the work of his hands, and his possessions have increased in the land. But stretch out your hand now, and touch all that he has, and he will curse you to your face." The Lord said to Satan, "Very well, all that he has is in your power; only do not stretch out your hand against him!" So Satan went out from the presence of the Lord.

Mark 1:12–13:
And the Spirit immediately drove [Jesus] out into the wilderness. He was in the wilderness forty days, tempted by Satan; and he was with the wild beasts; and the angels waited on him.

THE STORY BEHIND THE SCRIPTURE

One of the things that people *know* is important but easily forget is that the Scriptures are written in the ancient languages of Hebrew and Greek, languages incredibly different from modern English. Also, we don't have the original manuscripts for any of the books of the Bible. Rather, we have thousands of fragments and papyri; the only full copies of the text tend to come from hundreds of years after the originals were written. The difference between what's written in the ancient language and what survives in modern Bibles plays an enormous role in the development of satan over time. I say the development of satan because this figure changes dramatically from the earliest mentions to those hundreds of years later.

The first instance of satan in the Scriptures comes from the fabulous story of Balaam and the talking donkey. (I have found that Balaam's story is the favorite story of middle school boys, if only because they get to read about Balaam's talking ass.) But unbeknownst to most, there is a lot more going on in this story than meets the eye.

In the story, Balaam is a sorcerer hired by the Moabites to curse the Israelites. On the way to his dark work an angel of the Lord holds out a flaming sword and blocks his path. Balaam cannot see the angel, but his donkey does. Two times the donkey tries to stop and avoid this terrifying sight. Each time Balaam gets angry and beats the donkey until he continues. Finally, when Balaam is about to beat the donkey for the third time, the donkey argues with him, spilling the beans about the angel. After Balaam's eyes are opened to the angel, he realizes God does not want him cursing the Israelites.

It's a great story. Any guesses as to the identity of the angel? Surprisingly, the angel is, in Hebrew, *ha satan*, meaning "the adversary." There are a couple of things to note here. First, the satan doesn't start out as a person but a job description. The satan, the adversary, turns into Satan, the Evil

One, only after hundreds of years. Second, the role of the satan is actually to be helpful to God. The satan here is doing the will of God, blocking this sorcerer who would curse the people. So, the satan actually starts out as a good guy. Didn't see that coming, did you?

In the Job story, we are no longer dealing with "the satan" as a job description but just Satan, an angel running back and forth between heaven and earth. But unlike Milton's fallen angel who tried to lead a mutiny against God, Satan in the Book of Job appears to be quite chummy with the Holy One. God has a little chat with Satan, proudly boasting about his boy Job, "Isn't Job great? He's so faithful. He's incredible." "Yeah," responds Satan, "because you give him everything. Duh. Take everything away, and he'd curse you to your face." You can almost see God frown, as God realizes that God hadn't really taken that into consideration. So, God gives Job over into Satan's hands to do as he pleases, just not to take his life.

Satan is definitely becoming a darker figure, and it's jarring to see God and Satan as close chums. Although more devious, Satan in the Book of Job is still not the red-suited, sulphur-smelling, pitchfork-wielding popular media figure.

In the last text, Mark's brief depiction of the temptation scene, we finally see Satan more as we imagine him today: a personal figure whose main job is to tempt people and make our lives miserable.

It's important to remember that this character isn't some kind of immutable, fundamental reality independent of our depiction. Humans writing the Scriptures invent the satan and transform him over time. When we use Satanic imagery to render the others around us, whether they are political enemies or theological enemies or what have you, we must acknowledge that we are the ones constructing this opposition. We aren't seeing reality. We are seeing what we want to see. When we engage in Satanizing, we certainly aren't looking for the image of God in one another or the face of Christ in the least of these.

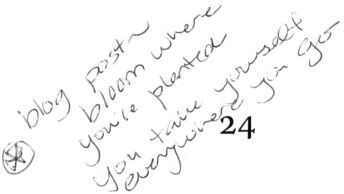

blog post ~
bloom where
you're planted
you take yourself
everywhere you go

24

Watering the Grass Where We Are

John 3:1–12

WATERING THE GRASS WHERE WE ARE

In response to these lines from David Whyte's "Sweet Darkness": "anything or anyone / that does not bring you alive / is too small for you."[1]

But what if it isn't them?
What if it's me?
My blindness and inability to see
my own predictable irrationality?

Fifteen and fleeing home
fighting in the flat driveway
beneath the blaze of an angry Texas sun.
Months later, new family, new house
I see the same old, tired problems start again.

---

1. Whyte, "Sweet Darkness," 346.

On the other side of forty he
was drowning beneath the depths of his life
exhausting kids, timid child-voiced wife.
He traded them in for a young thing needing saving
but after the heat of her dancing hips wore
he woke up as empty and less loved than before.

Nicodemus stumbled through the sweet darkness
having no ears for the truth that he heard.
The rabbi's words were not too little for him
he simply had too much to lose
to die and risk being born again.

It's so much easier to blame them all
to lay our restless hearts
on them being too small
but the greener grass always fades bit by bit.

The grass grows best
where you risk staying
showing up
and watering it.

THE STORY BEHIND THE POEM

For good reason one of David Whyte's most beloved poems is "Sweet Dark-ness." If people know any of Whyte's work, chances are they know it. It is a powerful, amazing poem. When we are tired, when we feel beaten down and broken, Whyte invites us to just settle into the darkness of ourselves and rest there.

In 2015, the church I serve offered our first healing and wholeness service during the Christmas season as a way to help people cope with loss and the difficulty of a season that seems to get crazier and crazier with every coming year. In the Pacific Northwest, the December sun goes down around 4:30 in the afternoon, which makes what can already feel like a dark season for so many feel like a veritable shroud. I opened that healing and wholeness service with David Whyte's poem, "Sweet Darkness," and it was really just perfect for that moment.

But. (You could feel the but coming, couldn't you?) As much as I love Whyte's work, and this poem in particular, I've always been troubled by the line: "Sometimes it takes darkness and the sweet / confinement of your aloneness / to learn / anything or anyone / that does not bring you alive / is too small for you."[2]

It is true that there are jobs and relationships that really do dimin-ish, in which case the most faithful act is to leave. My parents' divorce was absolutely the right decision for everyone involved. Nevertheless, it is all too easy to believe all the problems and challenges in our lives stem from the people around us. And how stunningly, seductively effortless it is to believe that if we just changed our relationships or jobs or locations, all would be well. (Remember when I was sixteen and left home only to discover that the same problems I didn't like at home started to reoccur?)

One Thursday morning I received a call from a couple who had been attending one of the churches I've served. It was an emergency, they said. They were in crisis and needed to talk to someone. I didn't know them well, but I dropped my usual Thursday sermon writing and made plans to meet with them.

I was not surprised to learn that the husband was having an affair. I *was* surprised to learn she was a young, exotic dancer with a drug habit. I was even more surprised by the conversation between the couple. After he complained about how she did not meet his needs in a hundred ways, I asked him if he planned to leave the marriage. No, he didn't think he did. They had kids after all. And he said he did love his wife. Confused, I asked,

2. Whyte, "Sweet Darkness," 346.

"So . . . and I'm just trying to understand here, do you want to stay married *and* have sex with this other woman?" Predictably, the wife said that wasn't going to happen.

We talked for a long time. I found them a marriage counselor skilled in dealing with such crisis situations. As these scenarios sometime play out, the couple wound up deciding to divorce. Even more fascinating was the phone call I received a few months later. The man had moved in with the young dancer, but now they were having problems. I met this new couple in my office just as I had met the man before with his now ex-wife. I sat and listened. In one of the most bizarre moments of pastoral déjà vu, I heard him complain about how his new partner did not meet his needs in a hundred different ways. And what was he really upset about? He had learned that while he was still married and having an affair with this young girl, she had the audacity to sleep with one of the men from the club. Again, I was just so confused: "So . . . and I'm just trying to understand here, you're upset because she cheated on you . . . while you were cheating on your wife with her?" Further, I brought to his attention the fact that just months before I listened to a very similar conversation, the only change being the woman sitting beside him.

Sometimes our problems really are due to toxic situations, and leaving those environments allows us to heal and become more whole. But so many times in my pastoral work the reality is that most of us come with baggage; examples of one-sided relationship problems are rare. It is more often the case that if we keep experiencing the same problems time and time again, the real solution lies within rather than without.

THE SCRIPTURE: JOHN 3:1–12

Now there was a Pharisee named Nicodemus, a leader of the Jews. He came to Jesus by night and said to him, "Rabbi, we know that you are a teacher who has come from God; for no one can do these signs that you do apart from the presence of God." Jesus answered him, "Very truly, I tell you, no one can see the kingdom of God without being born from above." Nicodemus said to him, "How can anyone be born after having grown old? Can one enter a second time into the mother's womb and be born?" Jesus answered, "Very truly, I tell you, no one can enter the kingdom of God without being born of water and Spirit. What is born of the flesh is flesh, and what is born of the Spirit is spirit. Do not be astonished that I said to you, 'You must be born from above.' The wind blows where it chooses, and you hear the sound of it, but you do not know where it comes from or where it goes. So it is with everyone who is born of the Spirit." Nicodemus said to him, "How can these things be?" Jesus answered him, "Are you a teacher of Israel, and yet you do not understand these things?

"Very truly, I tell you, we speak of what we know and testify to what we have seen; yet you do not receive our testimony. If I have told you about earthly things and you do not believe, how can you believe if I tell you about heavenly things?"

THE STORY BEHIND THE SCRIPTURE

Anyone who believes that the Bible should be interpreted literally has never read the Gospel of John.

I mentioned before that Matthew and Luke both had copies of Mark lying on their desks while they wrote their Gospels, which we know because of the way they copied some of Mark's work verbatim and then added their own material. You might have wondered about the Gospel of John. Well, if Matthew and Luke had the Gospel of Mark open on their desks, John must have had the Gospel of Cray-Cray spread out on his. Matthew, Mark, and Luke are known as the Synoptic Gospels because they share many of the same stories about Jesus in roughly the same order. In John, we're in totally different territory. The order of events is sometimes shifted entirely. Jesus cleanses the temple near the end of his life in the three Synoptic Gospels; it is probably one of the main reasons he is put to death. Conversely, in John the cleansing happens right at the beginning of Jesus' ministry. In the Synoptic Gospels, Jesus celebrates the last supper on Passover and reinterprets the Seder language: the wine now represents his blood rather than the Nile; the bread stands for his body rather than the matzah. In contrast to the Synoptic Gospels, Jesus dies on the Passover in the Gospel of John; thus, Jesus actually becomes the Passover lamb, at least on a symbolic level.

Perhaps the biggest difference between John and the Synoptic Gospels is how Jesus speaks. Jesus tends to speak in short, pithy statements in Matthew, Mark, and Luke. In the Gospel of John, however he speaks in weird, mystical ways. More than in any of the other Gospels, John's Jesus abandons literal, plain sense meaning and constantly talks in Yoda-like metaphors.

In the fourth chapter of John, Jesus approaches a Samaritan woman at a well and asks her for a drink. After a confusing exchange, Jesus finally tells her that if she knew who he really was, she would have asked him for living water. She replies that Jesus has no bucket and the well is deep. How did he plan to get this water? Of course, Jesus isn't talking about literal, physical water but is referring to himself.

Just after the living water conversation, the disciples become concerned that Jesus hasn't eaten and try to offer him food. He tells them he has food they don't know about. Puzzled, they wonder, "Did you order take out? Did someone bring you food when we weren't looking?" You can almost see Jesus' face palm when he has to explain that the "food" he is talking about is doing the will of God.

John alone records Jesus' "I am" statements: "I am the bread of life" (6:35), "I am the light of the world" (8:12), "I am the gate" (10:9), and so on. Not only are these sayings the very definition of metaphor (he isn't like a gate, he *is* the gate), but they also hint at God's self-disclosure to Moses back in the Book of Exodus; the "name" God gives Moses is: "I am who I am" or "I will be who I will be."

So, into the midst of this rich, poetic, metaphorical literary landscape slinks Nicodemus under the cover of night. Nicodemus, one of the leaders of the Pharisees, chooses rightly to come to Jesus at night. Not only can he avoid being seen with this trouble maker, but darkness also describes Nicodemus's state. Nicodemus comes to tell Jesus that he knows Jesus must have something to do with God because no one could do the things he is doing without divine help. Jesus, perhaps playfully, responds to the Pharisee that no one can see the kingdom of God unless they are born again, or born from above, depending on the translation. Nicodemus then seems to scratch his head, asking Jesus how can anyone enter again into a mother's womb to be born . . . again? Wah-waaah. As happens so often in John, Jesus is speaking in metaphor, and the people around him can't seem to move beyond naive literalism.

Looking at Nicodemus through the lens of David Whyte's "Sweet Darkness," I can imagine Nicodemus in his frustration walking away from Jesus—imagining that because he didn't feel more alive and enlightened after speaking with the young rabbi that Jesus was too small for him. In fact, the problem in the encounter between Jesus and Nicodemus, as it is throughout the Gospel of John, isn't that Jesus is too small but that his language is actually deeper than anyone wants to dive.

Again, it is true that sometimes people and situations are too small for us. But it's always worth asking whether it isn't them but us who might need to grow.

25

The Soul, *Ha Nefesh*
Psalm 63

THE SOUL, *HA NEFESH*

He said the soul, *ha nefesh*, is a baby
bird. Blind eyes, outstretched neck, gaping
beak. Always waiting, depending upon Her.
Screaming for food. Starving for love.
And somehow unknowing
aching to catch flight.

THE STORY BEHIND THE POEM

One of my favorite professors in seminary was Patrick Miller. I had Pat and the amazing Katherine Doobs Sackenfeld for Old Testament, which might have been the best duo ever. In one of our first classes I remember them lecturing on Adam and Eve, pointing out that Eve's pain and toil only occurred after their expulsion from the garden. The original dream of God for humanity, they argued, was one of men and women living together created equally in God's image. Right away, I knew I was going to like this class.

Pat at one point offered one of the images that has never left me. He said if we wanted to understand what a soul is in Hebrew, *ha nefesh*, we should imagine baby birds, their throats open to the sky, screaming for food. The soul as a hungry baby bird? I was baffled. We were talking about how different the Hebrew conception of being human was from the Greek and Western way of thinking that formed most of us in the room. For instance, we don't see the same kind of dualism between head and heart in Hebrew as we do in English. We, in classical Western thinking, imagine this enormous divide between thinking and feeling. Few bat an eye when the Myers-Briggs seeks to identify us as a thinker or a feeler. It makes sense to us that some are moved more by emotional appeals while others are drawn to logical arguments. But in Hebrew, the word for heart is *ha levav*, which connotes both feeling and thinking. When a language has one word to indicate two actions, it's a fantastic sign the culture sees these actions as unified rather than disparate.

An even more important difference exists between the tangible and intangible aspects of our reality, or our body and soul. In the West, we simply assume that the body and the soul are two different things. Ask any group of American Christians what happens to you when you die. Whenever I ask this question, the conversation invariably turns toward temperature. Are we headed for the up elevator or destined for the down? Everyone assumes that an immaterial, eternal part of us exists after we die—separate from this dull, mortal coil. People share all kinds of ideas about what heaven and hell are like, but all these people tacitly agree that there's a fundamental difference between body and spirit.

Pat Miller's point is that this fundamental assumption on the part of most American Christians is at odds with a biblical conception of body and soul. In the Hebrew imagination, body and soul are unified. The body is ensouled, and likewise, the soul is enfleshed. In the biblical imagination the soul is something you can touch. In *The Bible Doesn't Say That: 40 Biblical Mistranslations, Misconceptions, and Other Misunderstandings*, Joel Hoffman offers a fantastic exploration of this body/soul tension. As Hoffman points out, Jesus, when asked which commandment is the greatest, consistently quotes Deuteronomy and exhorts his listeners, in most English translations, to "love the Lord your God with all your heart, all your soul, and all your mind (Matthew 22:37; Mark 12:30; and Luke 10:27)."[1] In the English language we equate heart with emotion and mind with intellect. So, when Jesus tells us to love the Lord with all our heart and mind, this duality makes perfect sense to us. However, Hoffman notes that the words for heart—*ha levav* in Hebrew and *he kardia* in Greek—connote both thinking and feeling.[2] Similarly, Hoffman adds complexity to the word "soul," *ha nefesh* in Hebrew and *he psyche* in Greek. Whereas for English speakers the soul signifies some ethereal part of us that lives on after we die, in Hebrew *ha nefesh* refers to our flesh, blood, and breath.[3] The earliest Jewish traditions simply don't have a strong belief in life after death. The idea of an immortal soul and a mortal body came from the Greeks. Helpfully, Hoffman offers a better metaphor. When Jesus refers to our heart and soul, Hoffman suggests Jesus means something more like computer software and hardware: computer hardware, the physical parts, correspond to the soul, or *ha nefesh*. Computer software, the operating system and apps, correspond with our heart, or *he levav*.[4]

If you think all this heart, soul, and mind stuff is interesting, but kind of academic, I ask you to reconsider in light of the resurrection. Most Christians I know consider resurrection to be, to put it mildly, somewhat important. Yet, while many claim that the resurrection is an essential tenet, few Western Christians understand what resurrection entails and even fewer believe in it. Most Christians I know believe when you die your immortal soul goes somewhere and gets to hang out with all your friends and family who have gone on before you—something like the blue-tinged Yoda and Obi-Wan in Star Wars, hanging out together after their physical death. But this notion, while lovely, is emphatically not biblical resurrection. Resurrection, as evidenced by Lazarus, Jesus, and, according to Matthew, a bunch of dead guys popping up out of their graves on Good Friday, requires a body. When Jesus promises life after death through resurrection from the dead, he means we will live again—with bodies. If you have a hard time with this image, you are not alone. I honestly can't say I've run across many Christians in my tenure as a pastor who actually believe in Jesus' resurrection in the way he and others understood it in the first century. We say we believe in

1. Hoffman, *Bible Doesn't Say That*, 110.
2. Ibid., 111.
3. Ibid., 112.
4. Ibid., 114.

resurrection; but really, most of us assume we are spirits living, as Sting put it, in a material world. The Gnostics would have been cool with this spiritual/material distinction, but I wonder what Jesus would think?

THE SCRIPTURE: PSALM 63

O God, you are my God, I seek you,
  my soul thirsts for you;
  my flesh faints for you,
  as in a dry and weary land where there is no water.
So I have looked upon you in the sanctuary,
  beholding your power and glory.
Because your steadfast love is better than life,
  my lips will praise you.
So I will bless you as long as I live;
  I will lift up my hands and call on your name.

My soul is satisfied as with a rich feast,
  and my mouth praises you with joyful lips
when I think of you on my bed,
  and meditate on you in the watches of the night;
for you have been my help,
  and in the shadow of your wings I sing for joy.
My soul clings to you;
  your right hand upholds me.

But those who seek to destroy my life
  shall go down into the depths of the earth;
they shall be given over to the power of the sword,
  they shall be prey for jackals.
But the king shall rejoice in God;
  all who swear by him shall exult,
  for the mouths of liars will be stopped.

THE STORY BEHIND THE SCRIPTURE

Spiritual people get on my nerves. You know the people I'm talking about. They might be Christian, or Buddhist, or into energy and new thought stuff. But whatever their tradition, they talk to you in quiet, breathy voices, and they are, make no mistake about it, further along on the path than you are. They understand something about peace, or the mind of God, or the enneagram, or chakras, which the rest of us are totally missing. And this is fine, they will quickly assure us. This is totally fine, they say warmly, because we're all just at different places along the way—which is something you only say when you are sure you are further along on that way than everyone else. And then they offer us a well-meaning-but-condescending smile and apologize that they must be off to walk the labyrinth or do yoga with goats. (Don't laugh, yoga with goats is a real thing.)

It's not so much the gluten-free, non-dairy, non-GMO-ness of it all that I mind. (Although, as a "gluten-free-free" person, someone who can't tolerate food without gluten, I am finding fewer and fewer places left for me to eat in the Pacific Northwest.) It's the certainty that bugs me—especially the certainty that they understand what it means to be a spiritual person. I once cared for a woman who considered herself to be a very spiritual person; she came to me concerned about others in our congregation. Every Sunday in the church I serve, we observe a moment in worship when people bring their joys and concerns and ask for prayers. She was very bothered that other congregants prayed for certain outcomes. For example, if someone's father was in the hospital, they might ask for him to get well enough to come home. They shouldn't pray like that, she insisted. Nope. Instead, she offered, they should simply ask people to pray for God's will to be done.

Now, of course, I agree that God isn't a cosmic vending machine into which we insert our prayers and wait expectantly for positive outcomes. But I also believe people can voice their prayers in whatever way makes sense to them at the time—especially when they are troubled. I asked this very spiritual person what she thought I should do. Her advice was to correct people during worship, which would teach not only them but the whole congregation how to pray "correctly." As kindly as I could, I offered this counsel: it seems to me that any attempt to control the prayer life of another is as much of a concern as the prayer's inadvertent attempt to control God. She was disappointed and probably left thinking I was not as far along on the spiritual path as she had thought.

It's not only the sense of certainty about how others should think or pray that is problematic to me but also the certainty about what "being spiritual" even means. While there is a rich Platonic tradition that describes the soul as comprised of body, spirit, and mind, these days few make a practical distinction between spirit and soul. Today, to be a spiritual person is to be a person with a soul. Whereas the body is troubled by uncontrollable passions, the spiritual person is able to exert control over the tumult of the body and find inner peace in their soul. Indeed, as far as I can tell from hanging around very spiritual people, inner peace is the highest goal and mark of spirituality. While our bodies thirst and hunger and feel anger and desire, the spiritual person is somehow able to free themselves from all these appetites and emotions and just be at peace no matter what is happening around them.

These sharp distinctions between our bodies and our souls and between what's happening in the world and what's happening inside of us are problematic at best. As we've already discussed, the Hebrew word for soul, *ha nefesh*, admits no difference between body and spirit. To be spiritual is to be enfleshed. To be spiritual is to feel, to hunger, and to desire. When David sings of the soul in the Psalms, the soul isn't some tranquil inner part of him cut off from real life. In Psalm 63, for example, the soul thirsts and clings. And when the soul is at peace, it is satisfied like one who has enjoyed a rich feast—a deeply embodied image. I'm not suggesting that being spiritual never means being at peace, but a quiet, disengaged, inner peace certainly isn't the definition of what it means to be a spiritual person, either.

Let's consider the kind of privilege one must have to become a very spiritual person, as most people conceive of very spiritual today. Lululemon yogawear isn't cheap. And lest it sound like I'm just speaking about secular pop culture, this privileged Docetism infects the church as well. In-demand speakers can charge incredible amounts. Mainline congregations, largely populated by white professionals, design retreats and other gatherings with costs that effectively price out the very people with whom Jesus lavished his time.

Not only must one have sufficient money to get the "look" and/or enroll in enough classes to qualify as an enlightened person, one must also have enough time. Time, even more so than money, distinguishes today between people of privilege and the working poor. Thus, becoming a very spiritual person, as popularly defined, takes more time and money than many people have; this conception of spirituality also depends on the illusion that there is some kind of separation between a kind of personal inner peace and what is happening in the world around us.

I understand the need for people to turn off the news and take breaks from what seems like an increasingly unsocial media. But to pretend we can cultivate some kind of inner spiritual peace in isolation from the pain and suffering that our brothers and sisters can't simply turn off is perhaps the worst form of privilege there is. I know many church leaders who showed up in Charlottesville to support the counter-protest against white separatists in August 2017. In the way we commonly think of spirituality, there was nothing "spiritual" about what was going on in Charlottesville. Anger and hatred were on display. Bodies experienced terrible pain, and one, Heather Heyer, was murdered. None of the people I know who marched in Charlottesville experienced inner peace or tranquility. In fact, the fear they described was just the opposite. But when viewed through the lens of a more robust, more biblical understanding of the soul, an understanding of the soul that includes thirsting for justice and clinging to God in the midst of strife—in my mind those who marched against hate demonstrated the very epitome of spirituality.

When the Rev. Dr. Martin Luther King, Jr. invited Rabbi Abraham Heschel to join the march in Selma, Heschel had a problem. The march was scheduled to take place on the Sabbath. This was a real dilemma for him. On the one hand, the clear spiritual command was to rest. Heschel himself wrote an amazing book on Sabbath, calling it a "palace in time."[5] On the other hand, Heschel felt the pressing need to join King and others in solidarity. Ultimately, to the criticism of many, no-doubt-very-spiritual people, Heschel decided to march. In Or N. Rose's biography of Abraham Joshua Heschel, Rose includes Heschel's response to his critics: he said that when he was marching, he felt as if "his legs were praying."[6]

---

5. Heschel, *Sabbath*, 21.
6. Rose, *Abraham Joshua Heschel*, 58.

26

My Life with (and without) Baggage
John 20:1–18

MY LIFE WITH (AND WITHOUT) BAGGAGE

No one wants baggage today.
"He has . . . issues,"
we say with our noses held
as if our Philoctetes feet don't smell.

I once achieved a blissful luggage-less state
sitting at the airport gate:
"Will the owner of a green suitcase return to checkpoint one?"
And I noticed my bag was gone.

For the first time in my life
I didn't have baggage. I was free.
Just my laptop, exhaustion
and nervous cup of coffee.

I could have pretended not to hear.
I could have flown home past-free.
Instead I ran back to claim my case
this container of me.

And later I saw inside the bag
a jacket marred by a scar on one sleeve.
I could have replaced the coat
but never the mark, the memory.

When old Eurycleia saw the disguised beggar's wound
she knew Odysseus had returned home to his place.
When Mary saw the holes nailed through soft rabbi hands
and heard her name called again, his harvest
brown eyes bloomed through gardener face.

This baggage we carry with us:
These stretch marks. That scar.
Each one a broken gift
bearing the fractured story of who we are.

my body once loathed now beloved

Now I think even if I had tried to leave
that cartoon bright viridescent valise
would have caught up with me.
The past always does. Eventually.

THE STORY BEHIND THE POEM

Story time was one of my favorite times with our kids when they were young. Every night that I was home before their bedtimes, I would read at least a couple of stories. Mo Willem's Piggie and Gerald were favorites, along with a series of books I had as a child called *Sweet Pickles*. The town of Sweet Pickles was populated by large talking animals with strong personalities. Being a fan of accents, I voiced Goof-off Goose in a slow, southern drawl; Yakety Yak in my rendition of Brooklynese; and Smarty Stork in a New England dialect based on that guy from the old Pepperidge "Fahm" commercials. My personal favorite was Zany Zebra to whom I gave an extremely questionable 70s jive interpretation sounding like something out of the movie *Shaft*. (Shut your mouth! I'm talkin' 'bout Shaft.)

While the kids were happy with stories from books, what they really loved were what they called "tell stories." "Daddy, do a tell story," they would say, giving me their biggest eyes. And most nights, if it wasn't too late, I would oblige. Being a fan of ancient epics, I told my version of stories such as Gilgamesh and Beowulf. Those familiar with these stories know that these tales can be a bit dark and aren't always G-rated. So, I would customize them to make them as kid friendly as possible. Take Beowulf, for instance: in the original epic at the end of the fight between Beowulf and the monster Grendel, Beowulf tears the monster's arm off and sticks it up on the spire of Heorot, the mead hall, like a cocktail weenie on a toothpick. In our more age-appropriate version, Beowulf asks Grendel if he's going to make good choices or not. When Grendel refuses, Beowulf then takes him by the arm and swings him around and around and around. And, making a whooshing noise, I would pretend to swing Grendel around with my arm. Loving the idea of swinging around an ill-behaved monster by his arm, the kids would invariably join me in this behavior—complete with whooshing sound effects. And then, we would all throw Grendel. He would fly up through the chimney, soar out over the land, fly across an ocean, and continue sailing over another land and another ocean until finally, he would land buried in the sand. At this point, I would announce dramatically that Grendel got the longest time out ever.

Given the choice, my youngest child, Brynne, almost always wanted the same story: Philoctetes. Now, Philoctetes isn't the most familiar story these days. Thanks to the Percy Jackson series, most kids are at least familiar with Poseidon and Athena and think of Pierce Brosnan as possessing a horse's behind. But Philoctetes is hardly a household name. Even though he is instrumental in winning the Trojan war, Philoctetes makes only a brief appearance in Homer's Iliad and doesn't show up much in popular, modern

Greek gods and goddesses collections. In the ancient world, Philoctetes appears most extensively in a play named after him, written by the great playwright Sophocles. The version I tell draws mostly from this Sophocles tragedy, but like the playwright, I also embellish a few details along the way.

Once, I would begin, in the land of the Greeks, wily Odysseus set sail for Troy to fight alongside Menelaus and Agamemnon to rescue Helen, the most beautiful woman in the world. Running short of water along the way, however, Odysseus stops at an unknown island to search for water. Warning his men to stay on board, Odysseus goes off to search. But, after Odysseus was gone for a long time, some of the crew become impatient. One of these men is Philoctetes, who decides to leave the ship to find water himself. Instead of water, however, Philoctetes finds a small cave and stumbles into it. Lying at the bottom are poisonous snakes, one of which strikes and sinks its fangs deep into Philoctetes's foot. In incredible pain, Philoctetes manages to crawl his way to safety. But, Philoctetes is embarrassed because he disobeyed orders, left the ship, and ended up in a cave where he was not supposed to be. So, he doesn't tell anyone about his wound, and despite the searing pain, Philoctetes hides the bite in his boot where the wound begins to fester.

As the poison works its way throughout Philoctetes's foot, destroying all the flesh in its path, his foot begins to stink. The odor becomes so noxious and Philoctetes's cries so intense that the other men on board the ship can't stand it. They plot to throw Philoctetes overboard to relieve his suffering and theirs. When Odysseus gets wind of the plot, he knows he can't allow his men to murder Philoctetes, but neither can he order them to stop without facing a mutiny. So, wily Odysseus hatches a plan. He tells Philoctetes he needs him for an important mission and takes him to the uninhabited island of Lemnos. There, Odysseus suggests that Philoctetes seems tired and recommends a nap in the warm sun. Philoctetes agrees. However, when he wakes up, he discovers Odysseus has vanished along with the whole crew. Philoctetes has been left for dead.

Meanwhile, Odysseus and his men sail on toward Troy. But when they land and join the fight against the Trojans, the strangest things happen. No matter how skilled Odysseus and his fellow Ithacans are in battle, they have no luck. They meet defeat after defeat at the hands of the Trojans. One night, frustrated with failure, Odysseus falls into a fitful sleep. The goddess Athena (my girls' favorite) comes to him in a dream asking him how the fighting is going. Odysseus responds that it's terrible. No matter how hard they fight they can't win. Athena asks him, "Do you have everyone you need?" "Yes," Odysseus snaps. "We have all the men we need. That's not the problem. The problem is nothing we do is working." Repeating herself, Athena insists,

"Do you have *everyone*, Odysseus?" And immediately Odysseus remembers Philoctetes. "We do not leave men behind, son of Laertes," Athena chides. "Until you retrieve Philoctetes and his bow, you and your men will not win a battle."

Odysseus, heeding Athena's words, goes back to the island of Lemnos; it requires every ounce of cleverness for Odysseus to persuade the enraged Philoctetes to leave. He finally agrees to go with Odysseus and his men, and a son of the healing god Asclepius heals Philoctetes's foot when they arrive back in Troy. And now, made whole, Odysseus and his men finally find success against the Trojans. This is typically where I end the story with the kids, noting the connections between Odysseus and Philoctetes. In different ways, both of them hoped to avoid their problems by hiding them: Philoctetes tried to conceal his wound, and Odysseus thought he could leave Philoctetes behind without consequence. Yet, it is only when Philoctetes exposes himself and his foot to the light that he finds healing, and it is only when Odysseus brings Philoctetes out of exile that Odysseus and his men can fight effectively again. Often, that which we desire cannot be separated from that which we despise. In the brilliant essay "The Wound and the Bow," writer and critic Edmund Wilson saw a deeper psychological truth at play in this story. Wilson writes: "It is in the nature of things—of this world where the divine and the human fuse—that they cannot have the irresistible weapon without its loathsome owner, who upsets the processes of normal life by his curses and his cries, and who in any case refuses to work for men who have exiled him from their fellowship."[1]

This deep connection between the parts of ourselves we love and the parts we loathe is also a lot of what's behind my poem, "My Life with (and without) Baggage." Those who know me well know that I lose things. A lot. With a smile, I like to say my absentmindedness is due to thinking so many deep and important thoughts, but for some reason people seem to laugh a little too loudly when I say something like that. The truth is I can be careless, and this carelessness isn't a trait I like in myself. My thoughtlessness can rear its head at the most inopportune moments.

When I was a student at the University of Texas, our campus pastor and his wife, David and Liz Forney, were adopting a baby from China. Initially David was scheduled to go and pick Sammy up in China, but Liz made a last-minute decision: she wanted and needed to go. Unfortunately, you can't just decide on the spur of the moment to go to China. Liz needed a special emergency visa. We were all living in Austin at the time, and the only place to procure an emergency visa was from the Consulate General

1. Wilson, *Triple Thinkers, Wound and Bow*, 241.

of the People's Republic of China in Houston, a two-and-a-half-hour drive away on Interstate 290. Liz was desperate and needed help. I was a senior at the time and had a flexible schedule. Plus, I had taken two years of Chinese. Not that I would need to use it, but I kind of loved all things Chinese so I volunteered to drive to Houston. Waking up at what felt like the crack of dawn, I headed east with Liz's precious paperwork in hand.

Things went okay at first. I made it to the consulate, an odd, concrete building that looked something like a cross between a hotel and a prison. I pushed the buzzer on the imposing front doors, clearly built for security, and answered a series of questions before I was allowed inside the building. The protocol unnerved me, but I did my best to stay composed. After walking down a corridor and then waiting in line, I was greeted by a serious but not unkind woman. She repeated the questions I had already answered, but by that time I realized this was just part of the drill. I told her why I was there, handed her the papers, and then waited as she peered at them, reading them over closely. She stamped the papers and told me to come back in two hours when the visa would be ready.

So, two hours in Houston. What to do? It turns out I was about twelve blocks from the Houston Museum of Fine Arts. So, I headed south down Montrose Boulevard until I arrived at the museum. With only a short amount of time, I saw what I could of the galleries and then ate a quick lunch at the museum cafe. I love museum cafes. I had a fancier than usual chicken salad sandwich on a buttery croissant with a lime Perrier. I felt like the most cultured, suave guy in the world for at least an hour. Not wanting to be remotely late, I left in time to be back at the consulate about thirty minutes early. I arrived and parked.

I remembered that the serious visa woman told me to be sure and bring back all the paperwork because I wouldn't be able to pick up the visa without it so I reached for Liz's papers—her passport, her visa application, and all of her other papers. Nothing. They weren't on my passenger seat where I thought I had left them. Maybe they had fallen down on the side? I leaned over and checked. Nope. Beginning to panic, I started to look all around the car. I couldn't find them anywhere. My heart pumping, my blood pressure through the roof, I wondered if maybe I brought them with me somehow into the museum? I started the car and roared off for the museum, going way, way too fast. Making it to the museum, I ran to the cafe and asked the manager if any papers had been turned in. Looking at me with a puzzled glance, the manager said nothing had been turned in. Muttering under her breath, she said, "Nothing usually is." Terrified, I looked everywhere. Finding nothing, I realized I was getting very close to the time I was supposed to be back at the consulate. So again, driving way too fast, I tore back to the consulate hoping vainly that I might see the papers waiting for me in the parking lot.

Of course, the papers weren't there. I went through my car. Again. By this time, I was late. And by late, I mean it was past time for the consulate to close. Liz called me on my cell phone. Apparently, concerned Chinese officials called her worried about my whereabouts. Sobbing, I told her I had lost her papers. A complete mess, I told her it was my fault she wasn't going to be able to go to China to pick up her baby. In a voice that paired calmness with seething anger, Liz told me the consulate had all the paperwork. I just needed to go back into the building and pick up her visa. Shocked, I wasn't able to say a word. My memory of the woman telling me to be sure and bring back the papers seemed so vivid, so real. I struggled to grasp the truth: I hadn't lost the papers? I had given them to the official? The consulate had them the whole time? Again, Liz repeated her directions, snapping me out of my daze. I ran up to the imposing consulate door and rang the buzzer. Again, I went through the whole series of questions. Finally, I found myself in front of the same serious woman I had spoken with before. This time, however, instead of a kindly face, she glowered at me, her eyes shaming me. She handed me back all of Liz's papers and the emergency visa, along with a searing look I will never forget.

Everything turned out okay, but because of my absentmindedness, I came this close to causing a nightmare for someone I cared about very much. And unfortunately, my attention to detail hasn't improved over time. The story inspiring my baggage poem occurred almost two decades later. In 2016, I was honored to serve as spiritual mentor to a fresh cohort of DMin students at Duke Divinity School. (For some reason people also often laugh at the thought of me being a spiritual mentor as well. Go figure.) Duke is amazing. As a Presbyterian, I loved being part of an institution from a different tradition. When I was a DMin student at Duke Divinity School a few years back, I heard more about John Wesley than ever before in my life and learned how to say "trespasses" instead of "debts" during the Lord's Prayer. I think I stumbled over Jesus not going to hell in the United Methodist version of the Apostles' Creed every time. Now, as a mentor, it was an incredible privilege to walk alongside working pastors who were taking precious time out of their lives to continue their studies. I joined these DMin students on campus for one-week intensive sessions three times a year; we had time at the end of each day to go over what they were experiencing. Nearly every day I offered a poem—some of them from this collection as a matter of fact. In between these weeks on campus, I spent time with each of them over the phone, listening to what they were learning, their frustrations, and, hopefully, offering a helpful word now and again.

After the January 2017 intensive, I was headed back home to Portland, Oregon. It's always a long flight between Raleigh-Durham and Portland. To arrive home at a decent hour, I always tried to leave early in the morning. Apparently, this return trip was a bit too early for me to be fully awake. I flew from the Raleigh-Durham airport to San Francisco. With a little time before I departed on my next flight, I purchased a breakfast burrito and was hanging out. All of a sudden, a voice came over the loudspeaker inquiring after the person who left a bright green suitcase behind at the Raleigh-Durham arrival gate. Suddenly feeling lighter than usual, I looked down around me. Laptop bag? Check. Green suitcase? Not so much. I ran back just in time to retrieve my suitcase and make it back to my next plane right before the final boarding call.

In full disclosure, the green suitcase incident is not the only example of my airport forgetfulness. In early 2018, I was in Louisville for a meeting with a group of pastors. As there was an ice storm in the forecast, I rose even earlier to catch the first flight out of Louisville to Portland, which left me with a tight connection in Newark. In my sleepy haze and haste to make my next flight, this time I left my laptop bag under the seat in front of me. Hard to believe, even for me! Fortunately, the good people of United Airlines found the bag and shipped it back to me, with not one item missing. I just wish my ego survived as intact as the contents of my bag. I truly dislike this part of me that has a hard time keeping track of my belongings. But, at this point in my life, I have to admit that my propensity for losing things seems to be here for good so I'm learning how to make my peace with it.

THE SCRIPTURE: JOHN 20:1–18

Early on the first day of the week, while it was still dark, Mary Magdalene came to the tomb and saw that the stone had been removed from the tomb. So she ran and went to Simon Peter and the other disciple, the one whom Jesus loved, and said to them, "They have taken the Lord out of the tomb, and we do not know where they have laid him." Then Peter and the other disciple set out and went toward the tomb. The two were running together, but the other disciple outran Peter and reached the tomb first. He bent down to look in and saw the linen wrappings lying there, but he did not go in. Then Simon Peter came, following him, and went into the tomb. He saw the linen wrappings lying there, and the cloth that had been on Jesus' head, not lying with the linen wrappings but rolled up in a place by itself.

Then the other disciple, who reached the tomb first, also went in, and he saw and believed; for as yet they did not understand the scripture, that he must rise from the dead. Then the disciples returned to their homes.

But Mary stood weeping outside the tomb. As she wept, she bent over to look into the tomb; and she saw two angels in white, sitting where the body of Jesus had been lying, one at the head and the other at the feet. They said to her, "Woman, why are you weeping?" She said to them, "They have taken away my Lord, and I do not know where they have laid him." When she had said this, she turned around and saw Jesus standing there, but she did not know that it was Jesus. Jesus said to her, "Woman, why are you weeping? Whom are you looking for?" Supposing him to be the gardener, she said to him, "Sir, if you have carried him away, tell me where you have laid him, and I will take him away." Jesus said to her, "Mary!" She turned and said to him in Hebrew, "Rabbouni!" (which means Teacher). Jesus said to her, "Do not hold on to me, because I have not yet ascended to the Father. But go to my brothers and say to them, 'I am ascending to my Father and your Father, to my God and your God.'" Mary Magdalene went and announced to the disciples, "I have seen the Lord"; and she told them that he had said these things to her.

THE STORY BEHIND THE SCRIPTURE

Scars are strange things. On the one hand, we do everything we can to avoid them. Our son, Ches, was born with a Nevus Sebaceous of Jadassohn, a potentially pre-cancerous birthmark on his head, just above his right ear and running down the side of his face like a pink sideburn. Although it wasn't huge, it was noticeable. Once, when he was a baby and running a fever, I took him to an urgent-care clinic on a Saturday morning where a physician with negative people skills clumsily said, "What, did you miss with breakfast there, Dad?" Icily, I gave him the full name of the birthmark and quizzed him on how much he knew about it, which, it turned out, seemed to be less than I did. Worse, when Ches was a little older and we were consulting with a surgical dermatologist, we made the mistake of bringing him with us into the room as the doctor went on and on about how the birthmark was likely to grow, become hairy, and, I kid you not, "flappy." She even used a hand gesture to simulate what she thought might happen. I was caught off guard by a doctor who exercised so little tact and spouted such graphic details so quickly that I didn't have time to take Ches out of the room. He was more than a little traumatized.

When Ches was ten, we had the birthmark removed. Because it impacted his face, we did our best to find a surgeon who would remove the nevus with the least amount of scarring possible. Then, for months we applied scar gel, something I had never heard of before, that promoted healing and reduced the amount of scarring in the tissue. From Shakespeare's humpbacked Richard III to Scar in *The Lion King* and Le Chiffre in *Casino Royale*, our culture continues to link physical deformity with moral depravity. If possible, we wanted to avoid that fate for our son, but it didn't really work. In hindsight, we probably should have gone with a different surgeon. Ches ended up with a pretty solid scar from the surgery that will, in all likelihood, always be with him. He's had some fun with it by telling people wild stories involving knives or sharks or other forms of life-threatening struggles that tend to end with some variation of, "Yeah, but you should see the other guy."

On the other hand, for as much as our culture prizes blemish-free faces and new-car smell, we also have a certain nostalgia for older things. Vinyl records continue to make a comeback as we peruse the stacks in our distressed, torn jeans. I consider my cowboy boots barely wearable until the leather becomes worn and stretched. This fondness for older, familiar things extends to church services, too. An Englishman who worships at the church I serve complained to me once about the dynamic nature of our liturgy. At Tualatin Presbyterian Church, we call our worship style "creative traditional." While the order remains fairly constant, the language of the call to worship and prayer of confession changes from week to week. At the same time that we observe an ancient practice of declaring the assurance of pardon from the baptismal font, this congregation also invented a celebration for those who have had a recent birthday: the congregants rise, come forward to put an offering into a wicker basket (affectionately known as the birthday chicken), and receive a blessing. Suffice it to say, our liturgy is a bit of a mix. This Englishman, a former Anglican, sometimes finds this dynamic nature of our liturgy disruptive. Liturgy for him, he explains, is most useful when it becomes as known, comfortable, and familiar as a well-loved shoe. While we continue to create liturgy, I understand exactly what he means. While staying vital and fresh has its place, our lines, wrinkles, flaws, and scars make us who we are.

There is a lot going on in this John passage. Beyond the wonder of the empty tomb and the resurrection, there's a foot race between Peter and John that likely signals tension between early Christian traditions, some of which privileged Peter and others the beloved disciple. There's also the part about Mary clinging on to Jesus, or at least an idea of Jesus she once had, followed by Jesus' response: "Do not hold on to me" (20:17). Competition within the early church and the humility to admit that Jesus is larger than our individual ideas of him could both make for great sermons. What captures my imagination, though, is Mary standing outside of the tomb weeping and her inability to pick Jesus out from a line-up of one. When she sees a man standing there, she assumes he is some kind of gardener and accosts him, demanding to know if he did something with Jesus' body. Mary, like Cleopas and his friend on the road to Emmaus and like the disciples fishing together in John 21, stands face to face with Jesus without even recognizing him. I try to remember this as a preacher—that it's possible for people who walked with Jesus for years to not always be able to recognize him. How much more might this be so for people who never even met Jesus in the flesh? Would that more of Jesus' friends today would consider the possibility that we, too, might not recognize Jesus when he is standing right in front of us!

But then there's that moment of recognition for Mary. What is it that opens her eyes? With such spare text, John invites our imaginations to wonder. Perhaps it was simply deep grief that blinded Mary's eyes. Grief can profoundly impact our grasp on reality. Joan Didion's powerful and disturbing memoir, *The Year of Magical Thinking*, recounts her grief after the sudden death of her husband. With an unflinching eye, Didion examines the way she held irrational beliefs in the midst of her grief and how merely knowing they were irrational was not enough to break their spell. An elemental part of her believed, for instance, that her husband was still alive despite the fact that she watched him die in front of her eyes. Her persistent belief that he was somehow still alive caused her to be agitated by obituaries to the point where she couldn't stand to read them. Why? She explains: "I had allowed other people to think he was dead. I had allowed him to be buried alive."[2] Similarly, even though she knew she was expected to give his clothes away, and she made a valiant effort, she wasn't able to complete the job: "I stopped at the door to the room. I could not give away the rest of his shoes. I stood there for a moment, then realized why: he would need shoes if he was to return. The recognition of this thought by no means eradicated the thought. I have still not tried to determine (say, by giving away the shoes) if the thought has lost its power."[3] Grief causes us to believe things we know aren't true and can bring about auditory and visual hallucinations, which physically impact the way we perceive the world around us. Grief alone would have been enough for Mary to temporarily mistake Jesus for someone else.

2. Didion, *The Year of Magical Thinking*, 35.
3. Ibid., 37

But what broke the spell? What enabled Mary to recognize Jesus again? In the John text, Jesus calls her by name, and those steeped in the Scriptures know that nothing is more powerful than being called by our true name. Names signify our very being, which is why we need new names when we experience great change. After Jacob wrestled with the angel of God and Saul was blinded by a vision of Jesus, Jacob limped into the future as Israel and Saul became Paul.

I once heard Bishop Michael Curry preach on the importance of holding fast to our true names. He shared a story from a radio interview of Alex Haley talking about the adaptation of his novel *Roots* for the screen version. There's a scene in the film in which the slave Kunta Kinte is being whipped by an overseer until Kinte is forced to acknowledge his slave name, Toby. Again and again, the white man whips black flesh asking Kinte for his name. The overseer beats the young man within an inch of his life until Kinte finally says his name is Toby. Then, Bishop Curry related that Alex Haley said what happened next was a surprise to everyone including himself. The character Old Fiddler gets up and goes over to the young man in pain on the ground. Cradling Kinte's head in his hands, Fiddler improvises: "Your name not Toby. Your name Kunta Kinte!"[4] Knowing our names means knowing who we are. And when we are so devastated we can't even recognize the face of our beloved Jesus, hearing our names called again can bring us back home to who we truly are.

Reading between the lines of the text, though, I can't help but wonder if Mary noticed this strange man's hands. Did Mary notice this gardener's hands—and instead of seeing dirt under his nails—notice the holes in his hands instead? In the very next scene, John describes how Thomas places his fingers through the holes in Jesus' hands and touches the wound in his side. It is by Jesus' scars, in other words, that he becomes known to Thomas. Is it unreasonable to construe that it might have been the same for Mary? Discovering a stranger's identity through wounds has a long history in literature. When Odysseus finally arrived back home on Ithaca, his disguise as a beggar allowed him to safely check out the suitors courting his wife and feasting in his hall. But when his nurse, Eurycleia, bathes him and notices the scar given to him by a boar, she sees past the disguise and recognizes Odysseus for the king he is.

One of the beliefs that makes Christianity so powerful for me is that the resurrection did not cancel out the crucifixion. True, some Christians have a Ned Flanders-like cheerfulness bordering on the insipid that is all glory and light with no darkness. But authentic Christianity, Pauline Christianity,

---

4. Curry, "Someone Must Tell the Babies," par. 28–33.

preaches Christ resurrected and Christ crucified. The crucified, risen Lord has a body, and his body is scarred with wounds that will always leave a visible reminder. Through resurrection, Jesus overcomes these scars, these wounds—but this overcoming doesn't blot them out entirely. The scars remain. Was it the scars that opened Mary's eyes? Of course, I can't *know*. I can't know for sure that Mary knew Jesus by his scars, but I do know it's how we are known. The beautiful parts of us, which we love easily, and the scarred, misshapen parts of us, which are harder to own—these beautiful parts and scars shine together to make up who we are.

David the Broken-Hearted

27

David's Lament

Contemporary North American culture stands at odds with the biblical tradition in many ways. We trust in ourselves and innately believe the future lies within our own power, the very definition of functional atheism. We also trust in the American dream and tie our self-worth to what we can accomplish, purchase, and influence. Who needs free grace when we can have a Mercedes instead? When we view our national budget as a moral document, we the people value military security over all else—including educating our young people and the biblical mandate of caring for the poor, the widow, and the orphan. Perhaps the way we are most at odds with the biblical tradition, however, is our inability and resistance to lament.

Our American can-do optimism sees lament not only as pointless but also as dangerous. It is pointless because it is a waste of time—why cry over spilled milk? It is dangerous because we believe the gospel of the little engine that could: I think I can. We believe there's nothing we can't do if we set our minds to it. Success is simply a matter of desire. In sports, we unthinkingly assume the winner just wanted it more, for instance. Because of this faith in the power of mind over matter, lament isn't just a waste of time; it's focusing on, and therefore creating the conditions for, failure and loss. In our American magical thinking, grieving might actually bring about something worse.

And so . . . we don't. Today in America no one wants a memorial service. Everyone wants a celebration of life. Our collective hymn: "don't worry;

be happy." And believe me, not only do we want to be happy, but we want you to be happy, too. Just decades ago we as a people expected and allowed people a season of mourning to observe grief. People wore black. People were sad. People weren't expected to "just get over it." But today, if you aren't moving on and moving on quickly enough, you are making someone else uncomfortable. You might be seen as "dwelling on it" and risk being labeled, worst of all . . . "unhealthy."

Not only is our unspoken ban on lamentation cruel and inhumane, but it also blinds us from really seeing and experiencing what is happening in the world. Indeed, lamentation is not primarily about grieving; lamentation is about seeing.

In lamentation, we carefully observe and lift up—like construction cranes sorting through the wreckage of 9/11—the broken pieces of the world we cannot simply will back together again. In lamentation, we own the limits of our abilities. In lamentation, we recognize that sometimes the only actions from which we can choose are to sit and bear witness in the discomfort or to leave and distance ourselves from the pain of others and the world.

In my first pastoral call, our small new-church development decided to hire an intern. I remember sitting in a large conference room at Austin Presbyterian Theological Seminary with other pastors and seminarians for training on what this relationship might look like. Fred Morgan, an incredible, seasoned pastor who looked like a cross between Jerry Garcia and a grizzly bear, told the seminarians something I'll never forget. "Ministry is one of the hardest things you'll ever do," he said, "because ministry means learning how to become impotent." I am not kidding you when I tell you that the male seminarians in the room visibly shifted in their seats when they heard the word "impotent"; the women were clearly uncomfortable as well. Fred went on to explain that ministry is not primarily about fixing people. While once in a blue moon someone will come in with a challenge a pastor can actually do something about (it's rarer than anyone thinks), our primary job is to be present and bear witness to the love of God in situations that are beyond fixing. I have sat with parents who lost a three-year-old girl. I have sat in an attorney's office with a woman who was facing the undeniable fact that her marriage was over. I have listened to people caring for the dying, torn between the half of them who wished their loved one would just die and the other half of them who wished they would live forever. There is no fixing going on in those moments. No amount of saying "I think I can" will improve any of those outcomes. There is an impotence, literally meaning a lack of power, with which a pastor must learn to make her peace if she is going to discover how to stop fixing and start seeing and hearing what is really going on around her.

David knows how to lament. David knows how to lament because David knows how to see and listen to the world around him, which is slightly surprising at first. David is so confident, so sure of himself. When Goliath towers over the men of Israel, David doesn't hesitate to claim, "If I can kill lions in the fields, I can slay this unclean giant." When Saul sets Michal's bride price at one hundred Philistine foreskins, David doesn't blanch but brings back double. David is brilliant, bold, and brash—not the qualities we expect in someone who is also sensitive to those around him and open to all that is taking place in the world. Nevertheless, David is a listener. He hears and sees the people around him.

It is only because David listens to Saul that he is sensitive to his moods and knows when and what music to play. It is only because David listens that Abigail enjoys one of the longest, uninterrupted speeches of any woman in the Scriptures. It is only because David listens that Nathan can convict David's conscience by merely spinning a parable.

David listens even when you might imagine he would not. David listens when Shimei, a man of the same clan as Saul, curses him. After Absalom dethrones his father, David finds himself on the run again; Shimei curses David as he retreats, pelting him with rocks, and calling him a man of blood. One of David's men, Abishai, is infuriated and wants to kill Shimei for his disrespect—even in disgrace a king is still a king, after all. But David, ears wide open, absorbs the curse, acknowledging that it might well be from God. And later, when David returns, grieving the death of his son Absalom, Shimei comes crawling to him, begging his forgiveness. For the second time, Abishai wants to cut off Shimei's head, but David listens and again spares Shimei's life.

Because David listens, he laments the death of Saul and Jonathan. For all his brutality toward David, Saul did act as a kind of surrogate father to the boy. And Jonathan and David always had a special bond. When he receives the news of their deaths, David doesn't pretend that everything is okay. He doesn't put on a happy face. He grieves. In the first chapter of Second Samuel, we find David's lament over Saul and Jonathan: David tearfully sings, "How the mighty have fallen." He lifts up in song all his excruciating memories of these men he loved. He remembers Saul's shield, anointed with oil—the one too heavy for David to carry into battle against Goliath. He remembers Jonathan's deadly aim with the bow. He remembers their speed and strength. And in lamentation over Jonathan's death, David is finally able to express the great love he felt for Jonathan that was so difficult for him to articulate in life.

In biblical lamentation, we acknowledge there is no going around grief. There is no hiding from pain or wishing it away. In lamentation, we discover the only path leading away from pain is the path leading directly through the darkest heart of it. Perhaps if we recover our ability to keen, to vocalize our lament, we will be strong enough to hear the voices of those crying out in pain—even when these voices indict us as people of blood. Just as David opened his ears to Shimei's curses and heard the word of God, so too should we listen for those voices that indict us—perhaps these voices, too, are the very ones speaking to us the word of the Lord.

28

The Mistake of Christmas
John 1:1–14

THE MISTAKE OF CHRISTMAS

Sometimes God seems to make mistakes.
What else to say of the ten thousand Syrian families
a day washing onto Grecian shores?
Some of them still breathing. That one boy,
barely more than a baby, his body
limp and lifeless on sandpaper bed.
Red shirt, blue shorts, and those tiny shoes
holding onto him longer
than he could hold onto life.

How else to think of the man
hands up on highway, white shirt on black skin
a broken-down SUV his mortal sin and
fifty thousand volts searing flesh
his body convulsing like my brother's

did when that seizure threw him to the ground.
Then, her bullets filling his chest
silencing his now still, muted mouth
that will never ask for help again.

Sometimes God, you seem to make mistakes.
Yes, the rain falls on the just and unjust alike
and we know it isn't our place to say
who should leave and who should stay
but why? Why should Karen face the clean
white room, needle in arm? Chemo's poisonous cure
bringing more harm than good until she is gone
the ghost of her piercing, bright eyes
urging us to choose joy
when there is no bringing her back?

Of course, the egregious error
your great mistake took place in the Galilee
when you showed up in the wrong place
at the wrong time and chose the wrong body.

To rule our world? To be king?
We know you need to be huge
a larger than life colossus, a winner's winner
the boss of bosses. You'd live in
the tallest of towers, go to all
the right schools. You'd have every
advantage. Every angle cornered.

But for you an animal's cave seemed to do.
A manger, a stable. No angle
only angels, and their singing
as soft, as subtle, as miss-able as the night wind
sweeping slowly across the face
of a hill-country sky.

Instead of suits and ties
the armor of power
you chose our thin skin
able to be touched
able to be torn in the ninth hour.

Incarnation will always seem
like a mistake to our calculations
a story out of step, a perturbation of how
we know the world to be.

Your Advent seems an error
to we who are right
but what we miss is it's exactly
the kind of tear in time's fabric
into which steals the unexpected
and unstoppable light.

Tearing a rent in ordinary time
like Becky's fierce, glittering birds
beating emerald wings
seventy times in one second
fighting the pull of gravity's envy
jealous to tear down
their dance of splendorous resistance.

Tearing a rent in ordinary time like
our children casting Jesus' nativity
in their own native way
with shepherds in sneakers
a donkey cat argument
and spinning Christmas sloth
all part of the play.

Tearing a rent in ordinary time like Craig
and his students taking Christmas on the road
beneath the blaze of an African sky
the only presents they offer
their healing presence bearing
the gift of sight to the blind.

Incarnation tears a rent in ordinary time like you
not wholly sure why but
gathering anyway
in this holy place
on this sacred day
to own your part in the one body
who throughout time
lives to proclaim
that as long as we're standing
and have love left to fight
this growing darkness will
never extinguish the dawning of the light.

THE STORY BEHIND THE POEM

The first theology class I ever took was Feminist Theology and Christology, taught by Cindy Rigby at Austin Presbyterian Theological Seminary. I was a "special student," meaning I was not enrolled at the seminary but was allowed to take classes. (Of course, some have said I've always been a "special" student.) The registrar discouraged me from taking this class; she recommended I start instead with a basic theology class. But Feminist Theology and Christology is what fitted in my schedule, and, looking back, I'm so glad it did.

At one point Cindy introduced us to the Christology of the Eastern church. If the preacher in the tent revival meeting in the West gets all excited about the cross and Jesus dying for us, she said, dramatically, the high moment for Athanasius and the Eastern church is the incarnation—God becoming flesh of our flesh and bone of our bone. This emphasis on the body, on the flesh, and this insistence on the scandal of particularity paired especially well with the feminist theological project we were pursuing.

In the West, men have been, and often continue to be, associated with reason; whereas women have been linked more with feeling. (Clearly, whoever came up with this notion hasn't paid much attention to the comments in sports blogs or observed what a screening of *Rudy* can do to a roomful of guys.) Culturally, we have associated men with the mind while we have paired women with the body. While men were acknowledged to have bodies almost as an afterthought, women were somehow imagined to be tied to their bodies almost exclusively—more subject to the needs and whims of their corporality. To resist and refute this dichotomy, feminist theory helpfully confronted embodiment head on in a way that has been helpful for men and women alike.

In Christian feminist thought, nothing is theologically more significant than the incarnation when it comes to embodiment. That God, the Holy One of Israel, descended and became bone of our bone and flesh of our flesh emphasizes just how important and fundamentally good our bodies are. Jesus laid his hands on sick people and healed them—he touched their bodies. Jesus affirmed his own flesh by plucking grain on the Sabbath to feed himself when he was hungry. Even after his resurrection Jesus eats real fish and welcomes Thomas to touch his actual flesh.

One day Cindy asked a question I'll never forget: "After the ascension, where is Jesus now? Does Jesus have a body or not?" I was perplexed: "Does Jesus have a body or not . . . what kind of question is that?" But, according to our tradition, she pointed out, Jesus is sitting on the right hand of God the Father Almighty, and Jesus himself sits there *incarnatus*, in the flesh. Our tradition, in other words, places an extraordinary amount of emphasis on the body—on Jesus' body and, therefore, on our own.

This emphasis on the body not only discourages any attempt on the part of men to somehow align ourselves more with mind than body, but it also elevates the importance of all bodies—especially bodies made particularly vulnerable in a world still dominated by white men doing as much as we can to escape from our own limited flesh. It means seeing and caring for the integrity of women's bodies, and it means seeing and caring for the safety of brown and black bodies as well.

In the searing prose of *Between the World and Me*, Ta-Nehisi Coates lifts up how European immigrants to America, "the people who believe they are white," have increased their power by decreasing the security and safety of brown and black bodies.[1] He writes:

> These new people are, like us, a modern invention. But unlike us, their new name has no real meaning divorced from the machinery of criminal power. The new people were something else before they were white—Catholic, Corsican, Welsh, Mennonite, Jewish—and if all our national hopes have any fulfillment, then they will have to be something else again. Perhaps they will truly become American and create a nobler basis for their myths. I cannot call it. As for now, it must be said that the process of washing the disparate tribes white, the elevation of the belief in being white, was not achieved through wine tastings and ice cream socials, but rather through the pillaging of life, liberty, labor, and land; through the flaying of backs; the chaining of limbs; the strangling of dissidents; the destruction of families; the rape of mothers; the sale of children; and various other acts meant, first and foremost, to deny you and me the right to secure and govern our own bodies.[2]

Especially this Christmas of 2016, I felt incarnation's scandal of particularity requiring me to see, really see, and care about bodies that would be easier to ignore. The incarnation's scandal of particularity demanded I watch the killing of Terence Crutcher, an unarmed black man shot while he was already lying face down on the highway. The incarnation's scandal of particularity demanded I remember Aylan Kurdi's tiny Syrian body washed ashore. And closer to home this Christmas of 2016, the incarnation's scandal of particularity demanded I face the death of a young woman, beloved to the congregation I serve, after her battle with cancer.

1. Coates, *Between the World and Me*, 42.
2. Ibid., 7–8.

But, as heavy as it is to focus on the loss of these specific and particular bodies, the incarnation also lifts me up as well. The way one of our members, Becky Backen, copes with the painfulness of life is by photographing birds set amidst the aching beauty of the Pacific Northwest. In particular, Becky loves taking pictures of hummingbirds, their tiny, vulnerable bodies so full of energy and fight. When times have been the darkest, Becky posts these incredible images of God's beauty and fierceness in the flesh. These images help her, and they are part of what keeps our community going when we find ourselves mired in the darkness.

And our Christmas play for 2016? I don't know how Christmas plays go in your church, but in our church Family Ministry Director Sarah Beck empowers our kids to be kids—to tell the story of Christmas in ways that make sense to them. When one of our children, Jackson, told her he would like to be a sloth in the play, we were probably all thinking, "A sloth? A Christmas sloth?" But Sarah, who knew this child well, realized a Christmas sloth was exactly what we needed. And it was. Right in the middle of the traditional story, Jackson turned up; as he performed a kind of spinning move, he explained to the congregation's delight that he was the Christmas sloth. I'm still smiling as I write about it, months later.

The stanza featuring Craig and his students refers to one of our members who, for the last two years, followed a sense of call to bring his skills as an optometrist and a contingent of students to Tanzania, where they quite literally bring sight to the blind. Working in a region that has little to no eye care, Craig and his students spend hours a day checking people for conditions that, without attention, would lead to blindness or loss of sight. So many of these conditions are easily treated but only with access to healthcare. Our congregation raised money to buy tools and supplies for Craig's mission trip, and I can say with certainty that these were some of the best Christmas presents we bought in December 2016.

THE SCRIPTURE: JOHN 1:1–14

In the beginning was the Word, and the Word was with God, and the Word was God. He was in the beginning with God. All things came into being through him, and without him not one thing came into being. What has come into being in him was life, and the life was the light of all people. The light shines in the darkness, and the darkness did not overcome it.

There was a man sent from God, whose name was John. He came as a witness to testify to the light, so that all might believe through him. He himself was not the light, but he came to testify to the light. The true light, which enlightens everyone, was coming into the world.

He was in the world, and the world came into being through him; yet the world did not know him. He came to what was his own, and his own people did not accept him. But to all who received him, who believed in his name, he gave power to become children of God, who were born, not of blood or of the will of the flesh or of the will of man, but of God.

And the Word became flesh and lived among us, and we have seen his glory, the glory as of a father's only son, full of grace and truth.

THE STORY BEHIND THE SCRIPTURE

The prologue to John's Gospel is yet another most well-known and, at the same time, least understood texts in English. I say English, because the English translation is particularly deceptive: "In the beginning was the Word, and the Word was with God, and the Word was God." English speakers can be forgiven for imagining a giant Bible spinning in space when they read this text. I have found when most people hear the phrase "in the beginning was the Word" they suppose John is talking about the Holy Scriptures. But this is not what John is referring to at all—not even close.

In the *koine* Greek of the New Testament there are various words for words. While *ho logos* can refer to spoken or written words, in this context it points to something far deeper and more expansive than mere "words." *To rhema*, the word from which we derive our words "rhetoric" and "orator," would have been a better choice if the author of John had wanted to signify spoken and written words. Here, *ho logos* points to the logic or deep meaningfulness of the universe, that unseen realm below the level of the seen world, that enables mere words to have meaning at all.

One of the great tasks of ancient pre-Socratic Greek philosophy was discerning this logos, or logic of the universe. Famously, Heraclitus, heir to the shifty sophists Plato detested, argued that change is the fundamental logos of the universe. Heraclitus saw that while a river is one, it is constantly changing. As Socrates puts it in the Cratylus: "[Heraclitus] is supposed to say that all things are in motion and nothing at rest; he compares them to the stream of a river, and says that you cannot go into the same water twice."[3]

---

3. Plato, *Cratylus*, Kindle location 1473.

Countering Heraclitus's insistence that change represents the logos of the universe, Parmenides offers even more of a head scratcher: "Is is, and is not is not." Let me translate: Parmenides makes a distinction between the world as it appears to us and the world as it actually is. Parmenides affirms unchanging being as the logic, or underlying principle, of the universe. Is is. Is not, or the possibility of change, to Parmenides is not. Things may appear to change, according to Parmenides, but in reality there is an unchanging being underneath it all.

The pre-Socratics didn't all sound like fortune cookies, however. Perhaps an early fan of *The Last Air Bender*, Empedocles hypothesized that the logos of the universe could be reduced down to four elements: earth, air, water, and fire. These four elements, in different ratios, composed every facet of the natural world. Later, this view became the basis of medieval medicine. Further, we can see Empedocles and his four elements, along with Democritus and his notion of the atomic nature of reality, as early forerunners of a modern, scientific view of the world.

Now, when John writes "in the beginning was *ho logos*," he enters into this same ancient conversation about the meaning undergirding reality. Only, for John, this meaning, *ho logos*, isn't change, or being unchanging, or four elements. The logos, or the Word, is Jesus Christ. But Jesus Christ, a living person, is not what most English speakers visualize when they read: "In the beginning was the Word, and the Word was with God, and the Word was God." As I said, most people kind of imagine in their heads a ginormous Bible spinning in space beyond and before all things. But this isn't what John means at all. By equating Jesus with *ho logos*, the fundamental meaning of the world, he says Jesus is like a lens through which the world begins to make sense.

If Jesus is the one Word of God incarnate, though, this means that the actual words in our Bible are not. I have been significantly shaped by Karl Barth's understanding of the threefold Word of God; Barth imagines the Word of God as three concentric circles. In the center of these circles sits Jesus Christ, the Word of God incarnate.

The Holy Scriptures comprise the next layer out, and inasmuch as they point to Jesus Christ by the power of the Holy Spirit, they may be said to be the Word of God. Thus, the Holy Scriptures by themselves are not the Word of God. They are the imperfect record of God's revelation written by imperfect people interpreted by imperfect people. "Blessed are they that take their little one's heads and dash them against the rocks," the psalmist snarls in Psalm 137:9. "Slaves, obey your masters," Paul, or one writing in his name, commands in Ephesians 6:5 and Colossians 3:22. The truth is that the Holy

Scriptures have been used to harm as well as heal and can only be said to be the Word of God when they point to Christ's love.

Similarly, the word proclaimed exists in the final, outside circle. When preaching illuminates the Scriptures and points to Christ's grace and love, then these broken, human words may be said to be the Word of God—but only then. Robes and collars don't sanctify preaching that blames, shames, and disfigures the image of God in others.

So, can the Bible, the words of God, be said to be the Word of God? Yes. Sometimes. The same with preaching. But the one Word of God incarnate is Jesus Christ, a living, breathing, human mystery. Many have expressed frustration to me about this ambiguous view of the Bible; they say it isn't clear or easy enough to understand. For example, when are the Scriptures the Word of God and when are they not? And my response is to say, "Exactly!" This confusion is precisely why we need one another in community; we need one another to talk and converse and argue. We need to remember that the church did indeed support slavery and the subjugation of women by claiming churchgoers were just following orders. So, if we no longer believe that the Bible sanctions slavery, and I don't know any reasonable person of faith with integrity who still holds that slavery is biblically sanctioned, then it makes me wonder what else we sanction today that we might also be wrong about?

29

Theodicy

Lamentations 3

THEODICY

Above to clouds we cast our eyes
beneath an empty sky
calling out for help as to one
dead, deafened to our drowned-out cries.
Either you do not see, or could it be you
forgot the covenants you cut and promises you made and
gave to a stranger in a strange land.
He told her to be careful.
If he told her once he told her a thousand times to
just stay back from the edge, to
keep a safe distance from the
leviathan waters that finally tore her from the ledge
macerating her young body
now lifeless rag doll rolling in the waves while an
omnipotent, loving God looks on?

Painful was every face a
question mark. Worse the
religious attempts to
smooth over, console, and
tell him surely there was a reason, some good that would come.
Useless these sympathies designed to distance. No, what he
valued was the young friend who came and sank into silence
while he sat at his desk and stared, a hushed
xenia shared as the chasm between grace and hope
yawned and ten thousand dark animal feelings
zoo'd inside their cold, caged hearts.

THE STORY BEHIND THE POEM

I graduated from the University of Texas at Austin in 1998. That summer I married Melis; moved to New Jersey to take summer intensive Hebrew at Princeton Theological Seminary; and because we weren't sure we had enough to do, we welcomed a black lab pup named Rigby into our lives. (I'll say more about Rigby in the next chapter.)

Princeton was a challenging environment for me. I think of it as the Slytherin of seminaries, at least in the Presbyterian world. To be honest, I think most of us who attended, certainly me included, were at least somewhat attracted to the name and the power associated with it. These mixed motivations didn't always make for the easiest of classroom environments. Theological divides cut like razor blades. Students raised their hands seemingly to ask a question, but more often really to make a veiled point.

Once during Introduction to Systematic Theology, our professor, Dr. Sang Lee, had had enough. During a discussion about bad things happening to good people, arrogant young students who knew little of the world talked with breezy certainty about God's goodness in one tragedy after another. You could see Sang was doing his best to keep it together, but finally, he just said he wanted to stop class for a bit and tell us a story.

He told us about the time his family first moved to Princeton many years before. There were terrible storms, and the rains had swollen the rivers all around the area. His young daughter—his young, beautiful daughter—drawn by the power of the water, somehow ventured too close. She fell in, he said. And she drowned.

We sat there in utter silence.

Professor Lee, visibly angry, asked us what we would say to him. He asked us how we would tell him that a loving God was present then. No one said a word.

Dr. Lee told us in the days after his daughter drowned, countless people sent notes and flowers and stopped by his office with an encouraging word. It was a seminary after all. These people were, supposedly, experts in ministry. But the only person who helped, the only one who moved below the superficialities, he said, was a young professor named Bob Dykstra. Lee said Bob came to his office one morning and asked him whether he could just sit with him. Lee, dead inside, didn't have the strength to tell him to go away so Bob just sat there. At first Lee waited for him to offer prayer or to say "helpful" things, but Bob just sat there with him in that painful silence. He did this day after day until it seemed as if it was time to stop. Lee looked at us, and with emotion choking his voice, told us that the only person in that seminary full of experts who helped him was the one wise enough to keep his mouth shut and say nothing. Lee's story is the story I share in the poem.

Something to notice about the structure: the form is an alphabetic acrostic. Each line begins with the next letter of the alphabet. I did this to emulate Hebrew poetry. Hebrew poetry is interesting. Unlike Greek, Latin, and English poetry, Hebrew poetry doesn't employ meter or rhyme. Hebrew employs repetition and alliteration, and in some instances acrostic forms. Much lament poetry in Hebrew takes the form of an alphabetic acrostic: each line begins with a letter of the Hebrew alphabet, *aleph, bet, gimmel, dalet,* and so forth. It's as if in these times of terrible grief, we want to create order when the only thing we are experiencing is chaos. The text I pair this poem with, Lamentations 3, is just such an alphabetic acrostic.

One other thing to note about the poem is the phrase "beneath an empty sky" in the second line. This language comes from philosopher Emmanuel Levinas's 1955 essay "To Love the Torah More Than God." Levinas, a faithful Jew, writes largely in response to the *Shoah,* the Holocaust. Writing in the face of unspeakable evil, Levinas takes atheism seriously. An ever-present child's God who "dished out prizes, inflicted punishment or pardoned sins"[1] either cannot exist in the murder of six million Jews or cannot be good in any normal sense of the word good. For Levinas, however, atheism is not the only alternative. There is a kind of mature, adult faith in which God veils God's countenance, meaning God cannot be seen or felt in any empirical, provable way. This kind of faith follows the Torah, the law, beneath an empty sky, as it were: "It is the moment in which the just individual can find no help. No institution will protect him. The consolation of divine presence to be found in infantile religious feeling is equally denied him, and the individual can prevail only through his conscience, which necessarily involves suffering. . . . This condition reveals a God Who renounces all aids to manifestation, and appeals instead to the full maturity of the responsible man."[2] Levinas expresses a kind of deep faith that faces suffering, acknowledges there is no magic prayer that will make it all better, but continues to embody faith, nonetheless, through responsibility for the other. This is the kind of faith I saw in Dr. Lee. This is the only kind of faith I understand as a pastor who has seen more than enough good people experience needless, senseless suffering.

1. Levinas, "Loving the Torah More Than God," 143.
2. Ibid., 143.

THE SCRIPTURE: LAMENTATIONS 3

I am one who has seen affliction under the rod of God's wrath;
he has driven and brought me into darkness without any light;
against me alone he turns his hand, again and again, all day long.

He has made my flesh and my skin waste away, and broken my
    bones;
he has besieged and enveloped me with bitterness and
    tribulation;
he has made me sit in darkness like the dead of long ago.

He has walled me about so that I cannot escape; he has put
    heavy chains on me;
though I call and cry for help, he shuts out my prayer;
he has blocked my ways with hewn stones, he has made my
    paths crooked.

He is a bear lying in wait for me, a lion in hiding;
he led me off my way and tore me to pieces; he has made me
    desolate;
he bent his bow and set me as a mark for his arrow.

He shot into my vitals the arrows of his quiver;
I have become the laughingstock of all my people,
    the object of their taunt-songs all day long.
He has filled me with bitterness, he has sated me with wormwood.

He has made my teeth grind on gravel, and made me cower in
    ashes;
my soul is bereft of peace; I have forgotten what happiness is;
so I say, "Gone is my glory, and all that I had hoped for from
    the Lord."

The thought of my affliction and my homelessness is wormwood
    and gall!
My soul continually thinks of it and is bowed down within me.
But this I call to mind, and therefore I have hope:

The steadfast love of the Lord never ceases, his mercies never
    come to an end;
they are new every morning; great is your faithfulness.
"The Lord is my portion," says my soul, "therefore I will hope
    in him."

The Lord is good to those who wait for him, to the soul that
    seeks him.
It is good that one should wait quietly for the salvation of the
    Lord.
It is good for one to bear the yoke in youth,

to sit alone in silence when the Lord has imposed it,
to put one's mouth to the dust (there may yet be hope),
to give one's cheek to the smiter, and be filled with insults.

For the Lord will not reject forever.
Although he causes grief, he will have compassion
    according to the abundance of his steadfast love;
for he does not willingly afflict or grieve anyone.

When all the prisoners of the land are crushed under foot,
when human rights are perverted in the presence of the Most
    High,
when one's case is subverted—does the Lord not see it?

Who can command and have it done, if the Lord has not or-
    dained it?
Is it not from the mouth of the Most High that good and bad
    come?
Why should any who draw breath complain about the punish-
    ment of their sins?

Let us test and examine our ways, and return to the Lord.
Let us lift up our hearts as well as our hands to God in heaven.
We have transgressed and rebelled, and you have not forgiven.

You have wrapped yourself with anger and pursued us, killing
    without pity;
you have wrapped yourself with a cloud so that no prayer can
    pass through.
You have made us filth and rubbish among the peoples.

All our enemies have opened their mouths against us;
panic and pitfall have come upon us, devastation and
    destruction.
My eyes flow with rivers of tears because of the destruction of
    my people.

My eyes will flow without ceasing, without respite,
until the Lord from heaven looks down and sees.
My eyes cause me grief at the fate of all the young women in
    my city.

Those who were my enemies without cause have hunted me like
    a bird;
they flung me alive into a pit and hurled stones on me;
water closed over my head; I said, "I am lost."

I called on your name, O Lord, from the depths of the pit;
you heard my plea, "Do not close your ear to my cry for help,
    but give me relief!"
You came near when I called on you; you said, "Do not fear!"

You have taken up my cause, O Lord, you have redeemed my
    life.
You have seen the wrong done to me, O Lord; judge my cause.
You have seen all their malice, all their plots against me.

You have heard their taunts, O Lord, all their plots against me.
The whispers and murmurs of my assailants are against me all
    day long.
Whether they sit or rise—see, I am the object of their taunt-songs.

Pay them back for their deeds, O Lord, according to the work
    of their hands!
Give them anguish of heart; your curse be on them!
Pursue them in anger and destroy them from under the Lord's
    heavens.

THE STORY BEHIND THE SCRIPTURE

An unusual book, Lamentations defies easy attempts even to place it within the Scriptures. In the Hebrew Bible, Lamentations shows up in the last section known as the writings. In the Christian Old Testament, it follows Jeremiah due to the traditional belief that Jeremiah, known as "the weeping prophet," would have written such poetry.

    Lamentations collects five different songs of lament over the fall of Jerusalem and the Babylonian exile. Each chapter represents a different lament, and all of them are composed in the form of alphabetical acrostics. What I love about the third song here is that rather than each verse starting with a new letter in the alphabet, the poet triples the device: three verses beginning with *aleph*, three verses then beginning with *bet*, three verses beginning with *dalet*, and so forth. Technically breathtaking, it's hard enough to write beautiful, powerful poetry using an alphabetic acrostic one line at a time, but executing one in three line segments is truly astonishing.

At the heart of this lament beats the question: why is this happening? How can a loving, sovereign God allow such pain and devastation? Today we talk about the mystery, or problem, of evil as framed by the philosopher Gottfried Leibniz contrasted with the tragic 1755 Lisbon earthquake. How can a loving, omnipotent God allow awful things to happen?

While most people will frame this quandary as the problem of evil, it's important to call it a mystery. A problem is something that may be very complicated but ultimately has a solution. A problem is finite in nature. A mystery, however, is infinite. Just as it is complex to cross a swamp safely, there are many ways to cross through a mystery and myriad ways to become lost. There is no logical solution to the mystery of evil, but there are many ways to live with it.

When I lead discussions with church groups about evil, the first instinct is to avoid wading into the mystery in the first place. To avoid the mystery, the first thought someone lifts up is free will. We don't conceive of God as a puppet master with us on strings. So, we seek to absolve God of any responsibility for evil by shouldering all the burden ourselves. And, of course, there is truth to this self-guilt. Even the briefest tour through history (or your local middle school) is enough to know human cruelty knows no bounds. But for many, the free will argument breaks down in the face of natural disasters such as the Lisbon earthquake or unspeakably violent events such as the Holocaust. In the face of that kind of evil a loving God that could step in and doesn't cannot be considered loving in any normal sense of the word.

Within the mystery itself there are several common ways to make sense of the mystery. The most traditional way, and one you can hear in the Scripture text from Lamentations, is to acknowledge that what seems like evil may not actually be evil. Here's another way of saying it: from the human perspective something may appear evil, but God may have a larger plan of which we are not wholly aware. This way through the mystery gives God full credit for the painful things taking place. The poet here claims it is God and God alone who is besieging him and breaking his bones. And yet, the poet doesn't give up hope because of a sense of God's steadfast love and that God will, eventually, restore a state of justice.

Personally, I find this pathway through the mystery too much to swallow most of the time. While I appreciate the sense of humility and trust that God really may have a plan, for me this approach just feels like a way of denying the pain that we and others are experiencing. These days, a more popular way through the mystery questions God's omnipotence. Many are familiar with Rabbi Kushner's famous *Why Bad Things Happen to Good People*. Kushner lays out the classic view here: God is loving, evil is real, but God can't actually snap God's fingers and just change what's happening in the world. God isn't a lucky rabbit's foot. Thus, God will grieve with us, God's heart will break with ours, but God's job isn't to fix the world: we are the hands and feet of God and the ones we are waiting for. Of course, for some, this weakened image of God goes against the very notion of their concept of God. What's the point of a God who can only keep us company in our grief?

Finally, another common way we make sense of this mystery is to concede that maybe God, at least the way we were taught in Sunday school, really doesn't exist. To me, it's crucial that the church make room for this possibility. So many in the church seem to think the worst thing that could possibly happen to someone is not believing in God. I disagree. For one thing, a person can't truly believe in something or someone they aren't allowed to question. For another, belief and unbelief are natural rhythms. Just as marriage keeps two people in relationship as they fall in and out of love, generous and open faith communities can keep God's people in relationship as we fall in and out of faith. Churches must be sanctuaries for us not only when we're full of faith, but must also be refuges when, as the country song puts it: our head hurts, our feet stink, and we don't love Jesus.

30

Good Dog

Ecclesiastes 9:4–10

GOOD DOG

"A living dog is better than a dead lion."
So the Teacher tells us,
but even a dead dog will do
when the holy wants a word with you.

I lifted her tired body into the gray car
onto the seat she used to take with one leap
white muzzle on black fur
her sad brown eyes wondering why.

Why were we driving to the mountain
on that frozen February day?

The cold snow, uncaring, unsparing
to her house-sensitive paws
reminding me of South Sister's scoria
excoriating her pads and claws
and the withering look she gave me
when she waded into the relief
of Moraine Lake, silently glaring:
"How could you do this to me?"

I led her through the frost-filled firs
feeling the weight of the Ruger in my pack
the heavier weight of knowing two sets of tracks
were going in, but only one back.

In a cathedral of trees I laid her down
and gathered her into my arms.
I saw the bed she peed in Boston
              right in the middle.
The stick she shared with Paggo
and the bone my boy would borrow
as I told her, "Good dog. Good dog."

At sixteen now she was in pain
every minute of every day.
I knew what needed to be done
and felt this was the only way.

I don't know if there's a heaven
full of Christmas shoes to ruin
Hebrew Bibles to chew
and Jersey rabbits to chase
but I do know this:
She ate her food with satisfaction
drank from the toilet given any distraction
and enjoyed life with the people she loved
all the days of her vain life she was
given under the sun.

And then, red from black spilling out onto white
I held her, leaning against the frozen log
my hot tears filling her closing eyes,
"Good dog. Good dog."

THE STORY BEHIND THE POEM

Rigby was my first child. One week after Melis and I graduated from the University of Texas (Go Horns!) in May of 1998, we got married at University Presbyterian Church in Austin. We hopped in the car for a quick Colorado honeymoon and then moved to Princeton, New Jersey, where I took summer Hebrew and Melis started a new job with ExxonMobil. Not having turned our lives upside down enough, we decided we needed a dog. In August, we purchased a black lab pup and named her Rigby after our favorite theology professor from Austin Seminary, Cindy Rigby. (I'm still not sure how thrilled Cindy was about that "honor.")

I had a dog named Sandy as a boy growing up. Sandy was . . . psychotic. Sandy was a little yellow schnauzer/terrier mutt, and he really was not a good dog. One night my parents heard this wild noise in the backyard. Chucka, chucka, chucka! Chucka, chucka, chucka! The next morning it looked as if it had snowed. They had bought all these bags of wood chips to spread in the planting beds, and Sandy ran up and down the backyard all night long just flinging chips out of those chewed-through bags. Needless to say, my parents were not amused.

But Rigby, Rigby would be different. Rigby would be my dog. After learning about picking pups by comparing them with their litter mates, I knew I had a less dominant but not too submissive dog. But how to train her? Friends told us we had to get *The Art of Raising a Puppy* by the Monks of New Skete. They said it was the bible for dog raising. So, I did. Talk about a mistake. Every monastery has a work in which the monks engage; the Monks of New Skete train German Shepherd police dogs. Being monks, they train their dogs around the clock. For some reason I got it in my head that I had to follow their training methods exactly, and I adhered to their absurd regimen as much as my student schedule would allow. I nearly lost it. (In fairness, Melis would question the word "nearly.")

Puppies aren't easy. At one point, we were traveling up to visit Melis's aunt and uncle for a pig roast in Vermont. Unable to get away until Melis was off work, we broke up the drive and stayed over in Boston. It was raining buckets when we arrived in Beantown. While I tried to get this little dog to pee before settling into our room, Rigby just didn't want to be out there in that rain. Consequently, we went into the room and set her down on the bed for all of five seconds while I found my rain jacket so I could take her back out to try again. She peed all over that hotel bed. And the volume? Gallons flowed forth from this tiny dog. Melis and I wondered, "How can so much fluid even come out of something so small?" It didn't seem physically possible. And, of course, it was right in the middle of the bed so it wasn't as if we could sleep to one side or the other. But Melis was deliriously tired, and I wasn't too far behind her; contorting ourselves the best we could, we wound up getting enough sleep to avoid being too dangerous the next day.

If peeing wasn't the problem, her other bodily functions were. The married student housing when I attended Princeton was this cinder block complex named CRW, the Charlotte Rachel Wilson complex. The bathrooms boasted Pepto Bismol pink sinks and toilets, and you could always plan on at least an inch of standing water in the basement storage area. Now, all of this was fine. There would have been no way for us to afford living in that part of New Jersey without the benefit of reasonable student housing. The hard part for me was the block-or-two walk to get to the designated area for pets to relieve themselves. And unlike Austin, it snowed every winter we were in New Jersey. I remember taking Rigs out in the snow one night; I knew she had to poop. So, there we were, walking back and forth in the snow in the middle of the night. And she just would not go. I grew so tired and frustrated (this is not one of my better moments) I actually picked her up and squeezed her a little bit—as if she were a tube of toothpaste I might encourage with a little pressure.

But it wasn't all physical humor with her. She was a black lab, and labs can be mouthy and destructive. In her defense, she was always selectively destructive, and she had very good taste. One day I heard Melis gasp. Rigby had eaten her favorite pair of Christmas shoes—these fancy, expensive shoes with what I suppose were attractively shiny sequins. I might have chuckled a little bit although I shouldn't have. Soon after, I came home from class to find shreds of paper all over the floor. Rigby had shredded a book. No big deal, right? Seminarians are lousy with books. One fewer wasn't going to hurt, right? Wrong. It was my Hebrew Bible, my brand new, massive, and outrageously expensive Hebrew Bible—easily the most valuable book I owned at the time. And there it was on the floor doing its best impression of confetti.

If it sounds as if I'm complaining, I am. But it's only because I loved her with a love I had not known possible. I took Rigby everywhere with me. We explored the Delaware Water Gap on the Appalachian Trail. And when we moved to Oregon, we were in heaven. In the story behind my poem "The Table," I shared how Rigby received her "Jiffy Pup" trail name when a friend and I trekked around Mount Hood on the Timberline Trail. On my thirtieth birthday, I took her to hike South Sister in the Cascades of Central Oregon. The three sisters, like all the mountains in the Cascades are volcanoes. As you ascend above the tree line, the sandy soil gives way to this sharp, volcanic rock called scoria. We made it to the wind-howling top when I noticed she wasn't walking normally. I checked her pads; they were shredded. I felt awful. I would later learn they sell little boots for indoor dogs with soft pads. I took out my first aid kit and did my best to wrap her feet in bandages and make little boots, but I could tell she was in pain. As we headed down the mountain, there's a lake about two-thirds of the way back down, Moraine Lake. As soon as she saw the lake, she half hobbled and half ran to the water, plunged in, and then just turned and glared at me. It was one of the few times I was grateful dogs can't talk.

Rigby could also be a sweet dog. One day when our first child, Ches, was just starting to crawl, Rigby was chewing on a rawhide bone; Ches crawled over and took it out of her mouth. She looked at me and her eyes said, "Seriously, Dad? Can I bite him? Can I at least growl at him?" But she never did.

Of course, dogs don't live forever. At sixteen Rigby's muzzle was entirely white. Her bones were stiff. She was in constant pain. I realize now I probably should have made the decision to put her down earlier, but it was the first time I had to make that call. I can't tell you why I felt the need to put her down myself. I don't own a gun and have little experience using one. And I certainly didn't want to pick her up, put her in my car, and take her back to Mount Hood knowing I wasn't going to bring her home with me. But I did. All I can tell you is, for me, I just didn't feel right letting anyone else take her life. Everyone must make their own decisions regarding the animals they love. For me, this final act just felt like something I had to do myself. And while I still miss her, I like knowing that her body lies in a beautiful place, on a mountain we explored together—and that I was with her in her last moments saying over and over again: "Good dog."

THE SCRIPTURE: ECCLESIASTES 9:4–10

But whoever is joined with all the living has hope, for a living dog is better than a dead lion. The living know that they will die, but the dead know nothing; they have no more reward, and even the memory of them is lost. Their love and their hate and their envy have already perished; never again will they have any share in all that happens under the sun.

Go, eat your bread with enjoyment, and drink your wine with a merry heart; for God has long ago approved what you do. Let your garments always be white; do not let oil be lacking on your head. Enjoy life with the wife whom you love, all the days of your vain life that are given you under the sun, because that is your portion in life and in your toil at which you toil under the sun. Whatever your hand finds to do, do with your might; for there is no work or thought or knowledge or wisdom in Sheol, to which you are going.

THE STORY BEHIND THE SCRIPTURE

Some traditions encourage people to discover a "life verse"—a Scripture text they believe symbolizes who they are or what they value most deeply. I'm not really a life verse kind of guy, but if I had to pick just one I would go with these words from Ecclesiastes.

Ecclesiastes is a weird, weird book. Although, attributed to Solomon, the author only describes himself as Qoheleth, which means "the teacher." Normally, when people think about the Bible, they think about it as a book that is encouraging and positive, one that helps us focus on hope and joy and goodness. Not so much with Ecclesiastes. Ecclesiastes is one long existential crisis for Qoheleth. He tries to find meaning by becoming successful and wealthy only to realize that he is going to die just the same as the lazy, poor man. So, he seeks after wisdom and becomes incredibly wise until it dawns on him that even in his infinite wisdom, he is going to die just the same as any other ignorant rube. He chases after women and pleasure; every avenue he tries he discovers the same thing: the good and the bad, the righteous and the wicked, the faithful and the faithless all wind up food for worms.

Cheerful little guy, isn't he?

Finally, there is this amazing break in the gloom. In the ninth chapter Qoheleth acknowledges that all are going to Sheol, but not all hope is lost. (If you remember from our earlier discussion in the "Forts and Fires" chapter, Sheol is the Hebrew concept of a place of darkness to which all the dead go.) The hope, though, is not to be found in some kind of afterlife or some kind of imperishable accomplishment that might somehow bestow immortality. The hope is to be found in living life itself. Hope comes from living this life, living this simple life—as fully, as consciously, and as well as we possibly can. Hence, it's better to be a living dog than a dead lion. Dogs were hated creatures in the Hebrew world, but it's still better to be a living, hated dog than dead. Furthermore, Qoheleth says the simple joys of enjoying one's food, enjoying the time we have with the people we love—this is what life is about. These little moments of beauty, these little moments of heaven on earth, are as much as we get. And they are enough.

When I was a boy (and before I discovered Carl Jung), I loved Albert Camus. (Again, what boy doesn't?) One of the first serious books I can remember reading was *The Myth of Sisyphus*. In this series of existential ponderings, I was struck with the story of Sisyphus—the Greek god condemned to forever roll a rock up a mountain, only to reach the top, have the rock fall down, and then have to roll it back up again. Camus says this is pretty much what life is like: a series of repetitive actions that never quite satisfy and will never get us to some kind of imaginary promised land of pure happiness.

Like Qoheleth's earlier existential crisis, the fate of Sisyphus sounds gloomy, but for Camus true happiness lies in facing and rising above this absurdity. Sisyphus is a hero to Camus because he faces his fate—that there is no apparent meaning to what he is doing—without giving up or giving in. He even finds a kind of happiness in the work itself: "The struggle itself toward the heights is enough to fill a man's heart. One must imagine Sisyphus happy."[1]

Facing the facts that God's presence isn't obvious and there is no clear, unambiguous meaning to our lives and work doesn't have to lead us to despair. It can free us, like Qoheleth and Sisyphus, to embrace the life we know all the more, which was certainly true of Camus himself. Camus's philosophy didn't lead him to resignation but to engagement with life. An active member of *la résistance* in France during World War Two, Camus's philosophy led him to fight for goodness and life with determination and valor. I do trust in God—but with Qoheleth and Camus, I face the hard truths that none of us see God face to face, all of us die, and nobody has a real answer about what lies beyond. And rather than leap to an easy hope in some kind of heaven beyond or give up on God altogether, I prefer to embrace the struggle and seek the traces of God and glimpses of hope right here in the world we are given.

1. Camus, *Myth of Sisyphus*, 123.

31

Ashes to Ashes

Genesis 3:19

ASHES TO ASHES

"This is the time of tension between dying and birth
The place of solitude where three dreams cross"[1]
—T. S. Eliot

Ash-marked foreheads
tear-streaked cheeks.
"You come from the earth
and to the earth, one day
you will return."

---

1. Eliot, "Ash Wednesday," 94.

In a land where
everything is new
you stand in
ancient line
facing your end
searching, even, for
the blessing in it.

You can sense
the barren ground
rock and dust
and white bone
of wilderness tree
already buried
inside of you
the true wilderness
always within.

There is no escaping this
the only choice
to look up
as the ashes come
with welcoming, vulnerable
and brave eyes
or look away
denying the death
that somehow, alone
frees you to live.

THE STORY BEHIND THE POEM

The Lenten season culminating in Holy Week can be a hard time for those who serve the church. Most churchgoers think Advent and Christmas are a big deal, largely, I think, because a lot of folks are off work. Everybody notices us pulling out the stops on Christmas Eve. But Advent is just four weeks, and Christmas Eve? It's just one night. Yes, it's a big night to be sure. But still, it's just one night. Lent and Holy Week, on the other hand, last for six weeks—and instead of one night at the end, we finish off with Holy Week. The church I serve has, at times, celebrated the full Easter Triduum: Maundy Thursday, Good Friday, Holy Saturday, and Easter Sunday. By the end of a full-scale Holy Week, a lot of my colleagues joke that after we spent so much time getting Jesus into and out of that tomb, it's finally our turn to take his place in there for a few days.

I have known some challenging holy seasons in my time as a pastor. Some of them were painful on a personal level. Once, on a Palm Sunday, one of our couples, Jacqui and Roger, came early so Roger could practice with the choir. Jacqui stayed in the car, reading. Later, Roger would remember that she complained of not feeling all that well—she really didn't feel like going to church that morning. But, it was Palm Sunday, so there she was. Tragically, she wasn't well at all. Unbeknownst to her, Jacqui had a massive tumor growing in her lower back. That tumor ruptured as she sat there in the car, taking her life.

Now in our church on Palm Sunday, we throw a big pancake breakfast with an Easter egg hunt for the kids. And that's who discovered her out there in the parking lot—our children all dressed up in their finest. Needless to say, the egg hunt was cancelled. Then, so many police cars, fire trucks, and ambulances rolled in that it looked like a first responders' convention. We turned the basement of the church into a makeshift morgue. I sat with Roger in my office while the police went through the awkward, insulting questions the law requires them to ask in these situations. And after that long day was finally over, I realized it was only Palm Sunday. I still had all of Holy Week to get through, not to mention finding meaningful words to offer. Some folks actually told me how perfect it was that it was Holy Week: I could just proclaim the resurrection and how wonderful would that be? In my head I was thinking, yeah, but Jesus got to come back. Jacqui? She won't be coming back to her family. She may know eternal life in the sweet hereafter, but her family absolutely knows the pain and loss of her death here and now. There would be no easy Alleluias for our church family that Easter.

Oddly, what got me through that week was a ritual we observe on Ash Wednesday at the start of Lent: the imposition of ashes. Traditionally, the ashes used for the mark of the cross come from the palm branches brandished about by children on Palm Sunday. I'll be honest with you and tell you that burning palm branches to ashes takes too much work, smells like a cross between Oregon's newest legal intoxicant and burnt hair, and is difficult to apply. I've found charcoal and olive oil, in the right balance, vastly more user friendly. When the time comes for the imposition of ashes, I read a statement from our Book of Common Worship and then invite people to come forward. As they approach, some aren't sure where to look or how to respond as I smudge my thumb and make the sign of the cross on their foreheads and say to them, "You have come from dust and to dust, one day, you shall return." Some, however return my gaze with a fierceness, as if they are determined to stare death directly in the face. Still others tear up, perhaps feeling and remembering loss. But one person . . . one person did something that was completely new to me. When Jacqui approached, she looked straight into my eyes, almost smiling. And after I imposed the mark, she said, "Thank you." Thank you!

No matter how many times I heard her thank me, I was always taken by surprise. It seemed like such a strange response to what feels to me as if I'm killing off the congregation. It's as if every person steps forward, one after another, and I'm telling them: "Hey, don't get too comfy here. You'll be moving on soon." And Jacqui thanks me in response? It's possible she was just being polite. Every so often someone will thank me when I serve them communion. But it didn't feel like thin politesse. There was much more meaning in her response. She was really saying thank you.

I will never know what, exactly, she was thankful for. I never asked her, and now I cannot. For now, I can only venture a guess. When Jacqui thanked me, it felt to me like she was expressing gratefulness to God. She was expressing gratefulness to God for the life given to her. Ironically, the very act of acknowledging our death frees us to see what a pure gift our life truly is. We did nothing to earn our bodies and our place in this world. Neither, unless we choose to end our lives prematurely, is it up to us how long we stay. Some have asked me over the years if it isn't morbid to observe the imposition of ashes—if it isn't just dark and morose to focus on death? My reply: "It's quite the opposite!" At least for me it is, and I believe it was life-affirming for Jacqui as well. Remembering our days are numbered is precisely what spurs us to value the time we have, knowing we really have no idea how short it may well be.

These days when people remember Jacqui around here, it's mostly on Palm Sunday. Every Palm Sunday that rolls around makes it hard to forget that day. Folks often reminisce about Jacqui at the pancake breakfast or while the kids are gathering eggs. We remember the gifts Jacqui offered this congregation. But when I remember her, I remember her on Ash Wednesday. I remember her short, exquisitely cut hair, her eyes, open wide behind her thin, delicate glasses, looking up at me and smiling as I made the sign of the cross on her forehead—reminding her she came from dust and to dust, one day, she would return. And I remember her smiling and saying thank you, believing it wasn't me she was thanking at all but the one who was, is, and ever shall be.

THE SCRIPTURE: GENESIS 3:19

"By the sweat of your face
  you shall eat bread
until you return to the ground,
  for out of it you were taken;
you are dust,
  and to dust you shall return."

THE STORY BEHIND THE SCRIPTURE

My brothers and sisters who claim to read the Bible literally may love the Scriptures, but the first three chapters of Genesis highlight the fact that they don't always read them very carefully. For the life of me, I cannot understand how literalists miss the reality that Genesis offers two quite distinct stories of creation.

Seminarians learn about historical criticism: how scholars view the Bible like an archeological dig, only with different levels of recorded history mirroring the different layers of artifacts deposited over time. The earliest biblical accounts, J and E, are distinguished by the different ways they reference God: J refers to the "Jahwist" account; E alludes to the "Elohist" narrative. The Jawhist, or Yawhist, source tells the epic history of Israel using the unpronounceable tetragrammaton for God's name, which Christians insist on verbalizing as Yahweh. The Elohist account also tells the epic history of Israel but uses the term El or, more interestingly the plural Elohim, to refer to God or gods. With just a little bit of Hebrew then, a reader can see that in the first story of creation in Genesis 1—2:4, God shows up consistently as Elohim. But then, without warning, in Genesis 2:4—3, the writers now refer to God with the unpronounceable tetragrammaton, which Christians persist in turning into Yahweh, or Jehovah.

If you buy the historical-critical hypothesis, two different names for God is already solid evidence we're looking at two different stories. But maybe you don't go in for all this intellectual mumbo jumbo. Maybe you think scholars just read too much into things. Maybe instead the scribes just got tired of referring to God one way and then switched over to another term when they felt like it. After all, there are a lot of terms for God. So maybe this is an issue of style rather than substance?

I suppose the two names for God could be poetic license. Personally, I am persuaded by the general direction of the historical-critical school, but I also believe they don't have the answer for everything. But here in Genesis, even a plain sense reading makes it clear we're dealing with two very different and inconsistent stories. In the first account of creation, God first creates the heavens and the earth, then all the creatures in the sea, next all the animals on land and in the air, and then all the plants and vegetation covering the earth. Only at the very end of the story, at the pinnacle of creation, does God create humankind in God's own image.

However, after Genesis 2:4, the story is entirely different. In this second creation story, no plant yet exists because God hasn't caused rain to fall. Nor do any animals exist. In the midst of what had to be a very barren wasteland indeed, God reaches down, scoops up some dust, blows into it, and out pops the first living being. And notice it's only one living being, not humankind together as it is in the first story. In this second story, after creating Adam, God creates trees and plants and a garden and puts this man in the garden to keep it. Noticing that the male creature seems lonely, God creates animals for the man to name. When adding animals doesn't quite do the trick, God—acting like a psychopath at a barbeque—pulls a rib out of the man and fashions a woman from it. Of course, the lamentable business with the talking snake and the fruit ensues, and the man and woman wind up expelled from the garden to labor by the sweat of their brow "until you return to the ground, for out of it you were taken; you are dust, and to dust you shall return" (Gen 3:19). This second story begins what scholars call the primordial history, which goes from the bad expulsion from the garden to the worse murder of Abel, on to Noah and the flood, and finally to the tower of Babel, which establishes the need for God to do something new with Abram.

So, we have two entirely different stories of creation: the first is an orderly account with human beings created at the pinnacle, the second is a narrative in which human brokenness is on display. Our inability to read Genesis with care has caused massive problems, particularly about the ongoing rift between faith and science. While Darwin certainly didn't set out to create one of the largest conflicts of the twentieth and twenty-first centuries, his *Origin of Species* did so just the same. When Darwin was just a young adult aboard The Beagle, most people believed the Bible offered a single, orderly view of creation, and scientists backed them up, offering more and more detailed proof of God's hand at work.

But Darwin's theory of evolution challenged this worldview, setting off fiery responses not only from the scientific community in England but the theological establishment as well. If animals changed over time due to natural selection, then creation certainly didn't work in the way people in that era interpreted Genesis. Especially concerning was the possibility that humans weren't simply created as we are by God but evolved as well. Indeed, this suggestion that humans evolved from ape-like species seems to particularly enrage people. During the great 1860 Oxford evolution debate between Bishop Samuel Wilberforce and Darwin-supporter Thomas Huxley, Wilberforce bitingly asked Huxley whether his family was descended from monkeys on his grandmother's or his grandfather's side.[2] This same attitude prevailed during the famous Scopes Monkey Trial in 1925 in America. Despite all the evidence to the contrary, many still just rankled at the idea that we are animals and part of what David Whyte terms "the grand array"[3] in his poem, "Everything Is Waiting for You."

A friend and I saw this first hand. When I was a pastor in Austin, Texas, Ryan Valentine, of the Texas Freedom Network, and I attended the Texas State Textbook Hearings; that year they were evaluating new science textbooks. As much as I hate to say it, sometimes everything really is bigger in Texas. In this case, I mean both textbook sales and the crazy: textbook sales are a big deal because when Texas decides to buy a new textbook, several nearby states adopt it as well; and the crazy because, oh my goodness, did some fascinating people turn out to have their say. While Ryan and I were at the hearings to offer a Christian witness—affirming our support for faith and evolution—we soon found ourselves in a very small minority. A huge crowd, some in costume, turned out to blame everything from criminal behavior to teenage suicide on the evils of Darwinism. I have never been so uncertain what was comic and what was tragic.

How frustrating that all this uproar was based on a reading of Genesis that doesn't even make sense on the face of it. There can be no rift between science and "the Bible," when the creation narrative of Genesis doesn't offer a coherent, single narrative in the first place. It's not as if "the Bible" says one thing about God creating the earth and all within and godless scientists argue all manner of other crazy things. As we've seen, Genesis offers divergent,

2. Hesketh, *Of Apes and Ancestors*, Kindle location 1686.
3. Whyte, Everything Is Waiting," 359.

conflicting, and often incoherent stories that developed, or—if you will permit me—evolved over time. Cambridge theologian Sarah Coakley offers us a more helpful way to view the biblical creation accounts and the origin accounts offered to us by the scientific community. Coakley invites people of faith and the scientific community to acknowledge the various stories underneath both projects and to allow these different narratives to mutually inform one another.[4]

The first biblical account of Genesis lifts up the gorgeous order we can find in creation amidst the chaos. Our little corner of Oregon was privileged to see the full eclipse in 2017. Who didn't marvel at the phenomenal, sublime precision of the moon lining up perfectly with the sun, which caused a kind of weird, unearthly midnight at ten o'clock in the morning? The second account of Genesis dwells on why humanity, with all our good gifts, seems at once perfect and imperfect, flawless and flawed. All who are honest with themselves can't help but see our strengths paired with our weaknesses. Complementing the existential nature of the religious narratives, the scientific accounts of creation endeavor to explain how the world came to be rather than why it is the way it is. Instead of some sad competition trying to elevate *our* story over *theirs*, I live for the day we might celebrate these disparate, complex narratives and revel in what they offer all of us when we embrace them as two parts of the whole—believers and nonbelievers alike.

4. Coakley, "Reconceiving 'Natural Theology.'"

32

Heaven on Earth

Revelation 21:1–7

HEAVEN ON EARTH

Night drive. Light flooding
valley below. Small, gray, house.
Safest place I've ever known.

Mist hangs in tree line.
Gravel crunches under feet.
Climbing rose on door.

The smell of chocolate
chip cookies, warm, freshly baked
beckoning back home.

The untouched workshop.
Altar of order. A place
for every clean tool.

A cut-throat croquet
game. Balls sent down the hill.
Worn-grass badminton.

Lemon Blennd, lima
beans baked. Blue corn chips. Weird.
Doxology sung.

The kingdom is spread
out among you, on earth as
it is in heaven.

Heaven descending.
The New Jerusalem. Love
spreading out. Here. Now.

THE STORY BEHIND THE POEM

Earlier, I shared some of the instability and hard times of my growing up years, but it wasn't all chaotic. One of the anchors of my childhood was a little, gray house that my Grandfather Cashdollar built with the help of his carpenter brothers during the depression.

Every summer of my childhood I flew from the concrete expanse of the Dallas/Fort Worth airport to the lush, green, humid hills of Pittsburgh, Pennsylvania, to visit my grandparents. I didn't know it at the time, but it was ritual time. We went the same time every year to celebrate the Fourth of July. We did the same things every July 4th. We set up the badminton and told family members they must have a hole in their racquet when they missed the birdie. We created a unique croquet course on the lumpy green front yard that placed two side wickets on the edge of a steep hill. One of our favorite pastimes was hitting an opponent's ball near the edge of the hill, which gave the player two options: the player could take two shots and move ahead or place their ball right next to the one they hit, carefully step on their own ball, and whack it with the mallet to send their opponent's ball down the hill. I'm not sure this violent manner of play was exactly what the English had in mind with their lawn whites, but this is how my family rolled. (Pun intended!)

We ate the same foods. Around Pittsburgh, loyalists don't drink lemonade but Reymer's Lemon Blennd instead. Rather than baked beans, we had baked limas. I have no idea if this is a Western Pennsylvania thing or not, but it was tradition in our family. We had various potato and macaroni salads, an amazing peach Jell-O made with whipped cream, and simple turkey and ham sandwiches on the side. Every year my Aunt Donna made this decadent, fudge-topped chocolate cake that was so rich it was probably a good thing we only had it once a year. Before eating we always sang a slow, haunting version of the Doxology in full four-part harmony (we were all good Presbyterians, after all!) under the canopy of the cucumber magnolia trees, trees I have never seen in any other part of the country.

My grandfather had a shop in the basement that hadn't been touched after his death when I was a boy until we finally sold the house when I was thirty. He was a diesel engine mechanic in the Navy during World War II and continued to work on engines his whole life, first at the local Ford garage and then for an independent telephone company. A simple man with a humble job, he provided well for a family of five. He was a careful worker, and he kept a clean shop: nails and screws all sorted perfectly in small jars; and every tool in pristine condition, hung up on the pegboard exactly where it belonged. There was a smell in that workshop that was something between oil, wood, and peace. I didn't realize it at the time but going to Pennsylvania every year, doing the same things there every year, and being with extended family—this annual pilgrimage gave an enormous sense of rhythm and deep peace to an otherwise chaotic upbringing. Accordingly, I cast the lines of this poem in a strict haiku form. More importantly, whenever I think about Revelation's description of heaven actually coming down to earth, that little gray house with those special people always comes to mind—and I am forever grateful.

THE SCRIPTURE: REVELATION 21:1–7

Then I saw a new heaven and a new earth; for the first heaven and the first earth had passed away, and the sea was no more. And I saw the holy city, the new Jerusalem, coming down out of heaven from God, prepared as a bride adorned for her husband. And I heard a loud voice from the throne saying, "See, the home of God is among mortals. He will dwell with them; they will be his peoples, and God himself will be with them; he will wipe every tear from their eyes. Death will be no more; mourning and crying and pain will be no more, for the first things have passed away."

And the one who was seated on the throne said, "See, I am making all things new." Also he said, "Write this, for these words are trustworthy and true." Then he said to me, "It is done! I am the Alpha and the Omega, the beginning and the end. To the thirsty I will give water as a gift from the spring of the water of life. Those who conquer will inherit these things, and I will be their God and they will be my children.

THE STORY BEHIND THE SCRIPTURE

When I first arrived at the church I currently serve, I loved everything about the place except one thing: the youth director who has long since found her joy elsewhere. While I could look past her fake tan, platinum hair, and flash, I had a harder time when she told me she was really "into" theology. Really, I asked, kind of surprised and dubious, but hopeful all the same. She took me into her office where she had the entire *Left Behind* series on her shelf. See, she said proudly, something like a cat bringing a dead mouse and dropping it on your doorstep. The *Left Behind* series was her idea of theology? I didn't know whether to laugh or cry.

Revelation is the best book that no one reads. Fundamentalists don't read it, because they have Kirk Cameron and the *Left Behind* movies to tell them what they want to hear. The actual text would only confuse things. Liberals don't read it because it's weird and frightening. So, like a middle school boy awkwardly standing against the wall at his first dance, Revelation just kind of watches church members hang out with all the other cooler books.

To me the main thing to know about Revelation is that it isn't a crystal ball into the future. It's a book about the very real difficulties facing the Christian community in the first century: severe oppression by the Roman government. Thus, the book is written in coded language. Yes, the book makes use of unusual and even bizarre imagery to people who aren't well acquainted with the Scriptures. But for people who have read Ezekiel, Daniel, and other Old Testament prophets, John's Revelation is like a DJ sampling and mixing different elements and images from the Old Testament to spin up something entirely new.

For instance, the four living creatures in Revelation harken back to Ezekiel—only with a twist. In the first chapter of Ezekiel, the presence of God is heading from Jerusalem to the exiles in Babylon. In the midst of this presence were four living creatures that looked something like humans only each of them had four wings and four faces. One face was human, one face was a lion, another was an ox, and the final face was that of an eagle. These living creatures correspond directly with John's creatures in Revelation, but John splits the creatures into four individuals rather than one individual with four faces. So, these images in Revelation aren't crazy or drug addled; rather, they are deeply connected with the Hebrew tradition.

And the most significant thing in Revelation is that it is not about the destruction of God's good creation. It isn't. An apocalypse is not some kind of nuclear holocaust of destruction. Apocalypse means "taking away the veils" in Greek (hence, re-vealing), and it was written as a way of giving people courage. John was taking away the veils from a reality that looked hopeless by telling people that the living God was still acting in hidden ways—ways that were not always obvious or easily seen.

The most hopeful thing of all? The earth is being restored. In the beginning, God created the earth good, very good. And yes, there were a few weird turns along the way; but ultimately the message of Revelation, the final book of the Bible, is that God is restoring the earth by allowing the new Jerusalem, heaven itself, to descend right down to the good earth beneath our feet.

If the meaning of a work hinges on how it ends, the Book of Revelation is good news indeed. Through the lens of Revelation, we see once and for all that the message of the Bible is hope: we are not disembodied spirits who have to endure a terrible world and in the end, if we are good enough and believe enough of the right things, get to fly away to some place in the clouds on the wings of Yanni music. (Shudder.) The message of the Bible is that the world—this world that God made and this world for which Christ lived and died—is being restored to wholeness even now.

SECTION FIVE

Epilogue

33

The One Grain of Sand

THE ONE GRAIN OF SAND

Ocean's tears dry
on rough sand beach
the earth's wetness
pulling you into
her depths.

Eviscerated crab claw
torn sea weed
now flotsam in the white sticky
foam sprayed upon
the splayed body
of the beach.

This place of life
and death. Storm
and sex. This is where
life began. This
is life itself.

There is no pity
here. No mercy will
keep the waves from
crushing your body
onto the rocks below.

But there is this.
There is this.
There is a kind of comfort
in knowing you
are neither needed
nor required here
no matter what
you have been taught.

Your only task here
is to see the one grain
of sand. To feel
the harsh wind against
your cheek. To hear
the greedy cry of the gull
and to love it all
letting go of your
heavy ache to be
loved back
the way you
always thought you
needed.

THE STORY BEHIND THE POEM

I'm both fascinated with and challenged by these two Davids in my life, both King David and David Whyte. The image of King David as a leader who knows when to fight for his people and when to sing to them is incredibly powerful. The incredible faith David had in God—that God would show up no matter the circumstance and that David could trust himself to be in God's keeping—is profoundly inspiring and freeing. David, fully present in his life, knew how to lead by stirring the passions of people.

And yet, King David comes with such a dark side. At times, his passion for good seems to be balanced by, if not outweighed, by his lust and self-indulgence. Are these connected? Was David's darkness a consequence of his brilliance? Was it somehow not possible for David to be the man who inspired so many without at the same time being the David who destroyed so many others?

My feelings about David Whyte are also somewhat ambiguous. I am most drawn to Whyte's presence and comfort with himself in a room. I can't know what goes on in Whyte's head, but the feeling I get when I hear him read is that in the healthiest way, he trusts in the power of his work to such an extent that he really could care less whether listeners are moved by his poetry or not. Perhaps this perceived nonchalance isn't always true for him, but it is the feeling I get in his presence. While his scanning eyes at the end of a spoken-word piece and the way he draws his fingers through his long hair seemed to me, especially at first, the epitome of "the poet," there is nothing precious about David Whyte when it comes to his craft. He doesn't require perfection of himself. Rarely, I've seen him pause during a reading stuck on a word or phrase, and once, I've seen him consult a written version of an older poem when he was unsure of a line. But never have I seen him flustered or apologetic in any way in these moments. He is, in many ways, the embodiment of a non-anxious presence.

On the one hand, I'm deeply drawn to his detachment. As someone who desires to be liked and appreciated, Whyte's seeming lack of attachment is alluring. One of the worst challenges a pastor can face is the desire to be liked. When the main job of a pastor is to preach a Jesus who found a way to offend nearly everyone so much so that he wound up on a cross, the need to be liked can be a serious impediment to faithful ministry. But then, as I wrote earlier in this book about David Whyte's poem "Sweet Darkness," a part of me is suspicious of the willingness to move on, too quickly, from anyone or anything that doesn't immediately bring us alive. Arrogance and self-deception can lead us to blame others for our own deficits. My sense is David Whyte has found his balance between confidence and overconfidence, between following his own path versus making concessions for the sake of community—but I'm certainly still finding my way.

My final poem, "One Grain of Sand," touches on this balance between personal needs and the needs of those of others around us. When I have the chance, I love to walk along the sandy beach at Pacific City on the Oregon coast. Below the massive rock face of Chief Kiwanda, the surf relentlessly crashes to the shore, washing both life and death onto the beach. It is such a simple, elemental, and ancient landscape. Whenever I'm tempted, as I sometimes am, to think too highly of my own importance, the shifting sands remind me nothing is permanent. While I know that I am a valued child of God, the earth doesn't actually need me. And whenever I lament that my own needs aren't always entirely met in every way by the people around me, I'm reminded, looking at the torn crab legs and beached sea weed, that this is true for all. And, far from being sad or resigned about this, when the winds and my soul are calm, I am filled with a great sense of peace about my place in it all. Wrapped in this peace, I remember again my call to be present, aware, and attentive—to the one grain of sand, to the one who needs a word of hope, and to God's still, small voice.

Great ending

Bibliography

Anderson, Bernhard W. *Understanding the Old Testament*. 4th ed. Upper Saddle River, NJ: Prentice Hall, 1998.

Anderson, Gary A. "King David and the Psalms of Imprecation." *Pro Ecclesia* 15 (Summer 2006) 267–80.

Baden, Joel. *The Historical David: The Real Life of an Invented Hero*. New York: HarperOne, 2013. Kindle edition.

Brooks, Geraldine. *The Secret Chord*. New York: Penguin, 2016.

Brown, Brené. "Preface." In *The Gifts of Imperfection: Let Go of Who You Think You're Supposed to Be and Embrace Who You Are*, ix–xv. Center City, MN: Hazelden, 2010.

Brown, William P. *Seeing the Psalms: A Theology of Metaphor*. Louisville: Westminster John Knox, 2002.

Brueggemann, Walter. *David's Truth: In Israel's Imagination and Memory*. 2nd ed. Minneapolis: Fortress, 2000. Kindle edition.

Buechner, Frederick. *Wishful Thinking: A Theological ABC*. New York: Harper & Row, 1973.

Calvin, John. "Preface." In *Commentary on the Book of Psalms, Volume 1: Psalms 1–35*, xxxv–xlix. Translated by James Anderson. Calvin's Commentaries 4. Grand Rapids: Baker, 2005.

———. *Institutes of the Christian Religion*. Edited by John T. McNeil. Translated by Ford Lewis Battles. 2 vols. Library of Christian Classics. Philadelphia: Westminster. 1960.

Camus, Albert. *The Myth of Sisyphus and Other Essays*. New York: Vintage, 1991. Kindle edition.

Coakley, Sarah. "Reconceiving 'Natural Theology': Meaning, Sacrifice, and God." Paper presented at the Gifford Lectures at the University of Scotland, Aberdeen, May 3, 2012.

Coates, Ta-Nehisi. *Between the World and Me*. New York: Spiegel & Grau, 2015.

Cox, Harvey. *The Feast of Fools: A Theological Essay on Festivity and Fantasy*. New York: Perennial, 1972.

Curry, Michael. "Someone Must Tell the Babies." Sermon, Festival of Homiletics, Minneapolis, Minnesota, May 20, 2008. http://arc.episcopalchurch.org/myp/Ecce/Edited%20Transcripts/curry2_16.htm.

Darden, Robert. *Jesus Laughed: The Redemptive Power of Humor.* Nashville: Abingdon, 2011. Kindle edition.

Derrida, Jacques. *The Gift of Death.* Translated by David Wills. Chicago: University of Chicago Press, 1996.

Didion, Joan, *The Year of Magical Thinking,* New York, Vintage, 2007.

Eliot, T. S. "Ash Wednesday." In *Collected Poems, 1909–1962,* 83–95. Orlando: Harcourt Brace Jovanovich, 1991.

Evers-Hood, Ken. *The Irrational Jesus: Leading the Fully Human Church,* Eugene, OR: Cascade, 2016.

Faulkner, William. *Requiem for a Nun.* New York: Vintage, 2012.

Halpern, Baruch. *David's Secret Demons: Messiah, Murderer, Traitor, King.* Grand Rapids: Eerdmans, 2001.

Heschel, Abraham Joshua. *The Sabbath: Its Meaning for Modern Man.* New York: Farrar, Straus and Giroux, 1951.

Hesketh, Ian. *Of Apes and Ancestors: Evolution, Christianity, and the Oxford Debate.* Toronto: University of Toronto Press, 2009. Kindle edition.

Hoffman, Joel M. *The Bible Doesn't Say That: 40 Biblical Mistranslations, Misconceptions, and Other Misunderstandings.* New York: Thomas Dunne, 2016. Kindle edition.

Holmberg, Bengt. *Paul and Power: The Structure of Authority in the Primitive Church as Reflected in the Pauline Epistles.* Reprint. Eugene, OR: Wipf & Stock, 2004.

Jones, Alan. *Passion for Pilgrimage: Notes for the Journey Home.* New York: Morehouse, 2000. Kindle edition.

Jung, Carl G. "Preface" In *The Psychology of Dementia Praecox,* xviii–xx. Translated by Frederick Peterson and A. A. Brill. New York: Journal of Nervous and Mental Disease, 1909.

Kadvany, Elena. "Stanford Sex-Assault Victim: 'You Took Away My Worth.'" *Palo Alto Online,* June 3, 2016. https://www.paloaltoonline.com/news/2016/06/03/stanford-sex-assault-victim-you-took-away-my-worth.

Kapuściński, Ryszard. *Travels with Herodotus.* Translated by Klara Glowczewska. New York: Knopf, 2007.

Levinas, Emmanuel. "Loving the Torah More Than God." In *Difficult Freedom: Essays on Judaism,* 142–145. Translated by Seán Hand. Baltimore: Johns Hopkins University Press, 1990.

Lewis, C. S. *Mere Christianity.* New York: Touchstone, 1996.

Marcus, Joel. *Mark: A New Translation with Introduction and Commentary. Volume 2, Mark 8–16.* Anchor Yale Bible 27A. New Haven: Yale University Press, 2009.

Merritt, Jonathan. "Eugene Peterson Backtracks on Same-Sex Marriage." *Religion News Service,* July 13, 2017. http://religionnews.com/2017/07/13/eugene-peterson-backtracks-on-same-sex-marriage/#.

———. "Eugene Peterson on Changing His Mind About Same-Sex Issues and Marriage. *Religion News Service,* July 12, 2017. http://religionnews.com/2017/07/12/eugene-peterson-on-changing-his-mind-about-same-sex-issues-and-marriage/.

Moltmann, Jürgen. *Theology of Play.* Translated by Reinhard Ulrich. New York: Harper & Row, 1972.

Muir, John. *Our National Parks.* Vook Classics. Vook, 2011. Kindle edition.

Neale, Robert E. "The Crucifixion as Play." In *Theology of Play* by Jürgen Moltmann, 76–86. New York: Harper & Row, 1972.

Norris, Kathleen. "Incarnational Language." *Christian Century* 114 (July 1997) 699.

Oberman, Heiko A. *Luther: Man Between God and the Devil.* Translated by Eileen Walliser-Schwarzbart. New York: Image, 1992.

Perel, Esther. "The Secret to Desire in a Long-term Relationship." *TED Talks,* February 2013, 19.10 min. https://www.ted.com/talks/esther_perel_the_secret_to_desire_ in_a_long_term_relationship.

Peterson, Eugene H. *The Pastor: A Memoir.* New York: HarperOne, 2012.

Plato. *Cratylus.* Halls of Wisdom. Ozymandias, 2016. Kindle edition.

Rahner, Hugo. *Man at Play.* New York: Herder and Herder, 1972.

Ramo, Joshua Cooper. *The Seventh Sense: Power, Fortune, and Survival in the Age of Networks.* New York: Little, Brown, 2016. Kindle edition.

Rilke, Rainer Maria. *Letters to a Young Poet.* Translated by Joan M. Burnham. 2nd ed. Novato, CA: New World Library, 2010.

Robertson, C. K. *Barnabas vs. Paul: To Encourage or Confront?* Nashville: Abingdon, 2015. Kindle edition.

Rose, Or N. *Abraham Joshua Heschel: Man of Spirit, Man of Action.* Philadelphia: Jewish Publication Society, 2003.

Sanders, E. P. *Paul: The Apostle's Life, Letters, and Thought.* Minneapolis: Fortress, 2015. Kindle edition.

Semple, Kirk. "That Green Square (or Circle) in Mexico City Might Save Your Life." *New York Times,* July 20, 2016. https://www.nytimes.com/2016/07/21/world/what-in-the-world/that-green-square-or-circle-in-mexico-city-might-save-your-life.html.

Shakespeare, William. *Hamlet.* In *The Complete Works of William Shakespeare,* Volume 3: *Tragedies,* 1127–1170. Classics Club. Roslyn, NY: Walter J. Black, 1937.

Steussy, Marti J. *David: Biblical Portraits of Power.* Studies on Personalities of the Old Testament. Columbia: University of South Carolina Press, 1999.

Taylor, Barbara Brown. "Singing Ahead of Time," In *Home By Another Way,* 15–19. Lanham, MD: Cowley, 1999.

Trueblood, Elton. *The Humor of Christ: A Significant but Often Unrecognized Aspect of Christ's Teaching.* New York: Harper & Row, 1964.

von Balthasar, Hans Urs. *The Glory of the Lord: A Theological Aesthetics.* Volume 1, *Seeing the Form.* Edited by Joseph Fessio and John Riches. Translated by Erasmo Leiva-Merikakis. 2nd ed. San Francisco: Ignatius, 2009. Kindle edition.

White, E. B. "Bedfellows." In *Essays of E. B. White,* 99–111. New York: HarperPerennial, 2014. Kindle edition.

———. "Introduction." In *Onward and Upward in the Garden,* by Katharine S. White, viii–xix. Boston: Beacon, 2002.

Whyte, David. "Everything Is Waiting for You." In *River Flow: New & Selected Poems,* 359. Rev. ed. Langley, WA: Many Rivers, 2015.

———. "Faith." In *River Flow: New & Selected Poems,* 94. Rev. ed. Langley, WA: Many Rivers, 2015.

———. "Leaving the Island." In *The Sea in You: Twenty Poems of Requited and Unrequited Love,* Kindle location 438–43. Langley, WA: Many Rivers, 2015. Kindle edition.

———. "A Lyrical Bridge Between Past, Present and Future." *TED Talks*, April 2017, 20.15 min. https://www.ted.com/talks/david_whyte_a_lyrical_bridge_between_past_present_and_future.

———. "Sometimes." In *River Flow: New & Selected Poems*, 52–53. Rev. ed. Langley, WA: Many Rivers, 2015.

———. "Start Close In." In *River Flow: New & Selected Poems*, 360–61. Rev. ed. Langley, WA: Many Rivers, 2015.

———. "Sweet Darkness," In *River Flow: New & Selected Poems*, 346. Rev. ed. Langley, WA: Many Rivers, 2015.

———. "Vulnerability." In *Consolations: The Solace, Nourishment and Underlying Meaning of Everyday Words*, Kindle location 1090–1102. Langley, WA: Many Rivers, 2015. Kindle edition.

Wilson, Edmund. *The Triple Thinkers and The Wound and the Bow: A Combined Volume*. Boston: Northeastern University Press, 1984.

Wolpe, David. *David: The Divided Heart*. Jewish Lives. New Haven: Yale University Press, 2014. Kindle edition.

CPSIA information can be obtained
at www.ICGtesting.com
Printed in the USA
FFHW021251300719
53975080-59683FF

9 781532 636226